SERPENTS, GOATS AND TURKEYS

SERPENTS, GOATS AND TURKEYS
A CENTURY OF LIBERAL–LABOUR RELATIONS

DAVID LAWS

\B^b\
Biteback Publishing

First published in Great Britain in 2024 by
Biteback Publishing Ltd, London
Copyright © David Laws 2024

The publisher is grateful to Penguin Random House and Jane Ashdown for their kind
permission to reproduce extracts from *The Ashdown Diaries Vols 1* and *2*.

ISBN 978-1-78590-884-2

10 9 8 7 6 5 4 3 2 1

A CIP catalogue record for this book is available from the British Library.

Set in Minion Pro and Moret

Printed and bound in Great Britain by
CPI Group (UK) Ltd, Croydon CR0 4YY

FSC
www.fsc.org
MIX
Paper | Supporting
responsible forestry
FSC® C171272

For Jane and Paddy Ashdown

CONTENTS

INTRODUCTION

This is the story of the relationship between the Liberal Party/
Liberal Democrats and the Labour Party, from 1903 to 2019. It
is a story of both parties but is written from a Liberal perspective.
It is not a history of the Liberal or Labour Party, and the narrative
focuses on party development only to the extent that it sheds light
on the mutual relationship.

The book seeks to answer several questions. Are these two parties
natural allies, separate components of some 'progressive alliance'
that has been wrenched apart by historical accident and awaits re-
assembling? Or are they natural competitors, as they have been for
much of the past hundred years? What have been the overlaps of
policy and ideology, and where have the parties been most divided?
What explains the periods of co-operation but also the unwillingness or inability to work together for any significant time? And why
is it that if there is common ground between the two parties, the
Liberals have spent more time since 1915 working in government
with the Conservatives than with Labour?

Since 1903, the Liberals have been 'in government' with other
parties for twenty years – five in coalition with the Conservatives

(2010–15), one in a pact with Labour (1977–78), eight in National (wartime) Governments with both other parties (1915–18, 1940–45) and for six years in National Governments with the Conservatives, albeit with some Liberals remaining on the opposition benches (1918–22, 1931–33). Measured on this crude basis, the Liberals have been in government with the Conservatives for more years (nineteen years) than with Labour (nine years). No wonder some in Labour feel that the idea of a 'progressive alliance' is an illusion or merely an aspiration.

However, in addition to these years in government, there have been other periods in which Liberals enabled Labour minority governments to take and stay in power, while remaining largely independent of them (1923–24, 1929–31). If we include these years, we end up with the count being nineteen years of Lib–Con co-operation and twelve years of Lib–Lab.

Finally, if we utilise an even looser measure of 'friendliness/ co-operation', then we might also consider the years from 1906 to 1915, during which Labour was seated at times on the government benches and was generally supporting a Liberal government. We might even include (at a stretch) the period from 1997 to 1999, when Paddy Ashdown and Tony Blair were in close co-operation and established a Joint Labour–Liberal Democrat Cabinet Committee on Constitutional Reform. Adding these years (of very materially different relations) would give us a nineteen- vs 23-year split in favour of Lib–Labbery, over the 1903–2019 period.

This is a work of political history and not current affairs. The historical narrative ends in 2019. I have not considered the period since Sir Keir Starmer and Sir Edward Davey were elected, respectively, Labour and Liberal Democrat leaders. However, I have sought to reflect on the lessons of the past 120 years and how these might help inform and shape the future. I have also included a brief postscript to allow some early reflections on the possible implications of the landslide election of July 2024.

All the political parties mentioned in this volume have changed their names at different times over the period since 1903. The Liberals became the Liberal Democrats in 1988. From 1918 onwards, party splits also resulted in separate groups of Coalition Liberals, National Liberals and, finally, Liberal Nationals. The Labour Representation Committee became the Labour Party in 1906. Conservative candidates have stood under a wider range of party names, and I have tended to use 'Unionist' and 'Conservative' interchangeably, but I have generally favoured 'Unionist' before 1922 and 'Conservative' after this.

Electoral reform is, unsurprisingly, referred to throughout the book, and I have generally used initials to describe each voting system, rather than repeating their full names, which would become tedious for the reader. FPTP refers to 'First Past the Post', the current (2024) system used for Westminster elections, where the candidate with the largest number of votes is elected. AV refers to the Alternative Vote, where voters are asked to rank candidates in order of preference, with the preferences of the lowest-placed candidates reallocated until one candidate has a majority and wins. SV is the Supplementary Vote, another form of preferential voting, where if no candidate secures a majority, the top two candidates continue to a run-off in which the second preferences of the eliminated candidates are brought into play. STV is the Single Transferable Vote, which is a multi-winner system designed to deliver a 'proportionate' outcome by asking voters to rank candidates and transferring votes where candidates are eliminated or elected with 'surplus' votes. Finally, AMS is the Additional Member System, in which voters typically cast two votes, one to elect a local MP under First Past the Post and the other to elect a party representative from a local or regional list, to give a measure of proportionality. AV Plus is a system that mixes AV for electing constituency MPs with an AMS 'top-up'.

An interesting and important issue is how the relationship between both parties has been shaped and influenced by the significant economic, social and employment developments over this period of history. But attempting to do justice to this issue would have significantly added to the scope and complexity of this project, and I must leave that important question for other authors to consider.

In writing this volume, I have been able to draw on some unpublished material from my own time in politics, including in the period from 1994 to 2015. I am also hugely grateful to Jane Ashdown for allowing me access to the full and unpublished diaries of her husband, the late Paddy Ashdown. This has enabled me to shed more light on the period of Lib–Lab co-operation from 1994 to 1999 – unquestionably the most important period for Lib–Lab relations since Ramsay MacDonald and Herbert Gladstone agreed their electoral pact of 1903. I must also express my gratitude to Ian Patrick MBE, who for many years was Paddy's much trusted private secretary and who has enabled easy access for me to the key diary entries. The Ashdown diaries were published in abridged form in 2000–01, but there were some entries that Paddy did not wish to be made public during the lifetime of Roy Jenkins and while Tony Blair was still Prime Minister. These can now be properly considered.

I am grateful to others who have found time to read drafts of the book or talk through issues covered in this volume, including

Sir Nick Clegg, Lord Lipsey, Lord Oates, Lord Rennard, Lord (Jim) Wallace and Lord (William) Wallace.

My special thanks are due to Duncan Brack, whose encyclopaedic knowledge of Liberal and Liberal Democrat history was immensely helpful and saved me from quite a few foolish errors of both fact and interpretation.

Responsibility, of course, for errors, omissions and the conclusions lies entirely with me.

I am grateful to James Stephens of Biteback for commissioning the book and to my excellent editors at Biteback, Ryan Norman and Olivia Beattie, for their hard work and infinite patience. Thanks are also due to my fantastic publicist, Suzanne Sangster.

This book is dedicated to Jane and Paddy Ashdown, for the support, encouragement and wise advice that they gave me for twenty-five years, and in memory of the Liberal who may never have occupied government office but who was his party's most loyal, energetic and effective leader since Gladstone. Paddy would have loved to have survived to see the outcome of the 2024 general election, which saw seventy-two Liberal Democrat MPs elected to Parliament, and restored his own (former) Yeovil constituency to the Liberal Democrat family of seats.

David Laws
London
July 2024

CHAPTER 1

'NURSING INTO LIFE A SERPENT' 1903–14

The nurses at the Leicester Isolation Hospital on 6 September 1903 were almost certainly unaware that one of their patients was a 36-year-old man who had twice failed to be elected to Parliament and held the obscure-sounding title of Secretary of the Labour Representation Committee (LRC). His admission papers recorded him as Mr Ramsay MacDonald.

MacDonald had travelled to Leicester for the annual conference of the Trades Union Congress, but he was taken ill and admitted to the hospital. Today, he had a visitor (also unrecognised): a balding man with an impressive handlebar moustache who had travelled up from London. He was Jesse Herbert, political secretary to the Liberal Chief Whip in Parliament, Herbert Gladstone. Gladstone was the youngest son of the late Prime Minister, the most famous ever Liberal.

The two men were meeting in this unlikely setting to finalise a secret electoral pact that would soon assist in sweeping the Unionist Party from office. In time, it would contribute to destroying the Liberal Party itself. The 'Hospital Pact' changed the face of British politics for ever.

At the preceding, October 1900, general election, the Labour Representation Committee had secured the election of just two MPs. By 1906, the pact would enable them to win twenty-nine seats. Within twenty years, Labour had 191 MPs and over 30 per cent of the vote, pushing the Liberals into third position.

The 'Hospital Pact' now looks like one of the most ill-judged and disastrous political deals in British history. In 1970, the then Liberal leader, Jeremy Thorpe, wrote:

> The Herbert Gladstone/Ramsay MacDonald arrangement ... was an act of uncalled-for electoral generosity unforgivable in a Chief Whip ... At the very moment the Liberals needed no support from outside to win a smashing victory, they gratuitously admitted to Westminster ... a group of MPs whose only opportunity of expansion lay in replacing the Liberal Party.[1]

Was Thorpe right? And, if so, how did the mighty Liberal Party make such a blunder?

In 1903, the Liberal Party was one of the two great UK political parties. As recently as 1880, it had achieved 56 per cent of the vote. But the Liberals were now neither dominant nor confident of their future. The Unionists had beaten the Liberals in MPs elected in the last four general elections. The Liberal split over Home Rule in 1886 had boosted their Conservative and Unionist opponents, who secured 201 more seats than them in that year's election, forty-two more in 1892, a whopping 234 extra in 1895 and 219 more in 1900. Two short-lived Liberal administrations under Gladstone (1892–94) and Rosebery (1894–95) had ended in failure. After being in power so long, the Unionist grip should have been weak by 1903, but it seemed as strong as ever.

The Liberal Party organisation was in a fragile state. Its finances were poor, with many of the biggest donors having left over Home Rule. The 'grand old man' of British politics, William Gladstone, had stayed too long as leader, only stepping down in 1894 after a sixty-year career. He had failed to develop a policy agenda that responded to the new economic and social challenges and the expectations of the newly enfranchised elements of the working class. When Keir Hardie, first chairman of the Independent Labour Party but one-time aspirant Liberal MP, had led a deputation to see Gladstone to argue for the eight-hour working day, Gladstone refused to back the change on the basis that it was an infringement of liberty. It was a sign of how out of touch he was with the world of the working class.[2]

Now Gladstone was gone, but the Liberals had failed to find an imaginative, inspiring leader to replace him. And the party's broad-based coalition – so often a strength in a political party – looked increasingly challenging to weld together into a coherent whole. According to George Dangerfield: 'It was an irrational mixture of Whig aristocrats, industrialists, dissenters, reformers, trade unionists, quacks and Mr. Lloyd George.'[3] This is a little unfair. What is unquestionable is that the Liberal Party faced a huge challenge to transition successfully from what it had been in the nineteenth century to what it needed to be in the twentieth.

The Conservative and Unionist Party faced challenges too. But its image was increasingly sharply defined. It was the party of the social elite and the establishment. It was the party of finance and much of big business. It was the party of the Union, of nationalism, of the Empire and of jingoism. It was the party generally of timidity on social reform and of safeguarding the economic interests of the rich. Soon, for a while at least, it was to become the party of tariffs and protection.

The Liberal Party also had an identity, but too much of it was framed by the politics of the nineteenth century, and some was not terribly popular – including Home Rule for Ireland and control of the drink trade. And while the 'advanced' and 'radical' elements of the party were promoting policies such as social insurance and improved working conditions, many traditional Liberals saw these as 'socialistic' measures involving excessive state interference in 'private' matters. The future of the Liberal Party lay in providing a progressive alternative to the Unionist Party. But not all its members shared this vision.

A measure of the Liberal Party's parlous state was that in the 1900 general election, it allowed an astonishing 163 of the 402 Unionist MPs to be elected unopposed. Liberal candidates contested just 402 of 670 seats. In England, only 302 candidates stood for the 456 seats. By contrast, the Unionists deployed 569 candidates – fighting almost all the seats outside Ireland. And this was no aberration. From 1852 to 1874, the Liberals had consistently fielded more candidates than the Unionists. But in the four elections from 1886 to 1900, the Liberals fell well behind – standing just 1,830 candidates, compared with 2,326 Unionists.

The Liberal Party was also struggling to deal effectively with the issue of working-class representation. In the 1870s, a small number of working-class and trade union candidates were chosen to stand as 'Lib–Lab' MPs – the first two of these were elected in the 1874 general election. Local Liberal associations would support candidates who were receiving financial backing from the trade unions and who were willing to take the Liberal 'whip' in Parliament. This had the benefit of securing funding at a time when election costs often fell on the candidates themselves, who were not always able to pay. The advent of the Lib–Lab MPs was an ideal way for the Liberal Party to broaden its appeal while cementing its position.

But in many constituencies, the traditional Liberal membership was unenthusiastic about backing trade unionists – fearing that their political priorities and ideology wouldn't fit with traditional Liberal doctrines. Only in the coal-mining areas, where the miners were so large in number that they could impose their own candidates, did working-class men win selection. In other seats, working-class Liberals found themselves being snubbed, including by the senior industrialists who exercised influence in many constituencies.

Some important Labour leaders of the future suffered these rebuffs – including Keir Hardie in 1888 and Ramsay MacDonald in 1894. At a time when the Liberals needed to widen their appeal, they were cutting themselves off from the newly enfranchised classes and the trade unions. It was a disastrous error.

An increasingly assertive trade union and socialist movement now began to question whether they were best served by relying upon the Liberal Party. Many also doubted whether the Lib–Lab MPs were sufficiently energetic in advocating policies that would benefit the working class.[4] In 1888, Keir Hardie stood unsuccessfully for Parliament in a by-election at Mid Lanarkshire, as an Independent Labour candidate. He had been rejected by local Liberals as too left-wing. He was eventually elected to Parliament in West Ham South, also as an Independent Labour candidate, in the 1892 general election, without Liberal competition. Two other Independent Labour MPs were also elected this year – one in Battersea and another in Middlesborough. Friedrich Engels, the close friend and ally of Karl Marx, noted that 'the spell which … the "great Liberal Party" cast over English workers for almost forty years is broken'.[5]

The separate path for Labour had now been established, and the Independent Labour Party was formed in 1893, with Hardie as its first chairman. Its policy agenda was notably more radical than that of the Lib–Labs, including to 'secure the collective and communal ownership of the means of production, distribution and exchange'.

But breaking through against the existing duopoly would not be easy. Hardie lost his seat in 1895, fighting not just a Conservative candidate but an antagonistic Liberal press, in a general election which saw twenty-eight Independent Labour Party candidates stand without any successes. Moderate ILP members were angry with Hardie, feeling he had antagonised the Liberal supporters, whose backing they needed. Ramsay MacDonald, who also stood for the ILP in this election, wrote privately to Herbert Samuel, blaming Hardie for his own defeat.

Just as MacDonald could see the risks in competing with the Liberals, many Liberals now started to wake up to the threat presented by the new ILP. In a speech in Manchester in May 1894, Lord Rosebery noted: 'An independent Labour organisation will not catch a single Tory vote. Such votes as it does carry away will be Liberal votes … it may hamstring and even cut the throat of the Liberal Party.' As in much else, Rosebery was wrong. ILP candidates would not take only Liberal votes. But it was true that in the long term Liberals had more to lose.

The foundation of the Independent Labour Party was a clear signal that liberalism was failing to either smother or effectively embrace new working-class political aspirations. The 1884 Reform Act had extended the entitlement to vote to around three quarters of the adult male population. Political parties needed to appeal to the new electors. And by 1895, there were already hundreds of Labour councillors, and several councils were Labour-run.

In 1900, the Labour Representation Committee (LRC) was formed to help sponsor parliamentary candidates. Union leaders and socialists joined together with the aim of establishing a 'distinct

Labour group in Parliament, who shall have their own whips, and agree upon their policy'. But in a nod to the need to work with Liberals, the new group agreed to 'embrace a readiness to co-operate with any party which for the time being may be engaged in promoting legislation in the direct interests of labour'.

These were some of the political challenges which confronted Herbert Gladstone, when his party leader, Henry Campbell-Bannerman, asked him to take over as Liberal Chief Whip in April 1899. Today, a Chief Whip's role is tightly focused on parliamentary party discipline. But in 1899, the responsibilities were far more onerous – including electoral strategy, raising political donations and finding sufficient parliamentary candidates. In short, it was a dreadful job.

Gladstone represented a northern constituency – Leeds West – so he was already acutely aware of the risks and opportunities around working-class representation. He held the seat against the Unionists but, in the last three contested elections, by wafer-thin majorities. As early as 1892, he had advocated more working-class MPs – upsetting the then Chief Whip, Arnold Morley. Gladstone's personal manifesto of 1892 was also relatively radical, advocating payment of MPs, better housing and a cut in working hours on the railways.

Now, as Chief Whip, Gladstone realised that he had inherited a very poisoned chalice. It was difficult to find parliamentary candidates. And party coffers were empty. In 1900, he was so desperate for campaign funds that he felt obliged to write to thirty personal friends, asking them for £2,500 each. Only seven bothered to reply, and some of these – rather ahead of their time – wrote back to say that donating money to the Liberal Party was a hopeless cause.[6]

In 1899, Gladstone had been sufficiently desperate for cash that he had met with both the Social Democratic Federation and the Independent Labour Party. But they had nothing to offer financially and were risky politically, as socialist-inclined organisations. The meeting ended without agreement. What was more tempting was candidates who possessed the support of the trade unions. The unions had money, and their members and leaders were pragmatic and willing to work with the Liberals, as the Lib–Lab MPs were already doing. By 1898, there were eleven of these, all taking the Liberal whip.

It was a Liberal trade unionist with a mining background, Sam Woods, who took the first step that led to the pact of 1903. Woods had been twice elected as a Lib–Lab MP but was sympathetic to the LRC. On 14 March 1900, he told Ramsay MacDonald that he ought to approach Gladstone, who he felt would be open to a deal to allow LRC candidates a free run in certain seats. Woods was right. Gladstone was content for fifteen LRC candidates to stand in the October 1900 election, most without Liberal competition.

For Gladstone, the LRC arrangement seemed a rare glimmer of good news. He was struggling not just with candidates and money but with an undynamic party leader. During the run-up to the 1900 general election, Campbell-Bannerman insisted on taking his regular summer rest break in the mud baths of Marienbad. Just three weeks before voting commenced on 26 September, Gladstone was grumpily writing to the Liberal leader in the Lords stating that he hoped Campbell-Bannerman might return home soon and do something to show his party that 'he is still alive'.

In any case, only two of the fifteen LRC candidates were elected in October 1900 – Keir Hardie in Merthyr Tydfil and Richard Bell in Derby. Both stood in two-member constituencies. Bell, secretary of the Amalgamated Society of Railway Servants, faced only one Liberal opponent, rather than the usual two. Hardie won his seat because of a split between two Liberal candidates. One was a strong opponent of the Boer War, the other a jingoistic supporter. The jingoist lost. Bell was supportive of the Liberal positions on most issues, but Hardie was a committed socialist and still a member of the Independent Labour Party. So, the first LRC MPs embedded the tension that would exist in the Labour Party for its next 120 years – was it a vehicle for radical socialism, or a moderate ally of the 'new liberalism'? For now, the LRC was an uneasy alliance of the unions, preoccupied by their own interests and seeing Liberals as allies in supporting these, and the Independent Labour Party, which was much more interested in building a socialist movement.

Ramsay MacDonald was again one of the thirteen unsuccessful LRC candidates in 1900. He stood in a two-member constituency in Leicester and was unable to prevail, given the presence of two Liberal candidates. One Liberal finished first, but the second lost out to a Unionist by just over 500 votes. Given that MacDonald had polled 4,164 votes, his intervention had cost the Liberals a seat. Both parties took note. The LRC would find it difficult to win if they stood against Liberals. But a Labour intervention could cost Liberals dearly.

The Liberals had again lost badly in 1900. Some supported the war in South Africa, while others were bitterly opposed. They were so weak that in September 1900, Herbert Gladstone had publicly admitted that 'the opposition are not in a position to furnish a strong government'. They finished with 183 MPs to the Unionists' 402. And where no Liberal candidates stood, the local party organisations were decaying – many now in a moribund state.

While the Liberals were weakening, the LRC was becoming increasingly influential. The 'Taff Vale judgment' of 1901 removed trade unions' legal protection from strike-related damages and strengthened the case for getting more LRC MPs into Parliament.

The affiliated membership of the LRC rose by 238,000 in the first six months of 1902 and by September 1902 exceeded 700,000. In December 1901, the miners had introduced a levy to set up a parliamentary fund to support more LRC candidates. And in 1902, the LRC followed up the initiative with work on a common fund into which union political levies could be paid. Suddenly, the LRC was going to have money – and a lot of it.

But after the electoral disappointment of 1900, MacDonald determined that he needed Liberal co-operation to break through. In March 1901, he secured a meeting with Jesse Herbert – Gladstone's political secretary. Herbert was sympathetic to Lib–Lab co-operation. His salary was being part-funded by a £300 annual donation from George Cadbury, the well-known Liberal businessman and philanthropist. Cadbury had also contributed £500 to ILP funds and in 1901 took over the *Daily News* (later the *News Chronicle*), which from then on became an advocate of stronger LRC–Liberal relations.[7]

In September 1901, the Liberals ran a candidate in the North-East Lanarkshire by-election against a local miner, Bob Smillie, who was surprisingly being backed by the Scottish Liberal Whip. Smillie stood as 'Scottish Workers' party. A Unionist won the election, seizing the seat from the Liberals, by around 1,000 votes. With 2,900 votes going to the third-placed Smillie, it seemed clear that division on the progressive wing of politics was costing seats.

In October, Gladstone told his constituents that he could 'come to terms with the leaders of the Labour party in the course of half a morning'. This was music to MacDonald's ears, and in the same month, MacDonald wrote a letter to *The Echo* newspaper, rejecting a proposal to establish a 'New Party' of trade unionists, the ILP and pro-Boer radicals, stating instead that radicals and Labour

candidates should co-operate by 'securing for each other the opportunities of contesting seats unhampered by third candidates.'[8]

In August 1902, the LRC secured its third MP when it won an unopposed by-election in Clitheroe, after the Liberals were convinced
by the strength of Labour, and by their own national leadership, not
to field a candidate. Local Liberals were invited to London to meet
Campbell-Bannerman and Gladstone and leant on to back the LRC
candidate.

It was in late 1902 and early 1903 that Lib–Lab plotting came to a
head. MacDonald told Jesse Herbert that he wanted a deal in which
the LRC would be allowed an uncontested run at a limited list of
seats, with the assumption being that they would allow the Liberals
primacy in all other constituencies. On 25 February 1903, MacDonald and Herbert met. MacDonald negotiated hard. He was offering little to the Liberals but asking for a free run in seats that the
Liberals would otherwise almost certainly lose. He pointed out the
financial resources now at his disposal, through the parliamentary
fund, and highlighted the overlap in Liberal/LRC policy positions.
He claimed the LRC now had 1 million members and a £100,000
campaign fund. He argued that LRC candidates could win over
working-class Tories. He allowed the risk of LRC candidates standing against Liberals to hang over the meeting. It was a subtle mix of
tempting promises and barely veiled threats.

Herbert, clearly keen, asked MacDonald to send him a list of the
constituencies he had in mind. He does not appear to have thought
of putting to MacDonald a list of Liberal demands, including that
LRC members would follow the Liberal whip or be engaged in some
other Lib–Lab embrace.

Instead, on 6 March, he sent Gladstone a note of his meeting,
backing MacDonald's pitch while also briefly highlighting the risks:

The official recognition of a separate group unpledged to support of the Liberal party, a group which will harass every government and whose representatives in Parliament will probably decline the Liberal whip, is not lightly to be given. It would be the recognition of a vital change in the organisation of parties.[9]

It would indeed.

But Herbert then rapidly and excitedly warmed to his main theme, suggesting that the LRC was only asking for a 'friendly concession by the party of the liberty to run their candidates unhampered by the presence of official candidates'. This should have been a red flag to any self-respecting Chief Whip. However, in the miserable circumstances of 1903, Herbert was making a strong pitch to Liberal self-interest: 'Ought the Liberal party to prefer defeat rather than assist in any way to foster the growing power of the Labour Party?' He argued that the 'severe individualists' within the Liberal Party who might be upset were 'very few' and unlikely to cost the party much in votes and financial support. Instead: 'The gain to the party through a working arrangement would be great and can be measured best by a comparison of the results of "no arrangement" with those of "an arrangement".'

Herbert then rehearsed MacDonald's argument: 1 million votes under supposed LRC influence; the alleged £100,000 fighting fund – which he noted as 'the most significant new fact in the situation'; their candidates were generally former Liberals. These were all temptations. But there were threats too. Crucially, should LRC supporters

be advised to vote against Liberal candidates … the Liberal Party would suffer defeat not only in those constituencies where LRC candidates fought, but also in almost every borough, and in many of the Divisions of Lancashire and Yorkshire. This would be the inevitable result of unfriendly action towards LRC candidates. They would be defeated, but so also should we be defeated.

Finally, letting the LRC fund the campaigns in thirty-five seats might well save the Liberal Party £15,000, and Gladstone a lot of letters to reticent supporters.

Gladstone clearly found this analysis convincing. In a modest number of constituencies, he and his party would be spared the task of finding candidates and raising funds. And if he could limit the number of LRC candidates, he might avoid Liberals losing their seats to Unionists. It might even save his own seat. Finally, if the LRC and Liberals were allies, Liberal candidates might benefit from some of those working-class LRC votes in constituencies where it was a straight Liberal–Unionist fight. For a Chief Whip of a bat- tered party that had finished behind the Unionists in four general elections in a row, the deal was tempting. Whether it made any long-term sense is another matter.

A crucial meeting between MacDonald and Gladstone soon followed, and on 13 March 1903 Gladstone sent a secret minute to Campbell-Bannerman.[10] This started by noting there was 'no com- pact, alliance, agreement or bargain'. There were also 'no material points of difference' in the policies of the two parties. Instead, 'we are ready to ascertain from qualified and responsible Labour lead- ers how far Labour candidates can be given an open field against a common enemy'. In an extraordinary statement of generosity, naivety or sophisticated political tactics, the memorandum stated in its third point that 'we are ready to do this as an act of friend- ship and without any stipulation of any kind'. This was 'because we realise that an accession of strength to Labour representation in the House of Commons is not only required by the country in the interests of Labour but that it would increase the progressive forces generally and the Liberal party as the best available instrument of progress'. This was very dangerous ground. It seemed to suggest that only Labour could represent a portion of the working class. It was, perhaps, to be the first and last occasion of unreciprocated generosity in the long history of Liberal–Labour relations.

The memorandum went on to explain what the 'non-agreement' might mean in practice. Essentially, Gladstone was offering to use the influence of the national Liberal Party to persuade certain local Liberal associations to 'abstain from nominating a Liberal candidate' and to unite in supporting the Labour candidate provided he was 'recognised and competent' and supported 'the general objects of the Liberal party'.

The memorandum noted that the LRC 'propose to run about thirty candidates'. This excluded Scotland, MPs connected to the Miners' Federation (who were proposing to run fifteen to eighteen candidates of their own) and candidates backed by 'socialist bodies'.

And then it was down to the brass tacks. There followed a list of twenty-three parliamentary seats 'where there is no difficulty'. Only one ('Merthyr') was in Wales, and most of the others were in the north and Midlands. Five seats were described as 'adjustable', and another five were 'claimed by LRC and difficult', alongside a helpful list of six that might be 'available alternatives'. Four seats were named that were 'Labour seats not recognised by LRC'. The memorandum considered it 'quite possible' that Labour be given an unchallenged run in thirty seats, with the miners having the same in another twelve.

In total, the list included fifty-five parliamentary seats where

Gladstone was considering some sort of arrangement to hand the seats to non-Liberal Party candidates. That amounted to 8.2 per cent of the MPs in the House of Commons. The document finished by noting that where Liberal candidates did stand, despite a pact, they would have to be supported by the party, 'but the Liberal Council will use every legitimate effort' to give Labour its unopposed run.

It all looked like a fantastic deal for the LRC and 'Labour', but it was not yet formally agreed. Over the next three months, there were at least seven further meetings between Herbert and MacDonald.[11] A revised list of seats was drawn up on 7 August.

While the talks were ongoing, there were two key parliamentary by-elections. In March 1903, Labour won Woolwich, with a solid majority of 3,000. There was no Liberal candidate, and the Conservatives had held the seat continuously since its creation. It looked like Labour had snatched away a Unionist seat by tapping into a vote that had not previously been Liberal – another argument for the pact.

On 24 July 1903, there was a by-election in Barnard Castle, County Durham. This time there was both a Liberal candidate and a Unionist, but the LRC's Arthur Henderson (a former Liberal election agent) beat the Liberal into third place. Henderson won by only forty-seven votes, with the electorate split three ways – LRC 35.4 per cent, Conservative 35 per cent and Liberal 29.6 per cent. The seat had previously been Liberal for several decades, and this was the first LRC seat ever won against both other parties.

Gladstone was content to see the LRC gain the seat. He ensured some low-key Liberal support for Henderson and would have preferred no Liberal candidate. This caused the angry chairman of the Northern Liberal Association, Samuel Storey, to complain to the *Daily News* on 7 July that Liberal leaders had 'cheerfully cast

Barnard Castle to the wolves in the hope, perhaps of keeping them from their own doors'. He went on to warn that they were 'nursing into life a serpent which would sting their party to death ... The effect of surrendering to this new party will be the destruction of organised liberalism here in the North.'[12] Other Liberals, including Morley, were also doubtful of the tactics, and nineteen of the twenty-three presidents of Liberal associations in north-east England opposed any further deals.[13]

The LRC was now up to five seats. It was also becoming more independent minded. In February 1903, its conference had voted to insist that LRC candidates and MPs should not identify themselves with other parties and had even decided not to invite the Lib–Labs to join their Commons grouping. But despite this, the long period of secret Lib–Lab talks bore fruit, and the Leicester Isolation Hospital meeting of 6 September sealed the deal that had been sketched out six months earlier.

MacDonald had told Keir Hardie what he was up to but had neither briefed nor consulted his LRC committee. It suited both the Liberals and LRC to keep the deal secret and relatively informal. MacDonald later wrote his own, undated, rather coy summary of the negotiations for his private record.[14] He claimed that 'there was no bargain struck', explaining:

I told them what seats we were determined to fight ... The impression they gave me was that they [agreed] that we should have a fair chance of representation. Their attitude no doubt did influence me in opposing wild-cat candidatures and in one or two constituencies I told them there would be no Labour candidates because there was no Labour organisation. I repeat, however, that information was not given in any way as a quid pro quo.

Once the deal was done, MacDonald acted quickly to get candidates in place. By the end of January 1904, the LRC had selected thirty-eight. Twenty-seven were in single-member seats, and seventeen of these would be unopposed by Liberals. Eleven would be in two-member seats, and only two of these would have Liberal opponents.

MacDonald was determined that he would finally make it into Parliament, and after months of scheming, the Leicester Liberals decided to run only one candidate in their two-member constituency, giving MacDonald a clear run. Leicester had appeared in the Gladstone memorandum of 13 March 1903 in the list of five 'adjustable' seats. It had now been 'adjusted'.

For MacDonald, all was going well. To deliver an LRC breakthrough, he had needed to deal with the Liberals and see off the tribalists in his party. But he did not want the LRC to get too close to the larger 'progressive' party. He set out his vision in the New Liberal Review, in September 1903: 'If the new Labour movement were simply an attempt of Trade Unionists to use their political power for purely sectional ends ... it would be a menace ... Trade Unionism ... must set [its] demands into a system of national well-being.' He argued that a Labour movement was not simply about representing 'Labour' in Parliament. It was all about 'opinions, not ... social status'. The old agenda of seeking to 'thrust working-men candidates upon Liberal Associations' was now dead.[15]

MacDonald saw the Liberals as a decaying and outdated political force – an ageing biological organism in which the 'structures of the body are hardened and thickened, the saps of life flow more and more slowly ... until at length motion ceases altogether'.[16] His view was that the Liberal Party was stuck in the politics of the nineteenth century. It had fulfilled its mission but now needed to give way to a bolder and more socially progressive party: 'Lower forms merge into higher forms ... socialism, the stage which follows liberalism, retains everything of value in liberalism by virtue of its being the hereditary heir of liberalism.'

David Lloyd George, by now a senior Liberal politician, began to see the risk to his party, noting in a speech in November 1904:

> We have a great Labour Party sprung up. Unless we can prove ... that there is no necessity for a separate party to press forward the legitimate claims of Labour, you will find that ... the Liberal Party will be practically wiped out and that, in its place, you will get a more extreme and revolutionary party.

In the Commons, the LRC MPs were now getting closer to the Lib–Labs, and in the last few months of the 1900–06 parliament, these members sat together in the Commons for the first time.[17] But the ILP socialists remained nervous that 'Labour' should not become too close to the Liberals. They saw the Liberals as just another 'capitalist' party. At some stage, the Labour grouping would need to decide. Was their future as a separate, socialist party? Or as the 'radical', working-class wing of the Liberals?

Gladstone, meanwhile, was doing what he could to create other Liberal allies – this time amongst the Unionists. He dined with Winston Churchill in January 1904, and Churchill reported to a friend that Gladstone was willing to help save the seats of fifteen Unionist free traders. Churchill would soon join the Liberals and decades later seek to reciprocate the tactical support offered, by standing down candidates against Liberal MPs.

By 1905, the Conservatives had been in office for most of the past twenty years. They were deeply split after Joseph Chamberlain launched his tariff reform campaign in 1903, which was soon adopted by the Unionist Party. This allowed the Liberals, and the LRC, to unite behind a populist campaign to resist 'food taxes'. In November, the Unionist leader, Arthur Balfour, resigned. Shortly afterwards, Parliament was dissolved. Voting would take place from 12 January to 8 February 1906.

These were not yet the days of the detailed fifty-page election manifestos. Instead, Campbell-Bannerman published his own short, discursive and underwhelming address. After a rant about the Unionist economic record, and high taxes, it eventually alighted on the issue of protection. And – other than a mention of 'the time-honoured principles of liberalism… peace, economy, self-government, and civil and religious liberty', that was about it. There was certainly no programme of social reform to compete with an upcoming Labour Party.

The LRC published a standard election address for all candidates, which was also brief, amounting to less than a side. Its case was simple – 'Labour' needed representation in Parliament. There was a strong but vague social policy pitch and clear opposition to protection. This might be a Labour Party in the making, but it was not yet the party of nationalisation and fully fledged socialism – 'The LRC's political positions were virtually indistinguishable from those of advanced liberals.'[18] And that is how Ramsay MacDonald wanted it – nothing to scare off Liberal voters, Liberal associations or the wider electorate.

MacDonald largely delivered his part of the 1903 pact. But it was still tough to get Labour to withdraw their candidates in all the non-target seats, and even Herbert Gladstone came close to facing an LRC challenge in his Leeds West constituency.[19]

Soon it was clear that the long era of Conservative/Unionist government was over. 1906 delivered a Liberal landslide, on a mighty swing of almost 12 per cent (measured in seats contested in both 1900 and 1906). The Unionists secured just 156 seats – their worst ever outcome and way down on the 1900 total of 402. Only three Unionist Cabinet members out of seventeen survived. With 43.4 per cent of the votes, they had just 23.4 per cent of the seats.

The Liberals boosted their vote share from 45 per cent to 49 per cent, and their seat numbers soared from 183 to 397. They had fielded 528 candidates, instead of the 402 in 1900. Only thirteen Unionists were elected unopposed, not the 163 of 1900. Gladstone's hard work in finding candidates, raising money and improving the party's electoral machine had all helped. And he targeted resources effectively – over half of the money raised was spent in just a fifth of the seats.

There was no doubt of the pact's value to the LRC. It wholly vindicated MacDonald's strategy. He had stood just fifty candidates, thirty-one with no Liberal opponents. Twenty-nine in total had been elected – all but five with Liberal co-operation. Twenty-three of the twenty-nine were trade union sponsored and six were Independent Labour Party candidates. Of the LRC members, around half could be considered socialists, and the others were trade unionists of less radical outlook. There were also now seventeen Lib–Lab trade union MPs, of whom thirteen were miners. It was a massive breakthrough.

The LRC vote share was just 4.8 per cent, but that had yielded 4.3 per cent of the parliamentary seats. MacDonald had ensured that votes for the LRC had really counted. By contrast, in most of the seats where three candidates stood, Labour finished last. The swing in the fifty-six seats Labour fought was 15 per cent on average – greater than the national swing away from the Unionists. But this was partly because many of these seats were in industrial areas where the swing was larger anyway. Only in Lancashire was there some evidence that Labour candidates were doing better than Liberals.

This time, MacDonald had benefited from his own work. He was elected in Leicester, with the Liberals giving full public backing to 'their good friend, Mr. MacDonald'. The love-in had delivered both seats – relegating the Unionist to third position, well behind the Liberal on 14,745 and MacDonald on 14,685. Of these votes, 13,999 had been cast for both the Liberal and LRC candidate. In Leicester, the Lib–Lab alliance was very real. It looked like a win–win for both parties. But the Leicester Liberals, assisted by the party's own Chief Whip, had just placed into Parliament the man who in barely fifteen years would become Labour's first Prime Minister and who would help reduce their party to political rubble.

If MacDonald was pleased with the election outcome, so were the Liberal leaders. Jesse Herbert wrote to Gladstone on 6 February, asking: 'Was there ever such a justification of a policy by results?' In Lancashire, the sixteen LRC candidates had won thirteen seats from the Unionists, in a county where the Liberals were weak and where there was a strong Unionist working-class voting tradition. Meanwhile, Herbert noted that only two seats nationally had been lost by the Liberals due to LRC candidates, and only one LRC-favoured seat had been lost due to Liberal intervention. It was a pact that had served both parties well. Herbert contrasted the results in England with the situation in Scotland, where there was no Lib–LRC deal. In Scotland, there were ten three-way fights, and Herbert argued that this had cost his party six seats.

Herbert also thought that the pact would solidify LRC support for the new Liberal government. He described the LRC MPs as 'strong-ly favourable to the Government. There are not more than seven irreconcilable ... they are very friendly with me.' Gladstone agreed with Herbert and wrote to Campbell-Bannerman on 21 January, concluding that the pact was 'the prime cause of the abnormality of the Liberal victory'. He was also content with the politics of LRC MPs, noting: 'There is no sign of any violent forward movement – the dangerous element does not amount to a dozen.'[20]

But while Herbert and Gladstone celebrated, other Liberals again questioned the wisdom of the pact. The agent at Clitheroe, where the party had again stood aside for the LRC, wrote to the chairman of the Liberal Election Committee to complain that 'if the Liberal Party can only be made strong by giving away its strongest posi-tions, all I can say is that its day of usefulness is gone'.

And six days after Jesse Herbert's celebratory letter to Gladstone, on 15 February, the twenty-nine LRC MPs and one Lib–Lab met at Westminster and established themselves as the 'Labour Party', with their own organisation and whips, and Keir Hardie as chairman. They took up seats on the opposition benches. The other Lib–Lab MPs, meanwhile, irritated by the partial theft of their branding, re-named themselves as the 'Trade Union Labour Group', within the Liberal Party.

Was the Gladstone–MacDonald pact the naive gift to an emerg-ing Labour Party that it looked to be? In the short run, the pact had helped the Liberals. As Searle has noted: 'Almost all the seats where Liberal candidates stood down in 1906 were seats where the Liberals had been unable to win in 1900.'[21] Indeed, in only two of the 'pact' seats did the Liberals give up seats they had won in 1900, and both had already been lost to the LRC in by-elections.

Brack concludes that:

In retrospect, it became clear that the Liberals would have won in 1906 without the … pact, and as twenty-four of Labour's twenty-nine members were to be elected in the absence of a Liberal, it was easy to argue that the party had made an unforced error in helping its rival to its first real foothold in Parliament. However, this was not foreseen at the time, and the fear of splitting the progressive vote was a real one…[22]

But it is not quite true to say that the 'unforced error' wasn't seen at the time – some Liberals were profoundly worried by the deal. In the short term, the Hospital Pact was a win–win for both the LRC and the Liberals. But in the longer term, it posed a major threat to the Liberal Party.

Early in the new parliament, Labour scored several policy successes. The Liberals accepted the TUC's proposed Trade Union Bill and overturned the Taff Vale judgment. Labour pressed for and secured a new Workmen's Compensation Act, as well as School Meals and Medical Inspection Acts. During this period, Labour did well in by-elections, winning several seats – including some from Liberals. But 1906–07 was the high point of Labour influence. Over the rest of the parliament, it was the Liberals who dictated the scale, pace and nature of progress towards economic and social reform. Labour MPs ended up providing ballast for Liberal-led battles on the 1909 Budget, Lords reform, National Insurance and (eventually) Home Rule.

By April 1908, a terminally ill Campbell-Bannerman had been replaced as Liberal leader by Herbert Henry Asquith. Asquith was an impressive politician who had the ability to unite the Liberal team and serve as a bridge between the Liberalism of the nineteenth and twentieth centuries. He would later describe himself as 'a financier of a respectable and more or less conservative type', and he was a good frontman for a government that would prove to be far more radical on social policy than past Liberal administrations.

Asquith appointed Lloyd George as Chancellor and sent Churchill (who joined from the Unionists in May 1904) to be President of the Board of Trade. Both were advocates of the 'New Liberalism' that would put social policy centre stage. Asquith and Lloyd George were the Tony Blair and Gordon Brown of their era – Asquith providing the safe, soothing and respectable leadership, while Lloyd George delivered the provocative radicalism. The Liberals had stumbled on a potentially winning team that might help fend off the Labour challenge. Beatrice Webb would soon observe that 'Lloyd George and the Radicals have out-trumped the Labour Party', with policies such as labour exchanges, pensions and National Insurance.

Lloyd George might have been the saviour who rescued his party from an era of irrelevance. But the Liberal Party's fate was now in the hands of a highly ambitious man with a rather casual attitude to political parties. As Hattersley has noted: 'Party solidarity was never a virtue which David Lloyd George admired. What loyalty he possessed was to ideas.'[23]

For now, the Liberal government would need to be bold and effective if it was to hold on to power. But by the winter of 1908–09, the House of Lords had blocked a large part of its policy agenda, while a slump in trade caused unemployment to double from 3 per cent to 6 per cent and then go on rising to 9 per cent by the end of 1908. Troubled economic times meant troubled political times. Liberals were suddenly losing by-elections – by mighty swings of around 10 per cent. Liberal knees were wobbling. It looked like the landslide of 1906 would be followed by a rout in 1910–11.

Lloyd George and Asquith now planned a comeback that would

lead to the famous Budget of 1909, which so angered the Unionist-dominated House of Lords that they would overturn usual practice and veto the new taxes on the rich. An election was needed to break the deadlock, and Parliament was prorogued on 3 December.

This time there would be no new formal Lib–Lab deal. The hope of the Liberal leadership in 1909–10 was that it could contain the growth of Labour – continuing informal co-operation but stopping Labour seizing new seats. In 1909, the Lib–Labs had moved over to join Labour after the miners had decided that their interests were not being well served by the Liberals. Many mine owners were Liberals, and tensions over wages and working conditions were rising. This was an important political event as the miners had major influence in around ninety constituencies, of which the Liberals still represented around sixty.[24] If the Liberals were losing the loyalty of the industrial working class, this would have serious implications. In any case, the Liberals were still willing to allow these Lib–Labs, and the Labour MPs elected in 1906, to go unchallenged.

Labour would also be permitted to stand unopposed in a further handful of seats where it had been the clear or only opponent of the Unionists in 1906. But if Labour tried to compete with the Liberals in other seats, they would be fought hard, and this might invite retaliation in some of the seats earmarked for Labour. The Liberals had figured out that with the Unionists now on the rise, any further Labour gains were likely to be at Liberal expense.

Labour had its reasons, in any case, for wanting the Liberals to prevail in 1910. Late in 1909, the House of Lords had decided, in the Osborne judgment, that it was illegal for a trade union to contribute financially to a political party. This was potentially a huge blow to Labour, and they needed a Liberal victory to reverse it.

The elections of 1910 – one in January on the issue of the Budget and another in December on the powers of the House of Lords – would not be easy ones for securing a big Labour breakthrough. Both were triggered by major clashes between the Liberals and Unionists, in which Labour was inevitably eclipsed and obliged to row in behind Asquith and Lloyd George. In their election addresses, Labour candidates almost universally led on the 'Liberal' issues of the Lords, free trade, pensions and the Budget. They were more likely than Liberal candidates to highlight the right to work, nationalisation, payment of members, electoral reform and Home Rule. But social reform and pensions were prioritised by a similar proportion of Labour and Liberal candidates.[25]

Asquith knew that one highly probable outcome of the January 1910 campaign was that his party would lose its majority and be dependent on Labour and the Irish Nationalists. He faced a highly partisan press that were heavily aligned with the Unionists. A nod and a wink during the campaign that Home Rule might be back on his agenda helped to secure the Irish flank. And there was little doubt that Labour would ally with the Liberals.

Asquith's pithy but impressive manifesto was complemented by a successful speech on 10 December 1909 at the Albert Hall. The former put the Budget, the Lords and free trade centre-stage, but it also mentioned pensions and social reform, funded by progressive taxation. The latter anticipated Clinton and Blair by talking of the state lending a 'helping hand' – a clear indication of the importance of the New Liberalism. The Liberals had begun at last to respond to the changed political context.

Labour's January 1910 manifesto was also pro-Budget, pro-free trade and anti-Lords. It positioned the party as the advanced guard of reform – claiming it had 'demonstrated the value of the Labour Party acting on independent lines'. In the first snappy soundbites to appear in a UK party manifesto, it concluded with: 'The land for the people. The wealth for the wealth producers. Down with privilege. Up with the people.' That was sounding more radical than in 1906 but was not yet parting company from 'New Liberalism'.

Labour's campaign was limited to just seventy-eight candidates for the 670 seats. These were largely in the industrial north of England. It was still acting essentially as a radical, working-class offshoot of the Liberal family. MacDonald continued to work to ensure that individual constituencies stuck with his strategy. The right of the party, including in many mining areas, wanted more Lib–Lab deals. But the radical elements sought a more independent line. In 1909, at the ILP conference, local branches had made clear they wanted freedom to run candidates against the Liberals, regardless of national understandings. MacDonald and others threatened to resign from the party if this occurred. The conference eventually followed its leaders, but the vote was 244 to 146, demonstrating how widespread concern was. A grumpy MacDonald stayed away from the conference for the next five years in retaliation.[26]

Of the seventy-eight seats Labour fought in January 1910, fifty-one had no Liberal opponents. This included the twenty-nine seats won by the LRC in 1906, nine seats won by Lib–Lab miners in that year, four won in by-elections, three seats not fought by the LRC in 1906 and six seats that the LRC had lost in 1906 but where Labour either fought alone or were in a strong second to the Unionist.

Of the twenty-seven seats where Labour stood but the Liberals also contested, three were previously Labour, eighteen had not been fought by the LRC in 1906, and six were in seats previously fought by the LRC but where they were not the obvious challengers to the Unionists. In these twenty-seven three-cornered fights, twenty seats were currently held by Liberal MPs, and six were Liberal–Unionist marginals. In all these seats, then, Lib–Lab competition risked letting the Unionists in.

When the results emerged, from 15 January onwards, it was clear that there were huge regional variations, with the Liberal vote holding up in the north, but the Unionists doing much better in the south and Midlands. There was a big 'southern swing' of up to 10 per cent in some counties, but the average national swing of 4.4 per cent was not enough to deliver a Unionist majority, and the two big parties ended with a photo finish – 274 Liberal seats to 272 Unionist. But there was good news for Asquith. Labour had failed to break through in every one of the twenty-seven seats contested with the Liberals, and in twenty-three of these the Labour candidate finished last. Meanwhile, both parties were benefiting from explicit mutually co-operative voting in two-member seats. In most seats, where such voting was possible, over 90 per cent of the Liberal–Labour vote transferred to the other party.

As Asquith had anticipated, Labour and the Irish now held the balance of power. With their support, Asquith still had a majority of 112. But the Liberals had lost many seats. Lloyd George had hoped that his campaign could mobilise the working classes against the wealthy landlords and Unionist House of Lords, without upsetting other voters. But Herbert Samuel noted that 'it was the abiding problem of Liberal statesmanship to rouse the enthusiasm of the working classes without frightening the middle classes. It can be done but has not been done this time.'[27]

Labour was down from the forty-five seats they held going into the election to forty. The increase from the 1906 total of twenty-nine was entirely due to the Lib–Lab miners having joined the Labour group. Labour gained one seat from the Unionists but lost six to them. With more Labour candidates, their vote share was up to 7 per cent. In the Commons, Labour continued to support the Liberals – indeed, during 1910, the Labour MPs moved from the opposition side of the House and took up seats on the government benches. MacDonald was happy to stay close to the Liberal Party, for now. Hardie was not, and amongst the wider Labour Party there was criticism that the Liberals were being given too easy a ride.

The January 1910 election settled the issue of the Budget. But it did not resolve the issue of the Lords. That led to a further general election in December 1910, which delivered an almost identical result. Labour won around the same number of seats as in the January election (forty-two), but this time had fielded only fifty-six candidates against the seventy-eight of January. It had learned to target its resources on seats where its organisation, finances and Lib–Lab relations were conducive to success. Of those forty-two Labour candidates who were successful, not even one had triumphed in a genuine three-cornered fight. Three were unopposed. Eleven were in two-member seats in an arrangement with a Liberal candidate. Twenty-six were in single-member seats, without Liberal opposition, and just two were in straight fights with the Liberals.

This was good news for the Liberals. Having 'nursed into life the serpent', they now seemed to be controlling it rather than being 'stung to death'. Perhaps, in time, the animal might even be tamed and become part of the Liberal Zoo? As Neal Blewett has written:

Labour had launched a cautious exploratory attack on Liberal territory in January, which was almost totally repulsed. The result was less than a dozen clashes with the Liberals in December, again mostly disappointing. Liberal–Labour relations in the elections of 1910 had been dominated by the Liberal tactic of containment. Few tactical operations in electoral history can have been so completely successful.[28]

The Unionists had, as in January, secured more votes than their opponents in the December 1910 election, polling 46.6 per cent to the Liberals' 44.2 per cent (and Labour's 6.4 per cent). But the continued informal Lib–Lab arrangements had ensured that the Liberals still had a microscopic lead in seats – 272 to the Unionists' 271. Pugh suggests that the Unionists would have had an overall majority this time had the Liberals and Labour not avoided many three-way contests.[29] Co-operation was much more important in December 1910 than it was in 1906.

Meanwhile, if Labour and the Liberals found the pacts messy and controversial, their opponents were fearful of them. After the January 1910 election, Austen Chamberlain had written to Balfour concluding:

> The combination of the Liberal and Labour parties is much stronger than the Liberal Party would be if there were no third party in existence. Many men who would in that case have voted for us, voted on this occasion as the Labour Party told them – i.e., for the Liberals. The existence of the third party deprives us of the full benefits of the 'swing of the pendulum'.

The only dark cloud on the horizon, for the Liberals, was the geographic distribution of seats. The Liberals and Labour held just 39 per cent of the seats in the south of England. The Unionists were strong in the south but weaker elsewhere. The Liberals were becoming more dependent on the working-class vote and on seats in Scotland, Wales and the industrial north. If Labour could capture more of this vote, the Liberals would be in trouble – squeezed between a Unionist Party mopping up the middle-class southern vote and Labour in the north. Could Liberalism adapt its leadership and programme to contain this risk? Or would Labour break away, outbid the Liberals on social policy and steal the support of the working class? In 1911, the answer to this question was not immediately obvious or inevitable.

Would the Liberals even concede some measure of electoral reform to Labour, perhaps the Alternative Vote, to seek to embed a system that simultaneously allowed for both competition and co-operation against the Unionist foe? Relations between Mac-Donald and the Liberal leaders – Asquith and Lloyd George – were generally good. MacDonald was still intent on pursuing his longer-term strategy of replacing the Liberals but, in the meantime, was willing to work with Asquith to secure social reforms, promote legislation helpful to the Labour and trade union cause and get more Labour MPs elected.

By late 1911, Labour had nudged the Liberals into introducing the payment of MPs – important for a party whose members generally lacked independent financial means.

But the agenda of the December 1910 parliament was again dominated by Liberal-led priorities – including Lords reform, the Insurance Acts of 1911 and the Home Rule and Welsh Church Bills of 1912. Labour had to wait until 1913 for the Osborne judgment to be overturned in a new Trade Union Act. But when the Trade Union Act was passed, it gave a huge boost to Labour, which the Liberals naively seem not to have considered – it restored the ability of the unions to fund the political activities of the Labour Party. Union members who disliked this had to actively 'contract out'.

From 1911 onwards, the Liberals were beginning to lose by-elections, and their position in the Commons was increasingly less secure. There was speculation that some senior Liberals favoured a coalition, and in June 1911 a press report claimed that Asquith might offer MacDonald the leadership of a newly established Ministry of Labour. This seemed without foundation. But by 22 October, MacDonald was confiding to his diary that he had met Lloyd George for breakfast, and the Chancellor had asked him whether he would contemplate joining a coalition government. 'Not just yet,' he noted.[30]

By 13 November 1911, the Liberal Chief Whip – the Master of Elibank – was also courting the Labour leader, asking if he would consider a coalition 'at the next election'. The very next day, the result of a by-election in Oldham was announced, in a seat that had elected two Liberals in December 1910. This time the national Labour Party backed a Labour candidate – feeling that the two-member constituency should be 'shared' with the Liberals. Labour picked the general secretary of the textile workers' union – a clever choice in a seat where thousands of textile workers lived. The divided Lib–Lab vote let the Unionist in. In his diary on 15 November, MacDonald recorded: 'Liberals very angry about Oldham ... Elibank says Premier very much upset ... Tells me he is to fight three of my men...'[31]

A decade later, Arthur Henderson would claim that in 1910 or 1911, MacDonald had been invited by Lloyd George to join a three-party coalition with him and with Balfour, to remove Asquith. There is no evidence that can show whether this is true, but from 1910, Lloyd George had been floating the idea of coalitions, and he was eventually to deliver one in 1916. And it would not have been at all surprising if in mid-1910 he had sounded out MacDonald about joining the Liberal–Unionist coalition that he was known to have floated at that time.[32] But it is also quite possible that the reference in MacDonald's diary of 22 October 1911 was to a different coalition pitch of Lloyd George's – a pitch for a Liberal–Labour coalition. Given Lloyd George's penchant for political scheming and coalition government, it would be unwise to rule out any possibilities.

Had a Lib–Lab coalition been formed, in 1911 or shortly afterwards, political history might have been very different. It could have been an effective way of smothering Labour, and seeking to fold it into the Liberal Party, before it became a major threat. But if this was the plan, it failed.

By 1911, real wages had been falling for five years, and strikes broke out in the docks and on the railways. Labour broadly backed the strikers. Churchill and Lloyd George did not, and their approach was increasingly bellicose. MacDonald ended up brokering a deal between the unions and the government. It angered some in the Labour Party, but MacDonald wanted to show that his party could act in the wider community interest.

By 1912, there were more dock and coal strikes. In March, Lloyd George again asked MacDonald to consider a coalition government. MacDonald would be in the Cabinet, with a small number of Labour MPs being given junior ministerial roles. MacDonald told him this was 'impossible'. But the Liberals persisted, and on 24 June 1912, MacDonald was again approached by the Master of Elibank, who ushered him into a small room behind the Speaker's Chair in the Commons. This was another forceful attempt at courtship. 'Are you not wasting your influence? Will you not join the Cabinet? Of course, it would be high office...' Elibank laid it on with a trowel. This time the pitch seemed to be more about MacDonald joining the government than delivering a Lib–Lab coalition. But MacDonald was firm. He was not prepared to give unconditional support to the government and noted it would be hugely damaging to Labour if he did. Indeed, it would have been, which is no doubt why the offer was made.

By 1912–13, MacDonald was exhausted – worn down by managing both wings of his party. In June 1913, the other MP in his constituency, a Liberal, stepped down and triggered a by-election. Leicester politics were now keenly contested, with the town council consisting of eighteen Liberals, sixteen Unionists and fourteen Labour. Labour had got used to local competition with the Liberals and did not wish to give any Liberal a free pass. MacDonald wanted the existing Lib–Lab arrangement to continue, but his local Labour Party met to consider 'whether or not the two sections of the Capitalist Army should be fought'. Given that billing, it can have been no surprise that they voted 67–8 to contest the election, undermining MacDonald's pact in his own backyard.

Labour's Arthur Henderson was now sent to Leicester to change the local party's mind. He made a robust pitch for loyalty. He warned of a split vote letting the Unionists in. He underlined Labour's interest in supporting the government to deliver the Trade Union Act and Irish Home Rule. He talked through the voting figures from the previous four elections. He warned that a government defeat might prompt an early election. It was a long meeting that didn't end until 11 p.m. And for Henderson, it was a complete waste of time. At the end, a motion was passed unanimously to ignore his views and fight the seat. Somehow, he even managed to mislay the votes of the eight people who had opposed the contest just two days before.

MacDonald was fuming and made clear that he would stand down as Labour candidate at the next election unless the decision was reversed. The news of his strong views leaked in the constituency, causing more anger and division. Labour's National Executive

Committee now refused to endorse the ILP candidate. Instead, a candidate for the British Socialist Party stepped forward. On election day, 27 June, the Liberal scraped back in, beating the Unionist by 1,584 votes, with 2,580 votes going to the Socialist Party candidate. MacDonald was relieved but angry. In July, he warned of the political consequences of unnecessarily splitting the vote – the Unionists would gain and most of their policies were much worse than those of the Liberals. But his party was getting tougher to manage, and Keir Hardie intervened to say it had been a 'great mistake' not to fight in Leicester.

Labour was growing in strength and the party was eager to fight more seats. But it was not yet strong enough to break through in three-party parliamentary contests, and if the next election was 'open season', then this could only benefit the Unionists. In 1914, Labour had only sixty-five robust local party organisations – it was still reliant on deals and understandings with the Liberals. Vernon Bogdanor has concluded that 'competing with the Liberals would have seen Labour eliminated as a serious factor in politics'.[33] From 1912 to 1914, Labour came last in every single by-election where all three parties stood – losing even the three seats they had held. By 1913, there was not a single surviving Labour MP who had won his seat in a fight with both other parties.

For the Labour leadership, this was the uncomfortable reality of their position. But for many Labour members, it was too much to accept. In April 1914, Labour's National Executive voted to reject any renewed electoral understanding and ramp up the number of candidates at the next general election to between 120 and 130. It is unclear if this was just a negotiating position, and MacDonald did not support it.

MacDonald wanted Labour to eventually displace the Liberals, but he was now unwillingly beginning to consider whether this might be through the radical forces in both parties coming together. He was an opponent of proportional representation, even though this was the policy of every other European socialist party, and even though both AV and PR were now widely popular across the Labour Party and the unions.

Electoral reform would be a defining issue in future Lib–Lab relations. And in 1908, Asquith had agreed to establish a Royal Commission on Electoral Systems. This proposed to move to the Alternative Vote, as the 'best method of remedying the most serious defect which a single-member system can possess – the return of minority candidates'. But the issue did not gain political traction – the Liberals were now doing well under the existing electoral system, and most Labour supporters were focused on breaking through under First Past the Post. The Labour Party was too divided to give evidence to the commission, but between 1908 and 1914, some key members started to take more interest in AV – it seemed to offer a greater prospect of them gaining seats while retaining an informal tactical arrangement with the Liberals.

MacDonald wanted to continue with his existing strategy. He was worried about empowering small parties and did not want PR encouraging a splintering of left-wing political groupings. Others, such as Labour MP Philip Snowden, disagreed, seeing PR as a way of ending dependency on deals with the Liberals and allowing Labour to campaign on its own socialist platform. At the 1911 conference, MacDonald's view prevailed – a motion backing PR was defeated by 1,255,000 votes to 97,500.

However, the TUC supported PR at its own 1911 conference by a majority of three to one, and the ILP gave backing to the policy in 1913. In the same year, Labour's National Executive Committee published a report on PR and AV. Roberts, Labour's Chief Whip, and W. C. Anderson, chair of the Independent Labour Party, both argued for PR. They were worried that the Conservatives and Liberals might use AV to gang up against Labour – two 'capitalist' parties uniting to defeat a socialist party.[34] They saw Single Transferable Vote (STV) as an opportunity to break away from the Liberals and argued that STV meant 'equality in value of the vote'. But at the party conference in Lambeth in January 1913, there was no clear decision on whether to back AV or PR.

MacDonald wasn't budging on PR, but he did now appear to back AV, noting it would 'enable us to fight every seat we had a reasonable chance of winning and in doing so we would not be hampered by the cry that we were splitting the Liberal vote'. Labour's 120-year dalliance with AV had commenced in earnest. However, in 1914, Labour debated electoral reform again and there was still no consensus for change. PR (in the form of STV) was defeated by 1,387,000 votes to 704,000. AV was also rejected by 1,324,000 to 632,000, though, on this occasion, MacDonald had supported it.

With Labour support and seats seeming to have peaked from 1910, the Parliamentary Labour Party now supported a Bill to deliver the Alternative Vote. But it did not progress. Labour in 1914 was still a small party, heavily dependent on Liberal co-operation for many of its parliamentary seats and playing second fiddle to a Liberal Party that was beginning to embrace much, though not all, of the social reform agenda.

Meanwhile, Lloyd George's overtures were persisting, and on 3 March 1914, the Labour leader received a letter from the Chancellor, marked 'urgent' and requesting a 'serious talk … about the relations of Liberalism and Labour'. The government was unpopular and grappling unsuccessfully with the problems in Ireland. In the ten parliamentary by-elections from November 1913 to February 1914, there were huge swings against the Liberals, and in seven cases this was because of the intervention of a Labour or Socialist candidate. Four of these seats had switched from Liberal to Unionist. Labour/ Socialist interventions had cost the Liberals both the Bethnal Green and Leith seats in February, and a Liberal intervention in North-East Derbyshire had cost Labour a seat. Gladstone–MacDonald was unravelling, and the Unionists were the beneficiaries.

It was no surprise that Lloyd George's March letter warned that 'if we go on as we have been doing ... both your party and ours will meet with the worst disaster that has befallen us ... I have talked the matter over with some very important people in the government and I have some suggestions to put to you...' MacDonald went to Lloyd George's room in the Commons that evening, at 6.30 p.m. He brought with him Arthur Henderson, and Lloyd George invited Illingworth, the Liberal Chief Whip.[35]

Lloyd George seemed to be acting with Asquith's consent, saying that he had a message from the 'inner Cabinet'. He highlighted the political divisions over Irish Home Rule. He noted that a general election would soon be necessary. He said that the Liberals were willing to offer more unopposed fights in key constituencies where Labour were better placed to beat the Unionists. In exchange, Labour should give the Liberals an unopposed run in as many seats as possible. Lloyd George also suggested that the two parties should agree a post-election policy programme. Finally, if Labour wanted representation in the Cabinet, they could have it.[36]

This was 1903 with bells and whistles on. And it could help change the whole future of Lib–Lab relations and of British politics. Lloyd George and MacDonald agreed to meet again in a week's time to discuss matters further, as the political crisis over Home Rule developed. It is not entirely clear what MacDonald thought about the offer, but he seemed sympathetic.

But within Labour were many who wanted nothing to do with any new Liberal pact – including Keir Hardie. Division broke into the open at Labour's Easter conference, where there were rumours about MacDonald planning a new Liberal deal. MacDonald now offered up what might be considered a classic 'non-denial denial' – saying that 'there is no approach between the Labour Party and the Liberal Party that means that the Labour Party is going to change its policy by one hair's breadth'.[37] That wasn't the claim, as MacDonald well knew.

Snowden lobbed a carefully fused grenade into the conference debate by asking whether Lib–Lab negotiations were taking place, casting doubt on his leader's honesty. He claimed that at a recent Labour executive meeting, the outlines of a possible deal had been discussed. Hardie intervened to clarify that there had been a discussion but no definite proposal.

But the prospects of an early election now faded, and the proposed Lib–Lab deal seemed to fade with it. In April, Labour's National Executive met and rejected any notion of a Liberal pact. In May, the continuing failure to avoid three-party contests cost both Labour and the Liberals a seat. This time it was MacDonald's turn to be angry: 'If the Liberals run candidates against us … when that policy of stupidity has ended in devastation we will ask how it pleases them.' If this was the Liberal approach, Labour would go it alone and 'the fight … will then be between a great Labour Party and a strong reactionary party, with a small Liberal Party standing between, cut off from every source of inspiration and opportunity of growth'.

Lloyd George responded on 2 June in a speech at Criccieth, claiming that over the past two years, the Liberals and Labour had lost nine seats while standing candidates against each other – 'the great rock in front of us is dissension in our own ranks'. He was suggesting that he still saw Labour and the Liberals as part of the same progressive force. The Unionist vote was rising, while the Lib–Lab vote was falling. If the Unionists were to be kept from power, then a continued Lib–Lab pact seemed to be required.

And if the Liberals now had cause for concern, so did Labour. They had faced seventeen by-elections since the December 1910 election, and they had lost one seat to the Liberals, another to the Unionists and had finished third in fourteen of the fights. At Westminster, the party had a low profile and a limited impact, and its leaders were being courted by senior Liberals. Two Labour MPs had defected to the Liberals in early 1914 and three more would in 1915. Labour had won twenty-nine seats in 1906, had forty-two MPs by 1910, but in July 1914 was back down to thirty-six. At this rate, a majority Labour government would take a very long time indeed to arrive.

Had war not intervened, it is unclear how Labour's strategy would have developed. They were failing to build on the 1906 bridgehead, but they were still gaining votes at Liberal expense. This suggests either that Labour would have stood more candidates and possibly cost the Liberals the next election or that they would have bargained for a greater number of seats where they could fight the Unionists alone. Rowland concludes plausibly that Labour and the Liberals would have been driven by mutual self-interest into a new pact, along the lines of the 1903 deal – 'Lloyd George's speech of 2 June 1914 was certainly a tacit recognition of the fact that one was needed if the Liberals were to stand a chance … of winning the next election.'[38]

But in 1914, the Liberals still had the upper hand. And Tanner and Searle have concluded that Labour would probably have fielded just sixty-five candidates in a 1915 election – pushing for more local deals but not breaking away to compete head-to-head.[39]

It seemed, then, that the next election would deliver a modest evolution of the Lib–Lab arrangements of 1906 and 1910. And perhaps soon afterwards, Asquith might give way to Lloyd George, and the new more radical leader of the Liberals might seek to unite with Labour and bring their parties into coalition or some close partnership.

We will never know.

Because, on 4 August 1914, everything changed. At midnight, Royal Navy vessels across the globe simultaneously received a secret message from the Admiralty: 'Commence Hostilities Against Germany.'

British politics would never be the same again.

CHAPTER 2

'THE ERA OF THE GOAT' 1914–31

The Cabinet was meeting in 10 Downing Street on 22 May 1916 – almost two years into the 'Great War'. Two of its most senior members, War Minister Lord Kitchener and the Munitions Minister, Lloyd George, were soon due to sail on a secret mission to Russia. They would visit the Tsar and his government to try to keep a financially and militarily stretched ally in the war.

Sitting at the Cabinet table, Lloyd George was passed a folded note, which he opened and quickly read. It was written in the unmistakeable scrawl of the Prime Minister, Asquith. Headed 'Secret', it continued: 'My dear Lloyd George, I hope you may see your way to take up Ireland: at any rate for a short time. It is a unique opportunity and there is no one else who could do as much to bring about a permanent solution. Yours very sincerely, H. H. Asquith'.

This request, a few weeks after the Easter Rising, was to have momentous consequences. It would alter the course of British politics and shatter the Liberal Party. As a result of it, Lloyd George scrapped his plans to join the Russian visit. In consequence, he did not lose his life with Kitchener, when the vessel on which Kitchener was travelling, HMS *Hampshire*, sank with the loss of almost all 749 men on board.

Within six months, Lloyd George went on to mount a coup, replacing Asquith as Prime Minister. This fatally divided the Liberal Party, and by 1918, the Labour Party had replaced them as the main alternative to the Unionists. The Liberals would never again govern alone.

But we must first retrace our steps and consider the background to the great Asquith–Lloyd George split. When war broke out in Europe in early August 1914 and spread rapidly across the globe, problems over Ireland's future were dominating British politics. Initially, Asquith hoped that the UK could stand apart. But Germany's decision to violate the neutrality of Belgium brought Britain into the war on a wave of patriotic fervour. Ramsay MacDonald resigned his post as chair of the Parliamentary Labour Party, in opposition to his party's support for war.

Stalemate rapidly set in on the 'Western Front', and by May 1915, Asquith was facing criticism in Parliament and the press. Military operations in the Dardanelles had been a disaster and there was increasing focus on the government's apparent inability to provide the shells, equipment and manpower needed. Asquith's response was to establish a coalition government, on 25 May 1915. The new Cabinet included nine Unionists and one Labour member – Arthur Henderson. The Liberals maintained a grip on all the key posts.

A coalition might have seemed a natural response to a world war, but it split Labour and angered many Liberals. At a meeting of Liberal MPs, a motion was passed unanimously condemning the arrangement. Asquith was summoned and he explained that 'certain things had happened; certain things had been divulged; and certain things had emerged as probable'. Somehow reassured by this obscure revelation, the hostile motion was withdrawn.

By late 1916, and without recourse to a general election, there was pressure for a change in leadership. Asquith's laid-back style, more chairman than leader, which had been such a strength during the years of peace, seemed inappropriate for a time that required both dynamism and the appearance of dynamism. The offensive on the Somme petered out with Allied casualties of over 400,000. And there were difficult debates in the Liberal Party over the case for conscription – leading to the resignation of the Liberal Home Secretary, Sir John Simon.

In the last decade, Asquith had promoted Lloyd George to Chancellor, shielded him when the Marconi share scandal had threatened his career and then appointed him to replace Kitchener as Secretary of State for War. But politics can be a brutal business, and the energetic Lloyd George was not about to allow political debts to get in the way of his ambition. As long ago as August 1910, he had schemed behind his leader's back and pushed for a Liberal–Unionist coalition to grapple with the seemingly intractable issues of Lords reform and Ireland. His desire to work beyond the constraints of party politics dated back further to 1895 – 'he had been impatient with the petty orthodoxies of party controversy'.[1]

In August 1910, Lloyd George's secret coalition plan covered an extraordinary range of policies – from housing to drink, social insurance, unemployment, trade, the 'Irish Question' and foreign policy. It did not look like a scheme for a short-lived political truce to resolve one or two major constitutional issues. It was a clear signal that Lloyd George was more motivated by policies, projects and personal position than by party loyalties. He seems initially to have discussed his proposal with Churchill. Next, he met the Unionist leader, Balfour. Only after delicate and indiscreet talks, most with opposition leaders, did he deign to discuss the matter with Asquith, in mid-October. It was a breathtaking bit of freelancing and Asquith must have been surprised and concerned. Lloyd George generously made clear that he envisaged Asquith remaining as PM. What he did not dare tell his boss was that his plan would involve him being shunted off to the House of Lords.[2] On 29 October, he produced a second memorandum which covered Irish matters and even suggested an inquiry into the fiscal system, designed to open the door to reduced duties on trade with the 'colonies'. It was an attempt to sketch out a common programme for a national or coalition government.

Ultimately, Balfour sunk the plan. His concern was that both parties were being asked to accept the policies they most disagreed with – Home Rule and social reform for the Unionists, some form of imperial preference and conscription for the Liberals. In 1928, he would observe of Lloyd George: 'Principles mean nothing to him – never have. His mind doesn't work that way. It's both his strength and his weakness.'

So, in 1910, Lloyd George had made a first, unsuccessful, attempt to single-handedly redraw the party system. Now, in 1916, he would try again. He wanted a more aggressive prosecution of the war, and he believed he had the focus that Asquith seemed to lack (the fact the 64-year-old PM wrote some 560 letters over a three-year period to a 28-year-old lady who he was infatuated with, often giving away key war secrets, while chairing meetings of the Cabinet, did not help).

In late autumn 1916, Lloyd George seized his opportunity and secured the support of the Unionists for his plan. In theory, he was only asking of Asquith to appoint him to chair a small War Committee that would exclude the PM and turbo-charge the war effort. But Asquith was immediately suspicious, writing to the new Conservative leader, Andrew Bonar Law, on 26 November to note of Lloyd George:

> He has many qualities ... but he lacks the one thing needful – he does not inspire trust ... there is one construction and one construction only, that could be put on the new [proposed] arrangements – that it has been engineered by him with the purpose, not perhaps at the moment but as soon as fitting pretext can be found, of displacing me.[3]

He was right. And Asquith was unwilling to be reduced to a figurehead in his own government.

Unfortunately for Asquith, the Unionists backed Lloyd George over him, and he was forced to quit. Displacing a wartime leader was not something that many Liberals could forgive. Asquith himself, addressing his MPs and peers on the day after Lloyd George became Prime Minister, told them that he had fallen victim to 'a well-organised conspiracy'. Worse still, it was a conspiracy in which his Liberal assassin had made common cause with their political enemies. In politics, that's as bad as it gets.

Asquith did not believe that the new government could last. He remained Liberal leader and waited to return. The party was now deeply split. There were two Liberal groupings and two sets of whips. One grouping followed Lloyd George and remained on the government benches, the other backed Asquith and was seated on the opposition side of the Commons.

For the first year of the coalition, a low-key Liberal truce was maintained. But Asquith rejected Lloyd George's attempts to get him back in the government.[4] Lloyd George now began to contemplate a major recasting of politics. He imagined a future in which there might be a left-wing Labour Party confronting a new alignment of more moderate Liberals and Unionists, no doubt led by someone charismatic, Welsh and with the skills he uniquely (in his own mind) possessed. If this was how he saw the future, he was hardly going to invest huge efforts in bringing the Liberal Party back together. Churchill was another key supporter of this centre party concept.

By April 1918, Lloyd George was describing himself to Lord Riddell as 'nationalist-socialist'. No wonder he would later indulge in a brief and embarrassing flirtation with Adolf Hitler. He was 'a strong believer in nationality ... in the intervention of the state to secure that everyone has a fair chance and there is no unnecessary want and poverty...'

In May 1918, the bitterness between the old and new Prime Ministers increased when Asquith demanded a select committee inquiry into suggestions that Lloyd George had given an inaccurate account of British military strength in France. For Lloyd George, this was an issue of political survival. And for the first and only time in the war, the Liberal whips organised against the government. Although the coalition prevailed by 293 votes to 106, ninety-eight Liberal MPs opposed Lloyd George while seventy-one went through the government lobby. The day after the debate, the Liberal MP Cecil Harmsworth wrote to a colleague: 'There seems to be a dangerous likelihood of this division becoming permanent.' So far as Asquith and Lloyd George were concerned, this was correct. The two men would eventually work together again. What they would never again do is trust each other.

Deep division in any party is always dangerous. But the falling out between Lloyd George and Asquith was a disaster. It broke up the only pairing with a realistic prospect of evolving the Liberal Party from its nineteenth-century reality to its required twentieth-century form. It placed the radical Lloyd George in coalition with the Unionists for six long years, while leaving the much less radical Asquith, and his closest allies, out in the cold. As David Dutton has noted: 'The Liberal Party at this time lost much of its credibility as the standard bearer of the radical left in British politics.'[5]

But if Asquith was out of the government, Labour remained in. Arthur Henderson was the Labour Member of Lloyd George's small War Cabinet, as Minister without Portfolio. John Hodge became Minister of Labour, George Barnes Minister of Pensions, and J. R. Clynes took on the role of Under-Secretary in the Ministry of Food. Labour MPs were now occupying important roles in government.

As the war continued, the size of the state grew, as did its involvement in every aspect of the economy. And in Russia, war sparked a communist revolution. Across the world, socialist movements gained power and political establishments and the ruling classes looked on in fear. After the Bolsheviks won power in late 1917, socialist groups in Britain organised a conference to celebrate. Ramsay MacDonald and Philip Snowden were two of the Labour MPs attending – and MacDonald tabled a resolution specifically welcoming the revolution. Sweeping away the Tsarist regime may have seemed good socialist sense, but Labour was playing with political fire. Their support for Soviet Russia would come back to haunt them.

In late 1917, the British socialist thinkers Sidney and Beatrice Webb were working on a draft of a new Labour Party constitution, which was adopted in 1918. The famous Clause IV promised 'common ownership of the means of production, distribution and exchange'. What this meant was not wholly clear, but this was now a Labour Party that was parting company on policy and ideology with its former Liberal allies. State control seemed less controversial than it might have done in the pre-war era. But it was opening a vast new political battlefield – socialism versus the market economy, big government versus small. The old debates around free trade versus tariffs were being replaced by a new dividing line: free markets or state socialism.

At last, with the arrival of US forces onto the battlefield in large numbers in 1918, Germany and its allies collapsed. War ended on 11 November. Now was surely the moment when – eight years after the last general election – normal political service would be resumed. For a while, it seemed that way. In late 1918, an emergency Labour Party conference determined that the Labour members of the coalition should resign and approved a radical programme of nationalisation and 'democratic control' of key sectors of the economy. Labour wanted an immediate election.

But 'normal service' was not what Lloyd George envisaged. He might be Prime Minister, but he was not Liberal leader. Having in 1916 stabbed his leader, Asquith, in the back, he now, in 1918, did the same to his party. On 24 September, Lloyd George had extended an olive branch to Asquith, offering him the post of Lord Chancellor and the power to nominate two Cabinet ministers and half a dozen junior ministers. He was clear there would be a general election imminently – with the war about to conclude, he wanted to 'market his popularity'. As part of a deal with the Unionists, they would agree to Irish Home Rule, with the exclusion of Ulster. But Asquith was in an uncompromising mood. He didn't want to be pensioned off to the Lords. He didn't support the proposed Irish policy. And he didn't want a general election on Lloyd George's terms. Lord Murray, Lloyd George's chosen intermediary, concluded: 'Unless I am very much mistaken … I have been present at the obsequies of the Liberal Party as I knew it.'[6] He was correct.

Lloyd George ignored his former boss and ploughed on regardless. By 29 October, his Chief Whip, Freddie Guest, had concluded an agreement with the Unionists to avoid standing candidates against each other – this would cover 150 Lloyd George Liberals and any Labour candidates supporting him. The 'coalition coupon' letter, as it was dubbed by Asquith, signed jointly by Lloyd George and Bonar Law, was eventually sent to 159 Liberals, 364 Unionists/ Conservatives, twenty National Democratic and Labour, and two coalition Labour MPs. The letter confirmed that the designated candidate was standing with the backing of both Lloyd George and Bonar Law. But those not receiving the letter would be opposed by the coalition parties. This was treachery with bells and whistles.

In some cases, the allocation of 'coupons' was a little random. One strong supporter of Asquith, F. C. Thornborough, was astonished to receive an unsolicited 'coupon' letter through the post. It turned out that his constituency chairman had a friend on Lloyd George's staff who had fixed it for him.[7] He refused the offer.

Asquith, of course, received no coupon. For those Liberals left out, there could hardly be a more aggressive political act. Lloyd George would happily see them defeated. And he had signed an agreement that would benefit twice as many Unionists as Liberals. It was the greatest act of political treachery in British political history. In time, Lloyd George would pay the price.

The election was on 14 December, on a new franchise of all adult males over the age of twenty-one and most women over the age of thirty. Each of the three political parties was divided – in no party were the candidates either all coupon or non-coupon. Politics was getting very messy, under the self-centred oversight of the 'Welsh Wizard', or, as those who disliked him had dubbed him, the 'Goat', in reference to his loose personal conduct.

Lloyd George now fought a jingoistic campaign. On 11 December, he issued six pledges, which included putting the Kaiser on trial, 'fullest indemnities from Germany', 'Britain for the British' and 'a happier country for all'. It only served to widen divisions and increase bitterness. The campaign was a short one. By 15 December, the coalition had romped home, securing 506 seats in a Commons of 707. But the big, long-term winners were the Unionists. They emerged with 379 seats – a gain of 108, and more seats than they had secured during the landslide wins of 1895 and 1900.

Labour also performed well. It had fielded a mammoth total of 388 candidates, polled almost 21 per cent of the vote, and secured the election of fifty-seven Labour MPs (as well as four Coalition Labour and two Independent Labour). In December 1910, Labour had managed only 372,000 votes – barely higher than the 330,000 of 1906. This time, their vote had increased to 2,385,000. It was the huge breakthrough they needed, and with the Liberal Party shattered, they were perfectly placed to advance. However, there were significant Labour losses amongst those facing coupon candidates – Ramsay MacDonald and Arthur Henderson were both defeated.

As well as breaking through in the Commons, Labour's 1918 manifesto signalled clearly that the party was moving on from 'Advanced Liberalism' to a much more radical, socialist, agenda. The 1918 constitution had included the commitment to common ownership and the 1918 manifesto contained a 'demand' for the 'immediate nationalisation and democratic control of vital public services such as mines, railways, shipping, armaments, and electric power'.

Alongside this, it championed the abolition of unemployment, a legal limitation on working hours and tighter regulation of worker compensation. Beyond the domestic agenda, the manifesto argued courageously for a 'peace of reconciliation', 'freedom for Ireland' and the right of self-determination for nations within the British Empire. It also called for an immediate withdrawal of Allied forces from Russia.

All this was bold stuff. Some was simply fleshing out what Advanced Liberalism might mean in practice. But much was setting a new direction for the state. The 1918 election had pulled apart the Liberal Party. It also marked the end of the Liberal–Labour co-operation that dated back over forty years to the first Lib–Lab MPs. As significantly, these were no longer two parties travelling in the same broad policy direction.

The Liberal split, Lloyd George's alignment with the Unionists and the jingoistic campaign of 1918 all drove more 'radical' Liberals away from their party. Between 1917 and 1919, as many as 2,000 disillusioned activists and members left to join Labour.[8] Labour was picking up huge numbers of votes by virtue of being the clear opposition to the coalition government, and in the 1919 local government elections it saw a huge surge in support. In London, it took almost 34 per cent of the vote.[9]

In some parts of the country, in response to the Labour surge, the Liberals were now forming anti-Labour pacts with the Unionists – like the 'Hull Municipal Alliance' – or agreeing to more informal anti-Labour arrangements, as in Bristol, Merseyside, parts of Yorkshire and in west Scotland. Gone were the days when Liberals and Labour operated generally in partnership against the Unionists.

There were also signs that Liberal voters no longer heavily preferred Labour to the Unionists. In 1923 and 1924, there were still twelve two-member constituencies where it is possible to analyse how votes were split between the three parties. In most of these seats, Liberal supporters tended to divide their votes between their party and the Conservatives, rather than Labour.[10]

While Liberal and Labour MPs were no longer obviously aligned, nor were the Liberals ideologically closer to the Conservatives. If the party was forced to choose between these two, it was bound to split and risk division and defection.

If the Unionists and Labour were the big winners in 1918, there was no doubt who the losers were. Those who fought under Asquith, without the coalition coupon, had been wiped out – Asquith himself losing his seat in East Fife. After thirty-two years as local MP, it was a bitter rebuff. Asquith's election manifesto of 1918 had been distinctly underwhelming. It included a defence of his record during the war and a commitment to a policy of a 'national minimum'. But there was little detail on what this meant in practice. The truth was that Asquith had been leader of his party for ten years, was now sixty-seven, was angry and disillusioned and needed to give way to someone who could inspire and reunite the party. But he was re-elected to Parliament in Paisley in a by-election in February 1920 and would stay as Liberal leader until October 1926 – at least eight years beyond his political 'sell-by' date.

Every other ex-minister who had backed Asquith over Lloyd George also lost his seat in 1918 – McKenna, Samuel, Simon, Runciman and others. They, too, would never trust Lloyd George again. There had been 272 Liberal MPs in December 1910. There were now a mere thirty-six. The 276 Liberal candidates had polled just 13 per cent of the vote. It was the Liberals who stuck with Lloyd George and stood as National/Coalition Liberals who survived and thrived.

145 Coalition Liberal candidates stood, and 127 had been elected – with 12.6 per cent of the vote.

So, in total, the Liberals still had more votes and seats than Labour, but they were now in two divided blocks, sitting on different sides of the Commons. The Liberal Party, as an organisation, was shattered. The infrastructure was still in Asquithian hands, but the membership, finances and councillors were melting away. And a party distracted by war and division was much less capable of undertaking the challenging task of evolving the New Liberalism. The Liberals had gone from the dream team of 1908–16 to a leadership nightmare of 1918. And Lloyd George was now losing much of his progressive credibility, as leader of a coalition government dependent on 379 Unionists – 73 per cent of all coalition MPs.

Labour, by contrast, was largely united and (excluding Sinn Féin, who would not take up their seats) now the largest opposition party. Labour had gone in to the 1918 election as a party that had played second fiddle to the Liberals. It came out in a strong position to supplant the Liberals as the great progressive party of British politics. To deliver the killer blow, Labour would now need to consign the co-operation of the past to the political scrap heap. There would be no more cosy backroom deals. The serpent had escaped its cage and was indeed about to sting the Liberal Party to death.

For a short period after the 1918 election, the (Asquithian) Liberals bounced back, winning by-elections and benefiting from the swing that usually goes against the government of the day. Then they stalled, and Labour became the main beneficiary of government weakness.

Meanwhile, Lloyd George was leader of the new coalition government but by January 1920 was still considering forming a wholly new party. In February, he met with coalition Liberal ministers and told them: 'Liberal labels lead nowhere; we must be prepared to burn them.' He also argued that 'coalition' was no longer a politically useful asset and what was needed was unity of political command. He thought that reuniting the Liberal Party was impossible and that 'liberalism was not enough to govern the country with'.[11] His thinking was influenced by the Spen Valley by-election on 20 December 1919. The Coalition Liberals had previously held the seat but finished bottom of the poll. The result was seen as stunning and surprising, with *The Times* describing it as a 'political event of great significance'.

Churchill remained enthusiastic about Lloyd George's scheme for a new party, fusing Liberals and Conservatives. He believed that this was the only way to defeat the rising tide of union militancy and socialism. But in mid-March 1920, the whole plan fell through. Lloyd George discovered that Coalition Liberal ministers would not support his scheme – many still held out the hope that their party could be reunited, did not want to abandon their Liberal label and feared that free trade might be put at risk. At a meeting of all the Coalition Liberal MPs, Lloyd George had to perform a rapid retreat, talking only of the need for more co-operation with Unionists.[12]

The idea of a new merged party was now dead. For the next two years, the coalition would continue. But the economy was weak, and in Ireland unionists were angry about the Irish Free State Treaty. In the country and on the Unionist backbenches, the mood was moving against coalition. Coalition Liberals were nervous too. Since March 1920, Asquith made clear that Coalition Liberal MPs were fair game and would be offered no free runs in their seats. And most Liberal associations were sticking with Asquith.

In 1920, Lloyd George recognised his distance from old party

colleagues by starting his own, separate, National Liberal organisation. It even had its own magazine, modestly titled the *Lloyd George
Magazine*. This was published monthly until November 1923.[13] Lest
anyone mistake its allegiance, it contained wall-to-wall coverage of
his speeches, and its first issue included a poem to a 'D. L. G.', offering a moving tribute to

> A man whose soul is pure and strong,
> whose sword is bright and keen,
> Who knows the splendour of the fight and what its issues mean.

It is not thought likely that Asquith was a subscriber.

However much his own magazine was flattering him, by March
1922, H. A. L. Fisher, Lloyd George's Coalition Liberal colleague,
was warning him that 'the rank and file of the Tory party will never
be content until they have tried the experiment of a pure Tory administration. They want to get rid of you...' Lloyd George ignored
the suggestion that he should resign and leave the Unionists to fight
on alone. But it was clear that they would soon part company with
him. Where might he find the support to sustain him in office? Not
amongst the Liberals, still led by the embittered Asquith. And not
in Labour either. Through his jingoism at the end of the war, his
aggressive approach to the industrial action of 1919, when he was
ready to use force to end strikes, and in leading a coalition with the
Unionists, Lloyd George had burnt all his bridges. He had also been
willing to compare Arthur Henderson with Lenin and Trotsky and
raise the spectre of Labour support for a British Bolshevism.

While the patrician Asquith was never a likely ally for the new
Labour Party, the Lloyd George of the People's Budget might have
enabled Lib–Lab co-operation to continue. But by 1922, the 'old'

Lloyd George was a distant memory, and Labour leaders saw in him only a bitter enemy. An ambitious and infinitely flexible politician, Lloyd George would never have trouble in standing on his head to forge new alliances. But his political enemies were neither so flexible nor so forgiving.

In early 1922, a more pragmatic Prime Minister was pushing for diplomatic recognition of the Soviet Union, but this was vetoed by the Cabinet, including his de facto Coalition Liberal deputy, Winston Churchill. It did nothing for Lloyd George's credibility or for the loyalty of the Unionists. Unionists were also pushing for more economy in public spending. In August 1921, Lloyd George gave way, and – drawing on his First World War experience of bringing businessmen into government – established a 'business committee' and asked Sir Eric Geddes to set out a list of possible savings.

Coalition Liberals were concerned when in February 1922 the Geddes Committee outlined plans for £75 million of cuts to education, health, housing and unemployment insurance. The plan included children under six being excluded from school, and secondary education being 'confined to children whose mental calibre justifies it and whose parents cannot afford to pay for it'. Social housing would be flogged off. Health insurance benefits would be cut. It was even proposed to abolish unemployment exchanges and the Ministry of Labour. Lloyd George had thought that the views of Liberals and Unionists could be melded together in a new National Party. He was discovering the absurdity of this notion. It did not stop him from proceeding with many of the cuts.

The Honours Scandal of 1922 did even more damage to Lloyd George. It was revealed that he had been trading national honours in exchange for large donations. The practice had long existed, but not on the scale and with the lack of subtlety now displayed. As

Douglas has noted: 'They [the coalition] differed sharply from all modern governments in the scale on which it was done, the shamelessness of the touting system, and their total and cynical disregard for the worthiness and suitability of the recipient.'[14] The Unionist Party had shared in the practice 50-50, but this could hardly excuse Lloyd George. And while their proceeds seem mostly to have gone straight into party coffers, the Coalition Liberal share was retained by Lloyd George in a fund that was under his control. The row injected a new poison in the Liberal bloodstream. Many Liberals considered the sale of honours despicable. Others were angry that Lloyd George hadn't handed the cash over to their party. The bitterness lasted for the rest of his political career.

The government was now in trouble, and Unionist MPs wanted out. Lloyd George had been an asset. He was now a liability. In January 1922, he had been considering a dissolution, with the Coalition Liberals and Conservatives fighting together, possibly with a renewed attempt to form a centre party following on. But this was leaked and vetoed by the Unionist chairman.

The final straw came in summer 1922, when Lloyd George proposed deploying British troops to side with Greece in a dispute with Turkey. Just two years after the end of the First World War, there was no appetite for overseas adventurism, and Bonar Law spoke for many when he said Britain could not be the 'policeman of the world'.

Lloyd George did not see the crash coming. On 14 October, he was speaking in Manchester, rubbishing his former Liberal colleague (Lord) Herbert Gladstone and suggesting that he was 'the best living embodiment of the Liberal doctrine that quality is not hereditary'. This was a man still intent on burning old bridges. According to Campbell: 'The moral Lloyd George drew [from recent elections] was not so much the need for electoral reform – already a Liberal demand – but rather that no party on its own could guarantee stable government, and that the majority of moderate men of all parties should therefore stand together.'[15]

Austen Chamberlain, Conservative leader after Bonar Law's illness, hoped to rally support for Lloyd George and called a meeting of Unionist MPs at the Carlton Club, on 19 October. This came just hours after the results of a by-election in Newport, where the Unionist prevailed but on a platform of opposition to the coalition government, and with the Liberal coming in third behind Labour. Stanley Baldwin used the Carlton Club meeting to warn that Lloyd George was a 'dynamic force' – not intended as a compliment – who had 'smashed to pieces' the Liberal Party and who, given a continuation of the coalition, would ensure their party was 'smashed to atoms and lost in ruins'. It was probably not a bad prediction. Bonar Law, back after illness, also spoke against Chamberlain, and Unionist MPs decided by a margin of 187 to eighty-seven to end the coalition. Lloyd George resigned. Bonar Law was restored as Unionist leader, and an election set for 15 November 1922.

Labour would field 414 candidates. Their manifesto was similar to that of 1918 – progressive social policy, higher taxes on the wealthy and nationalisation of key industries. But it committed the party 'against revolution', stating that their programme was 'neither Bolshevism nor Communism' – an acknowledgement that they risked losing votes if seen as too radical.

Meanwhile, the Liberal Party was imploding. Asquith was still leader – now into his fourteenth year in post, at the age of seventy. The party of thirty-six MPs would field 334 candidates for the 615 available seats. Asquith's manifesto underlined his distance from the previous administration, which he described as 'the alliance between Mr. Lloyd George and the Conservative Party'. His statement that the coalition had left behind 'an unexampled record of extravagance and failure' and that 'both wings of the coalition are responsible for its misdeeds' was strong evidence of his continuing bitterness. But as Labour was moving leftwards, Asquith's manifesto struck a very different note, returning to more classically Liberal themes: 'The one Party in the State which has consistently fought waste, challenged estimates, moved reductions ... is the Independent Liberal Party.' Although there were references to a programme of social reform, the manifesto sought to create clear water with Labour: 'Liberalism is not socialism. Liberalism repudiates the doctrine of warfare against private enterprise.' The party stood instead for 'drastic Economy in public expenditure'.

A ten-point 'Programme for the Liberal Party' for the first time listed 'Proportional Representation' as a priority. In 1918, the Liberals had polled 13 per cent of the votes but had secured only 5 per cent of the seats. It is perhaps not surprising that a party that found itself in this position suddenly discovered a passionate and long-lasting commitment to electoral reform.

Meanwhile, Lloyd George was still leader of a separate grouping of 155 MPs that would field 151 candidates under a National Liberal banner. For the Liberal Party, it was a crazy outcome. The two best known Liberals were leading different groupings, fighting on policy platforms that the average voter would find difficult to tell apart. Some National Liberals were not opposed by Unionists. Other Liberals presented themselves as being backed by both Asquith and Lloyd George. It was a gruesome mess, and there were around thirty constituencies where Liberal candidates stood against each other – costing at least fourteen seats, ten of which were captured by Labour.

When the campaign was over, the Unionists emerged again as

winners. The disorganised opposition that they faced was a political godsend. They lost only thirty-five seats, electing 344 MPs for a modest 38.5 per cent vote share.

But Labour were the real beneficiaries of 1922. They gained eighty-five seats, emerging with 142 MPs and a vote share of 30 per cent. They were now the principal party of opposition. They had twenty-seven more seats than both Liberal groupings combined for the first time. And after four years out of Parliament, Ramsay MacDonald was back – this time as MP for Aberavon. Within a week of the election, he was again leader of the Labour Party, for the first time since August 1914.

And Clement Attlee, who was to become Labour's second Prime Minister, was elected for the first time.

The split Liberal vote was calamitous. The Liberals polled 18.9 per cent and the National Liberals 9.9 per cent – at 28.8 per cent combined, they were together only 1 per cent behind Labour. But Lloyd George's National Liberals lost seventy-four seats, including Churchill's in Dundee, and were reduced to just fifty-three MPs. His results would have been even worse, but in many National Liberal seats Bonar Law ensured there were no Unionist candidates.

Lloyd George had alienated the Liberals, infuriated Labour and hoped to fuse with the Unionists but had ultimately been ejected by them. Without some spectacular Houdini act, his time at the top of British politics was over.

Asquith's Liberals fared slightly better – gaining twenty-six seats – but they still only had sixty-two MPs. Overall, the Liberals were in a mess, but MacDonald was not complacent. He knew that if the Liberals reunited, and the dynamic Lloyd George took over, there was a risk that they could squeeze Labour. He was therefore determined to ensure that voters saw the political battleground as Labour versus

Conservative. This meant demonstrating that Labour could govern safely, responsibly and in the interests of the whole nation. Labour might be a socialist party. But it would be 'safety first' socialism.

The Conservatives similarly had an interest in building up Labour as the alternative government in waiting. They could then scare into their fold the middle classes and all who feared socialism and communism. And they could kill the Liberal Party, their potentially more dangerous opponents.

In the circumstances of the post-war period, a united and well-led Liberal Party, with a progressive and reformist New Liberal policy platform, might just have been able to contain the emergent Labour Party and win over the millions of newly franchised voters. But the Liberal Party was now neither united, nor well led, and its policy platform was timid and incoherent.

By March 1923, Lloyd George was angling for a reunion of the Liberal groups, based on their equal status. But even as he promoted unity, he could not resist having a subtle dig at his former boss. At the Scottish Liberal Club on 2 March, he warned: 'While we throw poisoned arrows at each other, Labour is walking away with the Ark of the Covenant.' He was willing to 'follow any leader who possesses the necessary vision, resolution, wisdom, courage and inspiration to lead the nation'. This was a poorly disguised job application and not an attempt to patch up differences with Asquith, who by 1923 possessed somewhere between one and none of the listed required attributes.

And as the new political landscape took shape, the national debate was becoming more polarised between left and right, public and private, pacifism and nationalism, big and small government. The Liberals were stranded in the middle ground, unsure which way to turn and increasingly divided between those who felt Labour was the main threat to the nation and those who still saw their principal enemy as the Conservatives.

In any case, the Conservatives had been returned with a healthy majority and were expected to govern for a full five-year parliament. Many National Liberal MPs continued to work with Bonar Law's government, and some of their leading lights, including Churchill, wanted a united front against Labour. There was, therefore, no 1923 reconciliation of the two Liberal factions, despite seventy-three MPs from both groupings coming out in favour of a reunion in March.

Within a year, Conservative Prime Minister Andrew Bonar Law had died from throat cancer, and Stanley Baldwin took over in May 1923. There had recently been rumours that Lloyd George – opportunistic, unprincipled and ambitious as ever – might mount a political comeback bid by uniting with two senior disaffected Conservatives, Austen Chamberlain and F. E. Smith (Lord Birkenhead), and leading their own campaign for protection. Lloyd George could certainly expect no outstretched hand from Baldwin, who by now despised him and wanted nothing more to do with coalitions.

In October, Baldwin suddenly announced that the economic environment, including sharply rising unemployment, required a new protectionist policy on trade. His predecessor had promised that such a policy would only be implemented after a specific electoral mandate.

For once, expectations of Lloyd George's breathless opportunism helped the Liberals. He may never have planned to back protection, but his scheming with leading Conservatives helped push Baldwin into a new policy direction, to unite his party.

Baldwin's lurch back to protectionism instantly healed Liberal divisions. About the one issue that united every Liberal was support for free trade. Within weeks, negotiations started for a reunited Liberal Party – with a single set of candidates, and a single policy prospectus, under the leadership of Asquith. Even Churchill now returned to the fold.

So, just over a year from the last election, Parliament was dissolved to fight a new one on tariffs versus free trade. Why a government with a large working majority would opt to hold an unnecessary general election during a period of economic crisis is an intriguing question. The period of unconventional, chaotic government that had begun in 1915 was continuing.

This time, the Liberal Party worked harder to get its act together. It would field 457 candidates – a similar number to Labour (427) but less than the Conservatives (536). And with Lloyd George back onside, party finances gained £90,000 from his ill-gotten fighting fund. The Liberal manifesto focused on the economic challenges, promising to defend free trade, tackle rising unemployment and deliver a programme of social reform. A section on 'bold and courageous use of the national credit', hinted at a Keynesian-style plan, promoted by Lloyd George, to use government spending to cut unemployment. The Conservative government was presented as the main enemy, but the manifesto attacked Labour's proposed Capital Levy and its policies of socialism and 'destruction of enterprise'. There would be no local Lib–Lab deals.

Labour's manifesto unsurprisingly also rejected tariffs. It was generally moderate, and its central plank was a programme to tackle unemployment, which was not dissimilar to the Liberal offering. The word 'nationalisation' seemed to have been banished, and on taxation the emphasis was on a reduction of income tax. One element of Labour tax policy had proved controversial – their 'Capital

Levy', which was now termed a 'non-recurring, graduated war debt redemption levy' – a fine, early, example of politicians' propensity to dress up controversial policies in deliberately obscure language.

Polling day was 6 December 1923, and as the results came in it was clear that Stanley Baldwin had gambled and lost. An unnecessary general election cost the Conservatives eighty-six seats and reduced their numbers to 258. Labour had polled 30.7 per cent, up just 1 per cent on 1922, but gained forty-nine seats and now had its largest ever total – 191.

The reunited Liberals finished on just 1 per cent less than Labour and ended in third position, with 158 seats – 'in the battle with Labour ... the battle that mattered, they only lost ground. The sense of recovery was therefore illusory, and the 1923 election merely another stage in the party's decline.'[16] The Liberals had done particularly well in the West Country, winning twenty-three of the thirty-six seats. But many of the industrial areas of the north and Midlands were swinging to Labour. Labour was also doing well in London.

Lloyd George claimed that the Liberals had 'killed protection' and that in the next election they would 'put before the people a programme of well-considered ... social reform which shall kill the crudities of socialism'. It all sounded marvellous. But it would be much tougher to deliver. The Liberals were in the superficially exciting position of holding the balance of power. But they were soon to discover that their power was more superficial than exciting. They had been delivered a very poisoned chalice.

With the Conservatives' tariffs policy rejected, it was clear they could not form a government. And Baldwin ruled out a suggestion from the King that he might seek a coalition with the Liberals. In any case, Asquith was not willing to prop the Conservatives up.

No party could command a majority. And Asquith seems not

even to have considered a minority Liberal government. Instead, he looked on with bemusement and amusement at the business, media and Conservative response to the prospect of a Labour administration – an 'epidemic of political hysteria', as he described it. He hoped Labour would take office. And then make a mess of things. Even Lloyd George consented. They would let Labour govern. The whole thing would be a flop. Then the Liberals would clean up.

Asquith was committed to Liberal independence. On 18 December, he told his MPs, gathered at the National Liberal Club, that there were no coalition negotiations between the Liberals and other parties 'directly or indirectly, officially or unofficially, above ground or subterranean, aerial or by wireless'. He argued that the Conservatives had to resign, as their protectionist agenda had been rejected. And if Labour was ever to take office, 'it could hardly be tried under safer conditions', given their lack of a majority. With a degree of optimism that would prove sadly misplaced, he observed that 'it is we, if we really understand our business, who really control the situation'. But Asquith was most definitely not in control, and if he had a plan, it is not obvious that it had been properly thought through.

At least one prominent Liberal, Winston Churchill, did not share Asquith's view. He had stood again but lost. He now saw socialism as the real enemy and had hoped for a Conservative–Liberal alliance to keep Labour out. For twenty years, protectionism had been his great enemy – from now until the end of his career, it was socialism. By March 1924, he was standing unsuccessfully as an independent anti-socialist candidate in the Westminster Abbey by-election. By the next general election, he would be back in the Conservative fold, after his twenty-year stint in the Liberal Party.

On 17 January 1924, a debate commenced in Parliament on Baldwin's King's Speech. It was soon clear the Conservatives were heading out of office for the first time since 1915. Four days later, the Commons moved to vote on the address and Labour's amendment. With the balance of forces in the Commons, the Liberals could not merely abstain. If they were willing to let Labour take power, they had to vote for them. Asquith made clear his acceptance of a Labour government. The amended address, expressing no confidence in the Conservative government, passed by 328 votes to 251. The Liberals had (mostly) sided with Labour to put them into power for their first time.

Austen Chamberlain claimed that Asquith had 'sung the swan song of the Liberal Party'. Some Liberals appeared to agree – ten voted with the Conservatives against Labour and seven abstained. In 1903, the Liberal Chief Whip had helped give Labour a solid foothold in Parliament. Twenty years later, his successor had shepherded his flock through the division lobbies to put Labour into power. If there was once a clever plan to use Labour to entrench Liberal dominance, it was not working very well.

Some in the Labour Party had been reticent to take office in these circumstances, but MacDonald pointed out that if Labour refused, it would be relegated to a minor position, with the Conservatives occupying the opposition front bench. It was government or obscurity. The party National Executive backed MacDonald but insisted there should be no coalitions. As neither MacDonald nor Asquith wanted a coalition, there would now be a minority Labour government, dependent on Liberal support or abstention.

The King sent for Ramsay MacDonald, who became the first Labour Prime Minister on 22 January 1924. Philip Snowden, a former Liberal and once an Inland Revenue clerk, was Labour's first Chancellor. Like MacDonald, he was another moderate, with conventional views about economic policy. One colleague described him as 'about as progressive as a member of the Junior Carlton Club', and Beatrice Webb saw him as 'chicken-hearted' and likely to favour cuts to public spending rather than programmes of public works.[17] Within months, Snowden was telling the attendees at the Lord Mayor's dinner that his job as Chancellor was like that of a 'man with his back to the wall, fighting off a pack of ravenous wolves'.

Labour was now in office, but with fewer than 200 MPs, they were barely in power. And MacDonald told C. P. Scott of the *Manchester Guardian* that the impact of the election had been to 'dig both deeply and broadly a ditch between Liberalism and Labour', claiming that the Liberal campaign had been 'dirtier than the Tory'.[18]

Asquith believed that Labour's electoral success was largely a function of former Liberal splits. If Labour did badly in office, the Liberals could overtake them next time. He thought Labour's new ministers were a 'beggarly array' and would struggle to run an effective government. Asquith also judged that the Labour left would not be satisfied with a moderate Labour government, and that this would prove fatal. That was his plan. Like many plans, it did not survive contact with reality. Asquith's wife, Margot, was closer to the mark, predicting that the new government would 'suffer from timidity and inefficiency ... rather than ... violence'. She was right that Labour would prove a relatively safe choice for the nation. What a Labour government was not safe for was the future of the Liberal Party. Asquith was an old man who was not in a hurry. But his party now needed more skill, urgency and ruthlessness to see off the Labour threat.

A government of only 191 MPs, and no coalition partner, is

never likely to last long. The Conservatives were already relishing the opportunity of being able to damn both their opponents at the next election – the Liberals for allowing Labour its chance. If they could kill the Liberal Party, the prospects for the Conservatives would be good – the electorate would face a stark choice between them and a socialist party. This two-party choice was MacDonald's vision too, though with an electable Labour Party.

However, one of the government's first actions was to recognise the new Union of Soviet Socialist Republics, and its manifesto had pledged to resume free trade and diplomatic relations with Russia. To some extent, this was merely a pragmatic recognition of new realities. But it was open to the criticism that this was a socialist government extending a hand of friendship to a communist regime. For Labour's many enemies, this exposed Labour's 'true' radical, left-wing agenda.

Baldwin speedily moved to exploit the issue. Just as rapidly, he dropped his policies of protection. The party's name was now changed from Unionist to 'Conservative and Unionist' – the conservative brand was intended to sound reassuring in the face of the new 'socialist' government.

Lloyd George was biding his time. In an article on 2 February 1924, he repeated his trick of subtly damning political rivals with one of his lists of the qualities they needed to possess but obviously did not. This time the target was MacDonald. His government would succeed if 'he has the clearness of vision, the judgement, the tact, the firmness and the drive…' As to whether he had – 'I dare not predict.' It was the sort of patronising drivel that irritated Labour MPs about Lloyd George. In any case, MacDonald would in time prove he possessed at least three of these 'necessary virtues'. From

1903 to 1923, he had exploited his opportunities well and had proved a far better party leader than Lloyd George – admittedly, a very low bar.

The government made it safely to the Easter recess on 16 April 1924. A Labour by-election gain from the Conservatives in West Toxteth on 22 May and a collapse in the Liberal vote in the Kelvin-grove by-election on 23 May suggested that Labour was doing well, the Liberals badly and the Conservatives treading water.

Lloyd George had always worried that if Labour succeeded in office, it would get all the credit, but if it did badly, the Liberals would get the blame for putting them in. It was to be a political law that plagued smaller parties in hung parliaments for the next hundred years. And by March, Lloyd George was already regretting supporting Labour, and he was attacking on a range of issues. Small-er parties in hung parliaments are either part of the government or become part of the opposition. Half-in, half-out is not sustainable for long.

The issue of PR might now just have created a bridge between the two parties. Since the pre-war debates on voting reform, there had however been very limited progress. As far back as 1916–17, a Speaker's Conference had considered a range of electoral issues, including PR. In late January 1917, the recommendations of the conference were published, and these included a unanimous pro-posal to adopt STV in all multi-member borough seats, alongside a majority recommendation to move to AV in the remaining single member (often rural) constituencies.

The Conservatives calculated that STV would help them in large urban areas, but they did not want AV, as it would likely cost them seats. By contrast, some in Labour saw AV as a great way (pre-1918) for the party to run many more candidates while maintaining some sort of Lib–Lab voting pact to keep the Unionists out. But Labour was not keen on STV for precisely the reason that the Conservatives saw some advantage. The three Labour representatives to the conference all supported AV instead.

A Bill was drawn up to deliver electoral reform, but there was inadequate support. Lloyd George failed to give government backing, and he did not make his views known. No doubt it was not a priority for him. Several PR amendments were debated in the Commons and Lords in 1917–18, with much cross-party voting. The Lords seemed to favour PR, but the Commons insisted on AV. Eventually, a compromise suggested STV in seven university constituencies with the status quo elsewhere, pending further review. Momentum for reform was then lost. The changes did not make it into the 1918 Representation of the People Act. Electoral reform is rarely a priority for those in power.

The issue of PR came up again in Parliament in 1921. This time it was a Liberal MP, Sir Thomas Bramsdon, who secured time for debate – an indication of the way the political winds were blowing. Bramsdon's Bill was debated in the Commons on 8 April. Perhaps surprisingly, twenty-five Labour MPs backed the call for PR, and five voted against. At this time, three senior Labour figures were vice-presidents of the PR Society (now the Electoral Reform Society) – J. R. Clynes, Labour leader from February 1921 to November 1922, Snowden and Lord Parmoor. The Bill, nonetheless, was defeated in the Commons.

The Liberals became supporters of PR in 1923–24, when they were losing out badly under First Past the Post. In late April 1924, a meeting of Liberal MPs agreed that co-operation with Labour would depend on their support for electoral reform. A Liberal MP, Athelstan Rendall, now tabled a Bill proposing PR for the Commons, which had its Second Reading in May 2024. The Cabinet, urged on by Asquith, agreed to support the Bill, but at an angry meeting of the Parliamentary Labour Party, it was decided by a large majority to grant a free vote instead. Most Labour MPs were not about to throw the Liberals a lifeline. When the vote took place, twenty-eight supported the Bill, but ninety-one went through the 'No' lobby. The Bill was defeated decisively by 238 votes to 144. Of Cabinet members, only six voted – four supported PR and two voted against.

Henderson, now Home Secretary, made clear that while the government might be willing to consider AV, it would not back PR. He pointed out that no party had included it in their manifesto and there was division in all parties on the issue. MacDonald was still an opponent of PR. In May 1924, speaking at the Tufton Street Labour Club, he said that the political system had not merely to reflect views in the country but deliver 'a workable government'.

So, Labour would not now give the Liberals any leg-up through voting reform. Worse still, they were planning to routinely stand candidates against all Liberals. Liberal MPs were furious. If they were getting nothing back from Labour, why should they sustain them in office? At a speech in Wales on 22 April, Lloyd George spoke out angrily on behalf of his party. It can hardly have helped that Labour had for the first time put up a candidate against him in Caernarvon Boroughs. MPs' perspectives on other parties are often heavily moulded by their own local constituency interests. Labour seemed to be treating Liberals, said Lloyd George, as 'oxen to drag the Labour wain over the rough roads of Parliament for two to three years, goaded along, and at the end of the journey, when there is no further use for them, they are to be slaughtered'. He was, of course, right. But his words did nothing to win over MacDonald, who loathed Lloyd George. He even mulled making a speech to attack how the 'cheap-jack' had degraded the honours system. In one of his regular reports to the King, he wrote with relish that the Liberals 'would appear to be finding their position to be one of growing difficulty and embarrassment'.

Meanwhile, Snowden delivered his first Budget on 29 April. It was so orthodox that the King sent him a message praising the substantial budget surplus. Lenin would not have been amused. Snowden explained that his key aims were to defend free trade, reduce the burden of indirect taxation and cut the national debt. Gladstone would have been most impressed.

Snowden was determined to resist pressures for higher public spending. MacDonald was pleased, noting that this surprised and wrong-footed other parties. Lloyd George was beginning to conclude that the problem with MacDonald's Labour was not left-wing radicalism but extreme caution and orthodoxy. It was at this time that he began to develop a new Liberal economic strategy, one that was designed to save the market economy from itself, rather than replacing it with socialism. This would be radical and new but firmly within the tradition of free markets, free trade and competition.

On public ownership, however, MacDonald was showing some socialist leg. He had appointed Manny Shinwell as Secretary for Mines, and in May Shinwell gave the green light to a Private Members Bill to nationalise the industry. Lloyd George, seizing joyously on the opportunity to oppose Labour, noted this was 'the first concrete example of the New Socialism'. The Bill was easily voted down by a combination of Conservatives and Liberals – 268 votes to 168. Lloyd George was now suggesting that the two parties might unite to bring down the government. But when a motion was tabled later in the month to cut the salary of the Minister for Labour, Asquith pulled his punch, and the government won the vote. Asquith did not want a general election yet – the party had too few resources.

There were further by-elections over the summer months, bringing good news only for the Conservatives. At Oxford, on 5 June, the Liberals lost a seat to the Conservatives, after Labour decided to field a candidate for the first time. The Labour vote of 2,769 was greater than the Conservative majority of 1,842. This was hardly calculated to improve Lib–Lab relations. A month later, on 9 July, another Conservative was elected. This time, a Liberal had wrecked Labour's chances. The old Lib–Lab pacts were dead and buried. On 31 July, there was yet another Conservative victory – this time overturning a Labour majority, after another Liberal intervention.

In mid-1924, Labour moved to normalise relations with communist Russia by presenting a government-backed loan and a trade treaty. Both opposition parties were opposed. Lloyd George sniffed blood in the political waters, warning that 'socialism is approaching skilfully under cover to the grand attack on the existing order of society'. It was opportunistic twaddle but a clear sign of his developing strategy. In July, Lloyd George tried again unsuccessfully to persuade his party to withdraw support from Labour. On 22 September, Asquith made clear he would seek to block the proposed loan, and Churchill joined the attack on 25 September, returning to his theme that the Conservatives and Liberals should unite against Labour.

MacDonald was in trouble, confiding to his diary that he was 'inclined to give the Liberals an election…' In the autumn of 1924, the government finally ran out of road. The trigger was MacDonald being accused by the opposition parties of deceiving the Commons over his role in withdrawing a planned prosecution of a left-wing journalist, John Campbell, the acting editor of a Communist weekly paper. Campbell was being accused of trying to whip up mutiny in the forces and a revolution.

The Conservatives tabled a censure motion in early October, and the senior Liberal MP Sir John Simon, no friend of Labour, presented an amendment to establish a select committee inquiry. Once again, MacDonald was angrier with the Liberals than the Tories – telling his party conference on 7 October that the Liberal amendment was 'conceived in the spirit of medieval crookedness and torture'.

When the motions were debated, MacDonald announced that a government defeat would mean a general election. Asquith, in what would be his last Commons speech, denied claims that a select committee investigation would be biased and offered to remove Liberal MPs from any committee. But the Cabinet was not willing to make concessions. And Baldwin now made his move, saying he would accept the Liberal amendment rather than pressing his own motion. He was cleverly snookering both the government and the Liberals. Sir John Simon's amendment passed by 364 votes to 198. Asquith hoped that his moment had come. Surely either Baldwin or MacDonald would see the light and offer the Liberals entry into a coalition?

But the Cabinet met – and decided on a dissolution. They were divided, but MacDonald's view prevailed. Snowden was furious, feeling there was no need for an election. And Margaret Bondfield, the first female Cabinet Minister, concluded: 'We fell just because Ramsay MacDonald lost his head.' Asquith seemed genuinely surprised and distressed. He also knew the election would not be easy for his party.

Both MacDonald and Baldwin felt they could benefit from the

election. MacDonald judged that the Liberals, rather than Labour, would be the big losers. He was right. Hung parliaments, and those with tiny minorities that necessitated further elections, would end up being damaging to the Liberals in 1924, 1931, 1951, 1966, October 1974, 1979 and 2015.

But MacDonald could not have bargained for the release of the forged Zinoviev letter, which sought to link Labour with Soviet Russia. Lloyd George had also not wanted an election on relations with the Soviet Union, which might only boost the Conservatives. But he upped his anti-Labour rhetoric, warning that socialism might lead to the existing order being 'overthrown'. The Conservatives decided not to stand a candidate in his seat, and he easily saw off his Labour opponent.

For almost a year, the Liberals had sustained Labour in office. What prize had they extracted for all the pain, internal division and opprobrium that would follow? The answer, bluntly, was nothing. As Dutton has noted: 'Overall, it seems unlikely the Liberals derived any benefit from their months of holding the parliamentary balance. The Conservative Party looked increasingly the natural home for those who feared the advent of socialism, while Labour enhanced its credentials as the vehicle for radical progress.'[19]

Lloyd George complained that Labour had missed the chance to create a progressive alliance that could dominate British politics for twenty years. But that was not what Labour was trying to achieve. It was seeking to kill off the Liberals. And it was now well on its way. Within a few years, John Maynard Keynes was asking whether it was the fate of the Liberal Party merely to supply 'Conservative governments with Cabinets and Labour governments with ideas'.

The 1924 Liberal manifesto attacked Labour for its policies of nationalisation, the Russian loan, and lack of action on unemployment.

It presented itself as the centre ground party rejecting both Labour 'experiments' and Conservative 'unthinking resistance to progress'.

But the manifesto was underwhelming. In an address to the 1925 Liberal Summer School entitled 'Am I a Liberal?', John Maynard Keynes was sharply critical, noting: 'Civil and religious liberty, the franchise, the Irish question, Dominion self-government, the power of the House of Lords, steeply graduated taxation of incomes and fortunes ... all these causes for which the Liberal Party fought are successfully achieved or are obsolete or are the common ground of all parties alike.'[20] The party needed 'to invent new wisdom for a new age'.

Liberals needed not just new ideas but money to fight the third election in three years. But Lloyd George was still refusing to hand over his private fund and would only donate £50,000 – half the minimum amount the party needed. Asquith wanted to field 500 candidates, but at a meeting in October 1923, Lloyd George questioned why they needed more than 300. He thought the party a 'disorganised rabble' and did not wish to waste 'his' money.

So, the Liberal Party was reunited, but its financial resources were not. It would field only 339 candidates – leaving 276 seats uncontested. Labour managed 514, just behind the Conservatives on 534. Labour's manifesto consisted of a robust defence of its record, a criticism of the other parties for blocking nationalisation, and a call to back moves towards a 'Socialist Commonwealth'. The Conservatives dropped their policy of protection. With their media allies and the Zinoviev letter they sought ruthlessly to associate Labour with the dangerous radicalism of the new Soviet Union.

When the results were in, the Conservatives had romped home with 412 MPs, a mighty net gain of 154. Labour lost forty seats and dropped back to 151. But their vote share rose to 33.3 per cent, its best ever. It was the Liberals who had gambled and lost badly. Their time as a party of government was over. They had polled a feeble 17.8 per cent – shedding 118 seats and finishing with just forty MPs. 'The blow intended for Labour laid the Liberals flat,' noted one newspaper. They had failed to win a single Conservative seat and had only been successful in seven seats in a contest against both Labour and the Conservatives. Crucially, other than these seven, all but two of their MPs had won without facing a Conservative opponent. This looked like the 1903 pact turned upside down. So weak were the Liberals that the Conservatives had concluded that Labour were now their main threat. Liberal MPs were increasingly dependent on Conservative goodwill for retaining their seats. The Liberal south-west stronghold had also crumbled and their twenty-three seats there had been reduced to just two – both of which were won by Conservative-friendly Liberals, without Conservative opponents.

The Zinoviev letter, designed to damage Labour, seems to have driven many Liberal voters to take flight and back the Conservatives as the most anti-Labour option. Even Asquith once again lost his seat. He would now head to the Lords but cling on to the party leadership for two more unproductive years. In his absence, Lloyd George was elected chair of the Liberal Parliamentary Party. He tried to blame MacDonald for the Liberal defeat, arguing that Asquith could not have known that the Labour PM would run his government 'like a jealous, vain, suspicious, ill-tempered actress of the second rank'. It was hardly the language to build bridges. And some Liberals would never be reconciled either to his conduct, his style, his lack of trustworthiness or to the 'advanced' programme he was associated with.

Baldwin was now back in Downing Street with a large majority. It seemed a good bet that the Conservatives were in power for at least two terms. But five years is a very long time in politics. The 1926 General Strike damaged the economy, and unemployment surged to 15 per cent.

The strike also delivered the final blow to the fragile alliance between Asquith and Lloyd George. Asquith opposed it, but Lloyd George favoured a more sympathetic line. The small parliamentary group was split, and bitterly so, but more (twenty versus ten) supported Lloyd George. As Campbell has noted: 'The Asquithians had been in 1923 the majority of a fairly large party, now they were the minority of a small one.'[21]

Asquith, who had a serious stroke at this time, resigned the leadership in October 1925. In a farewell speech on 15 October, he defended his decision to allow Labour to govern in 1923, without seeking (as Lloyd George was now suggesting he had favoured) a policy agreement with MacDonald:

> A great political party which is not for the time being in a majority should never allow itself to succumb to the temptation to degenerate into a bargaining counter. Independence is essential to self-respect and … it is the only way in the long run of securing the respect of the country … Keep the faith … Resist all the allurements of short cuts and compromises. Look neither to the right nor to the left but keep straight on.

A decade after he first stabbed Asquith in the back, Lloyd George had finally emerged as Liberal leader. It was the end of Asquith's political career, and he died in February 1928. He and Lloyd George were the most effective and impressive Liberal politicians of the post-Victorian era. But Lloyd George was also the most destructive leader the Liberals ever had.

While Lloyd George had divided his party, he was at least a restless force for new ideas and improved organisation. Even a critic, Masterman, acknowledged that 'when Lloyd George came back to the Liberal Party, ideas came back to it'. He now invested more time and money in party staff, set up policy commissions and reached out to influential economists such as Keynes to develop new policies to meet the challenges of the interwar years. He seized upon Keynes's proposals for a programme of state-funded public works to reduce unemployment, and the two men united to criticise Churchill's decision to revert to the Gold Standard at the pre-war parity.

According to his mistress, Frances Stevenson, in November 1926, Lloyd George now had a clear political strategy: 'D's idea is to go definitely towards the Left and gradually to co-ordinate and consolidate all the progressive forces in the country against the Conservatives' reactionary forces. Thus, he will get all the sane Labour as well as Liberals behind him. D will not leave the Liberal Party.'[22]

As ever, though, Lloyd George was keeping his options open, talking to all sides and being entirely straightforward with no one. On 3 October 1928, he was writing to Labour's Philip Snowden, warning that their two parties fighting each other would lead to 'another five years of Tory rule'. Nine days later, he was telling his party conference that there was little to choose between the other parties, and they should remain independent. By December 1928, he was confiding to a media friend that MacDonald could not take for granted Liberal support in any hung parliament – instead, co-operation with the Conservatives was possible.

He told the Labour-friendly C. P. Scott, though, that his preference was to work with Labour, but it must be 'a real coalition with a joint ministry'. But by 18 February 1929, he was confiding to Churchill that in the coming election the Conservatives might be forced into second place, in which case he was open to a deal to keep Labour out. He advised Churchill that if the Conservatives came second, the PM should not immediately resign but instead should talk to him – claiming 'we were just as anti-socialist as they were'. Lloyd George was even considerate enough to tell Churchill his terms. These were: electoral reform (which Churchill said he supported); no tariffs (Churchill said there would need to be an inquiry); a reconstruction of the government to 'remove several incompetents'; and a major drive to tackle unemployment. Churchill wanted a pre-election anti-socialist pact, but Lloyd George ruled that out. After the election, any deal would initially be for a two-year period. Lloyd George considered the meeting to be important enough to record a minute of it for his records, which was not his regular practice. Around this time, he also met with Baldwin, who wisely concluded 'of course I don't believe a word of what he says...'[23]

What was Lloyd George up to? He was keeping his options open. For at least fifteen years, he had been in the market for political deals with whoever would strike them. And he was astute enough to realise that his bargaining position would be stronger if both parties felt he could do a deal with the other. Did he have a preference? Quite probably not, but just as it would have been difficult to keep Baldwin in in 1923, after he had lost his majority over protection, it would also have been difficult in 1929 to prop up a Conservative government that had lost.

And as the election drew nearer, Lloyd George seemed to be heading back to his more traditional 'New Liberal' positioning. In March 1929, he formally launched his new policies of borrowing to invest in a short pamphlet – *We Can Conquer Unemployment*. The Conservative newspapers were appalled. *The Times* concluded: 'The money will doubtless be found at the end of the rainbow.'

Lloyd George was ushering in a century of elections in which right-wing parsimony would be contrasted with left-wing profligacy. The *Morning Post* rehearsed another criticism of the Liberals that was to be polished up and repackaged in every election since – noting that the boldness of the pledge was 'no doubt accounted for by the knowledge that it will never be put into practice'.

MacDonald, however, found it trickier to respond than the Tory press. In a speech in March, he claimed simultaneously that Lloyd George was 'talking through his hat' and that he was pinching Labour ideas. He continued, unconvincingly, to use both arguments.

Between 19 and 21 March, five by-elections were held – all in Conservative seats. Two fell to the Liberals, one to Labour, and the Conservatives just held on in the others. Liberal hopes of a break-through rose. Baldwin finally called the election for 30 May – campaigning on the theme of 'safety first', a strikingly complacent slogan for the times. Churchill suggested to Baldwin that the Liberals should be given a free run against Labour in additional seats, but Baldwin was not persuaded – his view was that Labour were in the long term less of a threat to the Conservatives than a revived Liberal Party.

With Lloyd George's money and organisational flair, the Liberals would now field 513 candidates – 174 more than in 1924. The Liberal manifesto put the economy and unemployment centre-stage, promising to break down barriers to international trade and deliver a programme of public works. During the campaign, Lloyd George was backed by Keynes, who published a pamphlet under the title *Can Lloyd George Do It? The Pledge Examined*. Keynes's conclusion was that the Liberal plan made good sense and was better than simply bearing the high costs of unemployment – which he estimated, in eye-catching terms, as the equivalent of providing the whole population with free cinema tickets 'to the end of time'.

Lloyd George was making the Liberals interesting again. But not all Liberals liked the new policies. The Liberal Council, formed to promote a more traditional platform, had declared its opposition to Lloyd George's new 'Yellow Book' in February 1927. It wanted the focus to be on 'free trade and sound finance'. The manifesto still included some old Liberal favourites, including 'temperance reform', 'cutting down of unproductive expenditure' and devolution. Oddly, electoral reform dropped off the list.

Lloyd George hoped that this was the moment they would sweep Labour aside and return to their rightful position in British politics. But ingenious new policies don't always cut through. And given the size of the Liberal Party, it could not easily present itself as a government in waiting. It appeared more a one-man band. Lloyd George needed a strong Liberal Party to recover his political career. But the vehicle of his ambition had been smashed to pieces by the disloyalty, selfishness and cynicism that he had displayed over the previous decade. He had inherited a tool that he himself had already broken.

On 21 March 1929, the Liberals overturned a Unionist majority in the Holland with Boston by-election. With the election just weeks away, this looked like an exciting omen. It wasn't. In fact, it was the last Liberal by-election win until Torrington in 1958 – almost thirty years ahead.

Labour's manifesto anticipated the right-wing attacks that would be deployed against it: 'The Labour Party is neither Bolshevik nor Communist. It is opposed to force, revolution and confiscation...' Tackling unemployment was the top priority. The mining industry would be nationalised, land put under public control, and there would be investment in a programme of public works. MacDonald still wanted to present Labour as moderate, and most Labour candidates followed his lead – only 8 per cent mentioning socialism in their personal manifestos. The manifesto's concluding pitch was simple: 'A Labour Government is the only alternative to the present Tory Government. The Liberal Party ... can be no more than a small minority in the new parliament.' The choice was between 'National Development and Reconstruction leading to the Socialist and Co-operative Commonwealth', or 'Reaction and Revolution'.

Labour was standing 569 candidates – its largest ever total. This time, MacDonald wanted to compete everywhere with the Liberals, to drive down their vote and smash their party. He and Baldwin were content to stand 'wrecking candidates' against Liberals, even if this handed seats to their sworn opponents.

When the votes were counted on 30 and 31 May, the Conservatives had suffered a big defeat, losing 152 seats on a swing of 8.7 per cent. But they still had 260 MPs – almost exactly their 1923 total. The question was whether Ramsay MacDonald or Lloyd George would benefit. And here there was no ambiguity. The Liberal vote was up by 5.8 per cent, more than the 3.8 per cent rise for Labour. But Labour now had 37.1 per cent of the vote and 287 MPs. The Liberals lagged far behind on 23.6 per cent of the vote and had only fifty-nine seats. Liberal strength was limited to north Wales, north Scotland and the far ends of south-west England. Labour was the party of the cities, including London, and the urban centres of the north, of south Wales and of southern Scotland. The national constituency map of 1929 would look instantly recognisable today.

In one seat, Spen Valley, Baldwin had intervened to persuade the Conservative candidate to step down. His action helped ensure the re-election of the Liberal MP Sir John Simon. It was to prove an astute move. Baldwin had kept in play a Liberal with no affection for Lloyd George, who would soon ensure a further disastrous division in his party.

From 1918 to 1929, the Liberals and Labour had slugged it out to secure second slot in British politics. Finally, Labour had emerged decisively as the winners. Liberal unity had come too late. To survive and thrive in the changed circumstances of British politics in the twentieth century, the Liberals had needed strong leadership, unity, tactical good sense and a fully modernised policy agenda. Instead, they had weak and divided leadership, disunity, tactical idiocy and a policy programme that still straddled both centuries. In 1903, they had 'nursed into life a serpent' and it had now, indeed, stung them to death, or at least into a state of paralysed incapacity.

The electoral system had doubled down on Liberal woes. The Conservatives had secured the largest number of votes – 8,253,000. But it had taken 31,740 Conservative votes to elect each Conservative MP. Labour had finished with 8,049,000 votes, but it had taken only 28,045 to elect each Labour MP. It was the Liberals who were the losers. They had secured 86,519 votes for each of their MPs. No wonder the party was increasingly attracted by electoral reform.

One Liberal could not resist gloating. Margot Asquith wrote to Baldwin to commiserate on his defeat, noting with relish that 'the British public was not taken in by Ll. G. and his silly promises and pledges'. The bitterness of 1916 would never be wiped away.

The split Labour–Liberal vote had now delivered another hung parliament. Once again, Ramsay MacDonald would become Prime Minister with no Labour majority. The year 1906 had seen the Conservatives poll 43.4 per cent of the vote but secure a miserable 156 MPs. In 1929, the Conservatives amassed just 38.1 per cent of the votes but ended up with 260 seats. The electoral system was now hammering the Liberals and helping Labour, but the split in the 'progressive' vote was assisting the Conservatives.

But could the 'progressive' vote be considered as some unified and coherent whole, divided between two different but fundamentally aligned parties? This had been largely the case in 1906 and in 1910. But the Labour Party of 1929 was a different and more radical beast. Labour was now a self-declared socialist party, committed to nationalisation. And the rise of the Soviet Union had hugely increased fears that economic stresses might cause an overthrow of the existing order that would be anathema to Conservatives and Liberals alike.

British politics had divided three ways – it had a nationalistic Conservative Party, which was largely the defender of the status quo and the interests of the upper classes; it had a relatively moderate socialist party in Labour, committed to both social reform and state control of important parts of the economy; and it had a Liberal Party committed to free trade, free enterprise, social reform and an uncomfortable mix of a distinctly modernist and interventionist fiscal policy, alongside some relics of nineteenth-century liberalism.

The Liberals were now in the centre ground of British politics – the only place they could be. But they were a small force stuck in a political no man's land and shot at by both sides. In 1929, they had an energetic leader, more money, more candidates and the only policy programme that seemed to offer creative solutions to the salient issue of unemployment. Their problem was that they did not seem like a credible party of government. They had spent the last decade divided and embittered – not an attractive image for voters. Unless they could find a better path than that taken in 1923, they now risked a miserable replay of their experience of 1924. If Labour did well, it would receive all the credit. In the more likely scenario in which a minority government failed, the Liberals would receive a huge part of the blame. It looked like another lose–lose scenario, unless the recent laws of politics could be rewritten. Or the rules of the electoral system changed.

In a 615-member House of Commons, Labour's 287 seats put them well short of the 308 they needed to form a majority. But adding the fifty-nine Liberal MPs to either Labour's 287 or the Conservatives' 260 would be enough to clear the threshold required for a majority.

Baldwin nonetheless resigned soon after the election. He despised and distrusted Lloyd George and was not going to negotiate with him. He regarded him as more dangerous than MacDonald – indeed both men were united in distrust and dislike of their Liberal foe. As far back as 1924, MacDonald had written to Baldwin from Chequers, oddly asking for a photo of the Conservative leader to put up in his study – 'Personally I should like very much to be reminded of you by your face looking at me.'[24] There was already a photograph of Lloyd George that made MacDonald 'see red'.

A coalition with the Liberal Party might have seemed the obvious solution to Labour's minority position. But MacDonald was determined to throttle the Liberal Party, not throw it a lifeline. And what sane PM would want to go into government with a partner like Lloyd George, who could hardly see a back without wanting to plunge a knife into it, and whose own colleagues had concluded that 'he would not recognise a principle if he met it in the street'? And what would be the Liberal price? Labour had at times toyed with the idea of the Alternative Vote. This might have seemed, tactically, a sensible system to adopt under the circumstances of 1903–14, when Labour and the Liberals had a highly complementary political programme and voter base. But in the circumstances of 1929, it was not obvious that every Liberal voter would want to select a socialist party as their second preference. And with an electoral system that now seemed biased towards Labour, change cannot have seemed attractive.

So, with Baldwin's swift resignation, Ramsay MacDonald was the new Prime Minister of a minority government – constructing his Cabinet without bothering to speak to Lloyd George. But the King's Speech, on 2 July 1929, promised an inquiry into the electoral system. MacDonald was keeping the Liberals hopeful, but at a distance.

If MacDonald expected a honeymoon period, he was to be seriously disappointed. In October, the 'Wall Street Crash' occurred, wiping away a huge proportion of world share values and leading to a mammoth economic slump. Labour had fought the election promising to address the problem of over 1 million unemployed, but by August 1931 unemployment would more than double to 2.8 million. The difficult economic circumstances drove MacDonald and Snowden, again Chancellor, to cut back on key parts of their social reform agenda and to fall back on the more orthodox prescriptions of their Treasury advisers.

The Liberals were also having a difficult time. Two MPs soon defected to Labour. And Freddie Guest, Lloyd George's former Chief Whip, left for the Conservatives. On some key votes in the Commons, the party would split and splinter – setting a pattern for parliamentary disunity that would continue for three decades.

By October 1929, Lloyd George was already writing to Churchill raising the possibility of a 'working understanding' with the Conservatives.[25] And in December, the Liberal leadership made clear it would block Labour's policy of nationalising the mining industry, preferring instead greater efficiency through compulsory amalgamation. In the Commons, Lloyd George and Churchill made their usual rollicking speeches of opposition. They had found some territory to attack Labour on and were going to exploit it to the full. MacDonald, tired and thin-skinned, confided to his diary that he might resign and leave the other parties to pick up the pieces – 'It would really be a relief. This office has no attraction for me.'

The Coal Bill survived Second Reading by a majority of only eight, with two Liberals backing Labour and six abstaining – more confirmation of Liberal disunity. Any little respect MacDonald had for Lloyd George had now gone, and in his diary on 19 December he let off a veritable blast of steam at the former PM: 'He made us victorious by bringing us to ruin … He degraded our public life and its honours; he was a friend who never felt friendship, a colleague who was ever disloyal; he never used a partner but for his own ends and sacrificed everyone who ever trusted him.'[26] This was not much of a character reference.

But Lloyd George had an ulterior motive for making life difficult for MacDonald. He now hoped to do a deal with Labour to deliver voting reform. The King's Speech had promised the inquiry into parliamentary elections, and in the debate on the address MacDonald had indicated in response to a question from Lloyd George that while he was still personally opposed to any form of PR, the inquiry might touch upon the issue. It was to become a strategy familiar to Labour and Conservative leaders for the next 100 years – keep the Liberals hopeful and string them along.

A three-party conference on elections was established on 4 December, under Lord Ullswater, a Conservative who had been Speaker of the Commons up to 1921. The conference had been agreed in July, but to Lloyd George's irritation had taken five months to get started. The remit was rather vague, perhaps because this suited MacDonald. The PM was not pushing for a speedy or clear set of recommendations, and Ullswater soon began to wonder whether he had been handed a poisoned chalice. The conference would consist of seven Labour MPs, seven Conservatives, four Liberals and four representatives from the Lords, including Ullswater. It was a recipe for indecision. In a letter to Ullswater, written in July 1929,

MacDonald wrote that the inquiry should consider whether any reform to the electoral system would 'sacrifice other requirements of an efficient democratic machinery'. Since that was MacDonald's established view about PR, it was, perhaps, a rather unsubtle hint.

But Lloyd George felt that Labour's weak parliamentary position was giving him some leverage, and in January 1930 he made a less-than-veiled proposal indicating that he might trade the Coal Bill for a deal on PR. MacDonald was not yet open to any deal. He wanted the Liberal Party dead – not sustained forever as the swing party in British politics. That Lloyd George was seen by MacDonald as an unprincipled chancer, and simultaneously his main challenger for leadership of the radical forces in the country, would not have made the Prime Minister any keener to throw the Liberals a PR bone.

But parliamentary arithmetic underlined MacDonald's weak position, and on 3 February 1930, he agreed to meet the Liberal leader. He included his colleagues Snowden, Henderson and Thomas, wisely deciding that witnesses might be handy. Lloyd George, the arch schemer, was ready with his latest plan. He was offering to give Labour support for two or three years, but the price was PR. MacDonald, predictably, was unimpressed, recording in his diary: 'The bargain proposed really amounts to this: we get two years of office from the Liberals and give them in return a permanent corner on our political stage.'

In a memorandum to senior colleagues the next day, MacDonald made clear that the deal he personally favoured was no more than that which held after the December 1910 election. The parties would remain separate. They would co-operate to keep the government going. He was clear that going any further would upset the Labour Party, concede too much power to the Liberals, help Lloyd George to unite his party and boost his credibility with voters, hamper

Labour freedom in by-elections, cede PR, which would not be acceptable to Labour and would mean abandoning his strategy of restoring two-party politics and marginalising the Liberals, and – finally – limit Labour's flexibility to exploit conflict with the House of Lords. It was not a 'maybe' to the Lloyd George plan – it was total rejection. MacDonald concluded instead that they should 'delay the conversation', keep talking to the Liberals and struggle on alone. He admitted that this was a real risk to the government's life expectancy, 'but the price we shall have to pay for a two years' security will be so high that we cannot pay it'.[27]

But MacDonald needed to stop Lloyd George moving into full opposition mode. On 20 February, the two men met for dinner. Lloyd George was still complaining about the Coal Bill, but despite his threats it again survived a vote on 27 February, by a majority of nine, with four Liberals voting with Labour and eight abstaining. It seemed that the Liberals could not even competently hold Labour to ransom.

In March, however, there were to be more votes on the Bill, and this time MacDonald's senior colleagues sensed defeat and wobbled. Lloyd George had been lobbying several of them behind MacDonald's back. The Cabinet finally agreed in March to tell Lloyd George that they would introduce an electoral reform bill. And on 5 March, Lloyd George was informed by a media contact that MacDonald was willing to meet him to negotiate 'a two year compact on terms of reasonable consultation pending electoral reform'.[28] It was all encouraging enough for Lloyd George to invent a bogus excuse to get his MPs to abstain on the tricky Coal Bill votes, on the eccentric and fanciful basis that the government ought not to be embarrassed during a critical stage of an international naval conference.

By 5 May, Lloyd George was optimistic. He wrote publicly and positively about Labour's willingness to consider electoral reform, and its 'shunning' of socialist ideas in its proposed legislation. On 8 May, the Ullswater Conference met again. The Conservatives allied with the Liberals and voted that if there was to be change to the voting system, it should be to PR. They knew this was unacceptable to Labour and wanted to avoid AV. The Labour representatives would only contemplate AV.

Some in Labour now concluded they might concede the Alternative Vote to the Liberals. The party's analysis, completed in June 1929, suggested that AV might have suited Labour very well in 1929 – handing it fifteen more seats and the Liberals forty-seven more, at Conservative expense.[29] This was based on several assumptions, including one third of voters not using their second vote and other voters dividing on second preferences such that Conservative voters split 60–40 for the Liberals, Liberal voters 60–40 for Labour, and Labour voters decided 75–25 in the Liberals' favour. If Labour was to have to concede electoral reform, it would be much easier if the system worked in its favour, and AV seemed to deliver that.

That, of course, was not the Liberal aspiration. They wanted something more proportionate. Their submission to the Ullswater Conference suggested a compromise, as envisaged in 1917, that would use two different systems – STV in urban areas and AV in rural seats. It was a system that Roy Jenkins would return to in 1998, while chairing Blair's Electoral Commission.

MacDonald had only proposed a deal to Lloyd George because his colleagues had insisted on compromise. He was now getting cold feet. In the spring of 1930, he wrote a confidential and 'very personal' memorandum. He was still worried that the deal on offer would come at unacceptable cost. His view was that the election in two years' time would be challenging and that the Liberal proposals on PR would lose Labour seats in industrial areas under STV, while any gains in the rural seats through AV would not make up those losses. The deal would be great for the Liberals, and bad for Labour. MacDonald could not be certain of the impact on the Conservatives but felt it would 'solidify' their position and leave them as the strongest of the three parties. He was, understandably, not up for a deal that might just hand Labour seats to his Liberal opponents. Nor did he want to have to forever rely on the Liberals. He was concluding that the best tactic might be to let a Bill proceed, and then allow it to fizzle out in the Lords in the face of Conservative opposition.

The shrewd tactician of 1903 was just as shrewd in protecting his party's advantage twenty-seven years later. MacDonald also came back to his earlier objection to a deal – it could not be sold to a Labour Party which would see it as a foolish concession to the Liberals and a capitulation on the strategy of killing off this competitor. He would need to get the deal past both his annual conference and his MPs. He judged neither likely.

Labour now sought to align the Liberals on the Ullswater commission behind their more modest AV plan, and other smaller changes including limitations on election spending.

But Lloyd George wasn't buying this. He met MacDonald again on 19 May 1930, and said he could not settle for AV, only PR – claiming his party wouldn't agree to AV. MacDonald dug in: AV or nothing. Neither would budge.

When the Labour National Executive met on 20 May, they took an even tougher line than MacDonald, voting 11–6 against proposing even AV to the Ullswater process. David Marquand has suggested that MacDonald may have deliberately involved the

National Executive, knowing they would torpedo a deal that he was only too happy to have junked.[30]

On 21 May, the talks between Labour and the Liberals broke down. The Liberals still wanted PR. MacDonald would hint at nothing more than AV. And Labour was still split. Some were opposed to any change. But Snowden favoured PR, Thomas was a vice-president of the PR Society, and Parmoor was its chairman. In July, the Ullswater Conference broke up without an agreement. The Conservative members voted with the Liberals that if there was to be a new system, it should be PR. The Labour members would still only support AV.

The Liberals now had to reflect carefully on their strategy. Many were deeply opposed to Labour but also feared a repeat of the 1924 electoral disaster. MacDonald played skilfully on these fears, and in late May he had also brought Lloyd George into discussions in government about the economy, including sharply rising unemployment. The Conservatives were also invited to the talks but declined. The new and rather over-large 'Economic Advisory Council' was not productive and mutual suspicion reigned. But MacDonald was being canny. He was trying to keep Lloyd George onside and engaged, without delivering anything on PR.

On 19 September 1930, Lloyd George met MacDonald again, and in an extensive three-hour meeting, they discussed the economy and electoral reform. Lloyd George was still pushing for PR or at least AV. Without this, he said it was too politically dangerous for him to prop up the government. He now also claimed that the Conservatives were willing to do a deal on PR, to turn out Labour. But he professed to prefer an agreement with MacDonald. He was offering to back Labour for at least as long as it would take to get the

Electoral Reform Bill through Parliament – probably two years or more, given likely Lords opposition.

MacDonald briefed the Cabinet on 25 September 1930, telling them that Lloyd George was threatening to ally with the Conservatives. After a long discussion, the Cabinet agreed that Lloyd George should now be offered AV. If he agreed in principle, they would work to convince the National Executive and party conference. In October, the King's speech included a reference to electoral reform, without specifying what this meant, and in his speech on the address MacDonald avoided giving further details.

It had always been a risk to Lloyd George that if he moved towards Labour, he would split his party. Late in October, Sir John Simon wrote to him, warning that if there was a confidence motion, he would vote against Labour. Simon was a Liberal of the 'old school', whose position in Parliament was highly dependent on Conservative support. He had faced no Conservative opponent in his Spen Valley seat since 1923, when his majority was just 1,075 over Labour, with a 7,390 Conservative vote. In 1929, he had held the seat against Labour and Communist candidates, with only 51.7 per cent of the vote. His constituency interests and personal views meant that he saw Labour as a much greater enemy than the Conservatives.

On 3–4 November, the King's Speech was debated. The Conservatives put down an anti-government amendment – effectively a vote of non-confidence. Lloyd George's line was a timorous and tactical abstention. But five Liberals voted against the government, including Simon, and four voted with Labour. The anti-government rebels included the Liberal Chief Whip – never a good omen for party discipline. He resigned and was replaced by Sir Archibald Sinclair, a future party leader.

Sir John Simon was now in open rebellion, publishing a letter to Lloyd George that claimed that the government was a 'complete failure'. Lloyd George's position was getting distinctly uncomfortable. He was giving vital support to Labour but getting nothing bankable in return. It was 1924 all over again: 'Once again, the lure of the balance of power was being shown up as a cruel deception.'[31]

Up to now, the Prime Minister was stringing the Liberal leader along. On 17 November, the Cabinet recorded that it had not yet settled its position on electoral reform. In the country, the Liberal Party was restless. On 5 December, Lloyd George met the Liberal Candidates Association. They were strongly opposed to propping up Labour. And their view was that unless Labour conceded PR, the Liberals should treat each vote in Parliament on its merits. Nor did they think that AV was sufficient. Lloyd George, now knowing that PR would prove too much for Labour, argued that they should consider settling for AV, which would help defeat the Conservatives and save the country from protection. But he got a rough ride and had to offer a reassurance that there was 'no deal and no pact'.

The Liberal Party feared proximity to Labour could be disastrous electorally. Lloyd George had a different view – if his party wanted electoral reform and to have real influence again in politics, it had to accept the risks and be willing to deal – 'If he could … bring the Liberal Party fruitfully to bed with Labour, he thought the result would justify the loss of independence.'[32]

On 17 December, the Labour National Executive again debated the issue. MacDonald had increasing reasons to deal with Lloyd George. Unemployment was surging. The public finances were a mess. Labour's political position was weakening, and the party was beginning to divide between supporters of the government and those who thought them too timid. The National Executive now voted 16–3 to include AV in a coming Electoral Reform Bill, but it wanted no pact with the Liberals. The following day there was a joint meeting of the Executive and Labour MPs. By 133 to twenty they also supported AV. Lloyd George was finally making progress and calculated that AV would have delivered him fifty-three more seats in England in 1929, with Labour gaining twelve.[33]

The government now brought forward both an Electoral Reform Bill and a Trade Union Bill. The understanding was that in exchange for the former, the Liberals would allow the latter to pass – restoring the trade union political levy, which Baldwin's government had abolished in 1927. AV was clearly not PR, but being the 'centre ground' party, the Liberals hoped to benefit from a system which brought second preferences into play. It has been estimated that AV might have increased Liberal seat numbers from 159 to 217 in 1923, from forty to seventy-four in 1924, and from fifty-nine to 137 in 1929.[34] The latter is the key date and election, as this would have transformed the Liberal position and notably reduced the number of Conservative seats.

While Lloyd George thought he was about to deliver this great prize for his party, the old Asquithian Sir John Simon came out publicly in mid-December against AV. This time, it was Lloyd George who was being stabbed in the back. It was hardly helpful, but in early February 1931 the Electoral Reform Bill passed with a majority of sixty-five.

In the same month, MacDonald and Lloyd George dined together in the Commons and discussed the economic crisis. Lloyd George was increasingly despairing of MacDonald's timidity, telling Frances Stevenson on 4 February that pushing Labour to do more on the economy was like 'trying to roll a melting, sloshing, snowball up the hill'. He thought MacDonald and Snowden too cautious and complained to his mistress of the PM: 'This ranting hero of the Socialist hordes squealed with terror when he was invited to face the financial weasels of the City.' In the face of economic crisis, MacDonald and Snowden were seeking the safety of conventional Treasury wisdom and not the unorthodox Keynesianism that Lloyd George now championed.

Some Labour figures wanted Lloyd George to join their party, but he rejected that in favour of proceeding with electoral reform. Then, 'when the Dissolution comes ... through the agency of the Alternative Vote there will be such co-operation at the polls as will ensure a fresh opportunity for a progressive Government...'[35]

In March, Lloyd George and MacDonald agreed to regular weekly meetings. The electoral reform plan was progressing, and the Bill was carried in the Commons on Second Reading, on party lines, by 290 votes to 230. In March 1931, the clause allowing for AV was also carried by 277 votes to 253. Despite the parties being whipped, eleven Labour MPs and two Liberals had voted against AV, and twenty-seven Labour MPs had abstained. Liberal MPs voted on 23 March to continue to support Labour, while avoiding any formal pact. But the vote was 33–17; not a huge endorsement.

And if Lloyd George and MacDonald were working closely but cautiously together, Sir John Simon was heading off in completely the opposite direction. In March 1931, he hinted that even those, like him, who supported free trade might need to consider other 'fiscal methods' to tackle the economic crisis. Sinclair warned on 20 March that Simon and others were a 'nucleus of disloyalty and disaffection in the party'.

On 16 April, the Conservatives moved a motion to condemn Labour for its failures on unemployment. Lloyd George led thirty Liberal MPs in supporting Labour. But five Liberals, led again by Simon, voted with the Conservatives. The split was solidifying.

Finally, after Labour announced a new land tax in its Budget of 27 April 1931, Simon and two other prominent Liberal MPs resigned the whip. Lloyd George was learning how tough life was for leaders with treacherous colleagues. The rebel was facing rebellion. In a speech in the Commons condemning Simon's defection, he responded with his usual vitriol: 'Greater men … have done it in the past, but … they … did not leave behind the slime of hypocrisy in passing from one side to another.' He had not just burnt, but incinerated, another bridge.

The Conservatives were now raising protection again as the solution to the economic slump. MacDonald and Lloyd George were still committed to free trade. Relations were now improving between the two men, and in July they may even have discussed some more solid partnership to sustain the government.[36] Campbell thinks the two men were plotting a coalition, with Lloyd George and other Liberals joining the government, possibly with Snowden leaving the Treasury.[37] On 14 July, MacDonald wrote to Sidney Webb saying: 'We have not the material in our party that we ought to have. The solution will have to come, I am afraid, by moves which will surprise all of you.' Was he thinking of a Lib–Lab coalition? Or a National Government?

In Frank Owen's 1954 biography of Lloyd George, he cites a memorandum, now apparently lost, from Lloyd George to Frances Stevenson. It was written in the last days of July, after the Liberal leader had met the PM. The memorandum suggests MacDonald was contemplating a coalition, with Lloyd George as both Leader of the House and either Chancellor or Foreign Secretary. MacDonald would continue as PM. Nothing was agreed, but that seemed the likely outcome.

There are also indications at this time that Lloyd George was doing what he always did – talking to other politicians, including Churchill, and keeping his options open. And he is even in one account supposed to have speculated about a MacDonald–Baldwin National Government.[38] Could it be that MacDonald was also keeping his options open? It seems likely.

The AV Bill was still making progress, finally being passed in the Commons on 2 June 1931, by 278 votes to 228. But in the Lords, the Bill faced determined Conservative resistance, with peers questioning the lack of mandate for reform and tabling amendments that would delay the passage of the Bill until the autumn.

At this crucial point, a further economic crisis blew up. A slumping economy meant declining tax revenues and big budget deficits. In February 1931, a Liberal motion in the Commons had seen the establishment of a committee to investigate the budgetary crisis. In late July, the report was imminent.

And at this crucial moment, on 27 July 1931, Lloyd George was taken seriously ill. On 29 July, he had a major operation to remove his prostate gland. He had to temporarily hand over the leadership to Sir Herbert Samuel. Two days after his operation, the 'May' Committee on the public finances reported. It estimated there was a huge £120 million budget deficit and suggested large cuts to public spending – including slashing unemployment benefit. The orthodox Snowden thought the report might help him to impose austerity on his more spendthrift Cabinet colleagues, but the markets took fright. The pound plunged, and the country faced an economic crisis. Keynes wanted the pound devalued, but the Bank of England and Treasury favoured spending cuts and fiscal orthodoxy. MacDonald was by nature a cautious and risk-averse man. He plumped for the official advice. Senior ministers were called back from their holidays to agree a package of spending cuts. They needed to be able to satisfy the markets but also secure support in the Commons.

The bankers and the Conservatives were now telling Labour that the cuts were not big enough. Which way would the Liberals leap? When governments are in a mess, the incentive is usually not for opposition parties to throw them a lifeline, though fifty years later the Liberal Party was to take a different course. This time, they followed the usual playbook and sided with the Conservatives, demanding bigger cuts. That effectively ended Liberal support for the minority Labour government.

MacDonald thought he could go it alone, but he was running out of road. And Labour's union paymasters opposed even the cuts that the Cabinet had already agreed – suggesting that taxes should be raised instead. In a corner, the Cabinet now asked for a loan from New York bankers, in exchange for a 10 per cent cut to unemployment benefit. There could hardly have been a more divisive measure for a Labour government to consider, and the Cabinet was deeply split – with eleven voting in favour and nine against. Arthur Henderson threatened resignation if they proceeded. MacDonald was furious – the government was too divided to continue. He saw his thirty-year effort to make Labour appear respectable, responsible and electable going up in smoke. For a while, he even considered resigning and supporting a Conservative–Liberal coalition from the backbenches. But the wily Conservatives could see greater benefit in leaving MacDonald in place to deliver the unpopular cuts.

On 24 August, Lloyd George was allowed out of his house for the first time since his operation. While he was driving through the Surrey countryside, MacDonald's government collapsed, and with it, Lloyd George's political strategy and career. But when MacDonald visited King George V at Buckingham Palace on this same day to submit his resignation, the King persuaded him that at this time of crisis it was his duty to stay on as leader of a National Government. What better way to deliver political stability than to put a Labour leader in charge of delivering austerity?

MacDonald reported back to his shell-shocked Cabinet the result of the meeting – a National Government to see out the crisis, followed by a general election. The election would be a competition between the parties, with no 'coalition coupon' on the 1918 model. MacDonald remained PM in a new Cabinet of ten, alongside four Conservatives, including Baldwin, and two Liberals – the acting leader during Lloyd George's illness, Sir Herbert Samuel, and Lord Reading.

MacDonald was now even contemplating a new, breakaway Labour Party that might be free of the trade union link. But he was fast losing the support of his 287 MPs, and not many more than ten, including Chancellor Philip Snowden, were willing to back the National Government. MacDonald was shattering the unity of his party in a similar way to Lloyd George in 1916. And just as they had cleverly used Lloyd George from 1916 to 1922 and then discarded him, the Conservatives were now happily using MacDonald as the frontman of a Conservative-inspired administration.

On 26 August, Lloyd George wrote to MacDonald, praising his 'heroic attitude'. Intriguingly, he wrote: 'The alternative – or shall I say both alternatives – were disastrous; and therefore, when it was intimated to me that you would probably be forced to throw in your hand I was in despair.' But he welcomed the new administration while warning 'I sincerely hope there is nothing in this talk of an early dissolution. That would undo all the good work...'

Labour now moved into opposition and selected Henderson as their new leader. The party was moving sharply to the left, and there was much talk of a conspiracy by the financiers to destroy a Labour government. MacDonald had always been an opponent of PR and a lukewarm supporter of AV. He had only been willing to consider the latter to keep his party in power. But now, with the bitter Labour split, the whole idea of pacts, coalitions, electoral reform and deals with the Liberals went even more deeply out of fashion in the Labour Party. MacDonald, no enthusiast for coalitions or voting reform, had managed to toxify both in the Labour Party for at least the next sixty years.

In September, the National Government passed its Budget, including the spending cuts agreed by the Labour Cabinet and the 10 per cent cut in unemployment benefit. Lloyd George was recovering from his operation and Sir Herbert Samuel was still acting leader. Samuel was closer to Labour than the Conservatives and had led the engagement with Labour in the period from 1930 to 1931. He was not keen on perpetuating the National Government but was nervous about an early election. Lloyd George, trying to stay in touch from his home in the Surrey countryside, was bitterly opposed to an early election, which he feared could see the Conservatives return on a protectionist programme. The by-election omens were not good, with big swings to the Conservatives. Meanwhile, the end of the Labour government had meant the end of his precious Electoral Reform Bill.

Lloyd George wrote to Samuel and his senior colleagues on 30 September. He warned that an election would be a disaster and if the Liberals were to stay in the National Government during this it would 'sign the death warrant of the Liberal Party as a separate party'. Ironically, given his conduct in 1918, he wrote: 'Liberal members may save their skins, but they will be completely stripped of their feathers and after the election you may have Ministers who are nominally Liberal in the so-called National Government, but they will only be a miserable row of plucked boobies...'[39]

The Liberals now did what they seemed, since 1916, to do best. They split. One faction of twenty-one MPs, under Sir John Simon, decided to support the National Government as Liberal Nationals – even if this meant accepting protectionist policies. They also backed an immediate general election and concluded a deal with the Conservatives not to oppose most of them. Ironically, it was the old allies of Asquith who were this time aligning themselves with the Conservatives and against free trade. The rest stayed under the leadership of Samuel.

On 28 September, MacDonald was expelled from Labour for his disloyalty to his party. On 5 October, the King approved MacDonald's request – backed strongly by the Conservatives – for a dissolution, with an election on Tuesday 27 October. Lloyd George was furious. He thought Samuel had made a disastrous misjudgement in unenthusiastically accepting an election.

Labour went into the election without their former Prime Minister and Chancellor. MacDonald stood as 'National Labour', in a grouping of just twenty candidates. Snowden retired from the Commons. This Labour division might have been a heaven-sent opportunity for the Liberals to reunite and make a come-back. But in a striking display of their determination to out-split any other party and shoot themselves in the foot, and indeed any other available part of the body, the Liberals now divided three ways.

The more left-leaning Sir Herbert Samuel would lead a group of Liberal candidates who were broadly supportive of the National Government but committed to free trade. They were only 111 in number. Sir John Simon would lead a more Conservative-sympathetic group of forty-one Liberal National candidates, also supportive of the National Government and more willing to compromise on protection. And, if that was not enough, there would be a group of six Independent Liberal candidates, opposed to the National Government and to protection, of whom four were members of the Lloyd George family (Lloyd George himself; his son, Gwilym; his daughter, Megan; and Gwilym's wife's sister's husband).

If this all seemed like a recipe for a total and utter unmitigated, grade-A Liberal disaster, it most certainly was.

CHAPTER 3

'LIBERAL NATIONALS OR LIBERAL SOCIALISTS?' 1931–56

The election of 1929 had been a disappointment for the Liberal Party. The election of 1931 was a catastrophe. In 1929, they received 23.5 per cent of the vote and fifty-nine MPs. In 1931, they managed 6.5 per cent and just thirty-two MPs. For the next forty-three years, a party which in 1906 had won almost half the vote and 399 MPs was so small that it had almost no national relevance and was permanently at risk of extinction. Indeed, if the Conservatives had declined to give Liberal candidates an unchallenged run in a small number of seats, the party might well have ceased to exist.

Many Liberals felt that they now had to choose between Labour or Conservatives. Two of Lloyd George's children had followed him into politics as Liberals, but by 1955 Megan Lloyd George had defected to Labour while Gwilym Lloyd George had effectively become a Conservative supporter ten years earlier – when he stood as a 'National Liberal and Conservative'. Gwilym was a minister in the Conservative government between 1951 and 1957.

This was the era of Liberal irrelevance, in which the party's general election vote share was stuck resolutely at or under 10 per cent, and the number of MPs soon fell to as few as six. Even in 1970, after a modest Liberal resurgence in the early 1960s, the party still had only six MPs – of whom only three were regularly turning up to undertake their parliamentary duties. They had a 'terrible job keeping the [single] Liberal table in the [Members] dining room', because there were so few of them to justify its exclusive use (Slade, 2002).

These long years of irrelevance can be divided into two periods – 1931–56, and 1956–74. In the first of these, there was often a greater proximity to the Conservative Party. But from 1956 onwards, the degree of identification and co-operation with Labour increased, and bridges with the Conservative Party were burnt.

The election of 1931, held on 27 October, and fought against the background of economic crisis which followed the Wall Street Crash of 1929, delivered a landslide victory for the Conservative dominated National Government. The Conservatives alone won 470 seats. The Liberal Nationals, under Sir John Simon, secured thirty-five seats and National Labour another thirteen. The Liberals, led by Samuel, returned with only thirty-two MPs. Lloyd George's Independent Liberals won four seats of the six they contested.

With 554 seats out of 615 in the Commons, and 67 per cent of the vote, the National Government had secured the biggest landslide in UK political history. By contrast, Labour suffered its greatest ever setback – its number of MPs slumped from 287 to just fifty-two, and its leader, Arthur Henderson, lost his seat. But Labour's vote share fell much less – from 37.1 per cent to 30.9 per cent. It was now very clearly the largest, and only serious, opposition party.

Meanwhile, National Labour leader, Ramsay MacDonald, was re-elected and remained PM. This was a replay of 1918–22; MacDonald was effectively the Conservatives' chosen frontman for a government of national austerity. It was not a situation that seemed likely to last long. In fact, MacDonald would remain Prime Minister until June 1935. Like Lloyd George, in 1918, the Conservatives had happily given him a four-year stint. They were remarkably patient with those who would do their bidding.

The Liberals had only won fifty-nine seats in 1929, but their three separate groups now returned with seventy-two in total. This might sound like a success, in the light of their plummeting vote share. But their split was now permanent, and despite their increased parliamentary numbers, they were in a far more precarious position. Because of these seventy-two Liberals, only ten had won seats against Conservative opposition. And the Liberal vote had declined by over 3 million – for now, only the Tory pacts were masking the party's implosion. The Lib–Lab co-operation of 1903 to 1910 had been dramatically replaced by Lib–Con deals. Without these, the party would be decimated.

Where was the Liberal Party moving on policy? A glance at their 1931 manifesto shows that it was far less economically radical than that presented under Lloyd George in 1929. Gone was the plan for fiscal reflation, to 'conquer unemployment'. In its place were a series of recognisably Gladstonian themes, including a commitment to 'keep the Budget balanced' and deliver 'a lowering of tariff barriers'. There were no commitments to improved social policies. Instead 'the maintenance of sound finance … is the condition of the restoration of industry and commerce, the indispensable steps to the lessening of unemployment and the resumption of social progress'. In the face of the economic crisis, and without Lloyd George, the party had swung decidedly rightwards.

And if the party's Conservative partners were implicitly criticised over their policies of protectionism, Labour was explicitly attacked over its spending policies – 'the programme of expenditure to which that party has now committed itself must ... lead to financial disaster'.

The manifesto concluded with a call for electoral reform and presented the Liberals as an 'independent party ... forming a barrier against both reaction on the one hand and rash and injurious changes on the other'. The natural progressive fit between Liberal and Labour manifestos in the years before the First World War was at an end.

If the Liberal manifesto was now rather timid, that of Labour was increasingly radical. Shorn of its cautious leadership and determined to resist the orthodoxy of the National Government, Labour now moved decisively leftwards to present its most radical programme yet. It argued that 'the capitalist system has broken down' and called for 'socialist reconstruction', including 'the extension of publicly owned industries and services operated solely in the interests of the people...' It pledged that 'the banking and credit system of the country ... [would be] brought directly under national ownership and control'. While rejecting tariffs, the manifesto promised 'definite planning of industry and trade ... and as a first step to reorganise the most important basic industries – Power, Transport, Iron and Steel – as public services owned and controlled in the national interest, with such a regulation of prices as will enable British industry to compete effectively'. In 1929, the party had proposed only to nationalise coal. Now, many more industries would be publicly controlled, including the Bank of England.

Ten days before the election, Labour's Chancellor, Philip Snowden – still in post but not standing again – had used a radio broadcast to make an extraordinary attack on his old party. He criticised former colleagues for a lack of political courage and rubbished Labour's manifesto:

It is the most fantastic and impracticable programme ever put before the electors. All the derelict industries are to be taken over by the State, and the taxpayer is to shoulder the losses. The banks and financial houses are to be placed under national ownership and control, which means, I suppose, that they are to be run by a joint committee of the Labour Party and the Trade Union Council … This is not Socialism. It is Bolshevism run mad.

Labour's programme would 'destroy every vestige of confidence and plunge the country into irretrievable ruin'. Snowden followed this up in a newspaper article that accused Labour's new leaders of being 'Little Lenins'. The Conservative-supporting press lapped it all up.

When Liberal MPs met on 5 November, ten days after polling day, a letter from Lloyd George was read out. He was formally resigning the leadership, saying he was 'completely at variance with the disastrous course into which the Party has been guided.' Samuel was now elected leader. The Liberal Nationals declined the party whip.

It was the end of Lloyd George's time in front rank politics. In Campbell's assessment:

His reputation for deviousness derived from his indifference to the means by which progress was achieved – in other words, to party. The first loyalties of Asquith and Baldwin were to the Liberal and Conservative parties respectively, whose health they identified with the welfare of the state. MacDonald's first priority too, up to 1931, was to establish Labour as the natural and trusted alternative party of government.[1]

For Lloyd George, 'it was always the end which interested him', rather than party. And his party was paying the price.

The National Government began with the support of four groupings – the 470 Conservative MPs, thirty-five Liberal Nationals,
thirty-three Liberals, and thirteen Labour Nationals, under Ramsay
MacDonald. From November, Simon was Foreign Secretary and
Samuel Home Secretary. But by November 1932, Samuel had
led most of his Liberals out of the government, in revolt against
protectionism.

The Liberal Nationals under Sir John Simon were meanwhile
moving in the opposite direction. They considered socialism to be a
greater threat than conservatism, were more pragmatic over tariffs
and wanted to be in government. The Conservatives saw the Liberal
Nationals as allies and, except in a few seats in 1931, had not put
up candidates against them, and they were also generally spared
Liberal competition until 1945.

Overall, the Liberal position was miserable. The party split in two.
Finances weak. Party organisation crumbling. In many traditionally
Liberal areas of the north, the party disappeared and gave way to
Labour. Increasingly, those with ambition were choosing between
the two big parties. The political centre ground (free markets combined with social progress) was failing to hold. Liberal MPs became
preoccupied by positioning, not policy: 'They allowed themselves
to be torn to pieces because most of their leading men did not ask
themselves so much the question, "What is the Liberal answer to
this particular current problem?" but instead the question, "Would
I prefer a Labour Government or a Conservative Government?"'[2]

The Liberals also lacked a strong leader with the strategy and au-
thority to bring the party together. Samuel's Liberals might have expected to gain popularity from their decision to leave the National
Government, but this failed to deliver an electoral benefit. By-election results were dreadful. The economy was now improving, and

in June 1935 an increasingly sick MacDonald had to stand down as Prime Minister, to be replaced by the Conservative leader, Stanley Baldwin. Baldwin called an election for 14 November 1935 – once more under the guise of a 'National Government'.

The enfeebled Liberal Party again presented a thin, timid and traditionalist manifesto. This highlighted that the 'National Government' was in reality 'a means of securing another lease of power for the Conservative Party'. It argued that a strong Liberal Party was needed as 'the only alternative should not be a Socialist Party pledged to a reckless scheme of wholesale nationalisation'.

Labour stuck with its manifesto themes of 1931 – arguing for a 'bold policy of Socialist Reconstruction' – 'the nationalisation of banking, coal, transport, electricity, iron and steel, cotton and land', as well as 'the reorganisation of agriculture'. It committed itself to abolishing the House of Lords and to 'promote socialism at home and peace abroad'. Once again, the Liberal and Labour policy agendas were far apart. The parties were no longer the natural allies of pre-war Britain.

The election delivered another resounding victory for the National Government, but not on the scale of 1931. The Conservatives polled 47.8 per cent, and secured 386 seats, a fall of eighty-four. Labour, under its new leader Clement Attlee, saw a big recovery – polling 38 per cent, and gaining 102 seats, to finish with 154 MPs.

This was the election that effectively finished the Liberals as a national force. In 1931, the three Liberal groupings amounted to seventy-two seats, to Labour's fifty-two. Their vote share was tiny and their candidate numbers risible, but they were still just about in the game. But a divided Liberal Party could no longer hold its own against Labour. Sir John Simon's National Liberals finished with thirty-three seats. This seemed a respectable tally. But Simon's candidates had polled just 3.7 per cent and stood in only forty-four seats. They faced no Conservative or Liberal competitors and were reliant on the charity of other parties.

Meanwhile, the Liberals had fielded just 161 candidates. Their vote share was an enfeebled 6.7 per cent, up just 0.2 per cent since 1931, and they emerged with only twenty-one seats, down from thirty-two. Shortly before the election, their president had admitted in a letter that 'we are beaten in advance by the public's idea that we are done for'. Some Liberals now wondered whether the party was too weak to continue. Harcourt Johnstone, a leading Liberal who lost his seat in 1935, argued that one option was to 'decide here and now to disband the Liberal Party'. Their leader, Sir Herbert Samuel, lost his seat. He was replaced by Sir Archibald Sinclair. Sinclair was an old friend of Winston Churchill, and a decade earlier he had written to Churchill, praising a speech of his that argued that there were no differences of principle between Liberals and Conservatives. Sinclair stabilised his party, which David Lloyd George and his three other family members now rejoined.

Thankfully for the Liberals, the election of 1935 was to be the last for a decade. The Second World War began in September 1939, and Sinclair rejected an invitation from Neville Chamberlain to join his government. But in 1940, Chamberlain was ejected from office, and Sinclair now accepted an offer from the new Prime Minister, Churchill, to join what was a genuine National Government. Attlee became Deputy Prime Minister; Sir John Simon was appointed Lord Chancellor and Sinclair was Secretary of State for Air.

During the war, the usual political activities were suspended. But there was a debate within all parties about their post-war strategies. Liberal activists were still facing in two different directions. Some argued against war-time regulation and bureaucracy, supporting a

'Manifesto on British Liberty'. Others wanted a tougher line against the Conservatives and more emphasis on social policies. In 1941, a 'Radical Action Group' was formed to press for 'the revival of Radicalism within the Liberal Party', a clear anti-Conservative focus, support for equality of opportunity and for the proposals being developed by Beveridge for a system of 'social security'. Beveridge was persuaded to join the Liberal Party in July 1944 and was elected as Liberal MP for Berwick-upon-Tweed in October that year, in what was seen as a major coup for the party.

During the war, the coalition parties agreed not to challenge each other. But the Radical Action Group wanted to see an end to Liberal membership of the coalition and backed Independent Liberal candidates in several by-elections – two of which almost resulted in defeat for the incumbent party. It was clear that after the war, the Liberal Party would face a debate about its future orientation.

The one group of Liberals now under intense pressure were the Liberal Nationals. They had sided with Chamberlain in his policy of appeasement. Sir John Simon was replaced as leader in 1940 by Ernest Brown. In 1943–44, there were talks about possible reunion with the Liberals, but this came to nothing.

Before the war ended, there was yet another Speaker's Conference, in 1944, and this looked again at the issue of electoral reform. Labour and the Conservatives were even more opposed than they were in the 1920s and 1930s. STV was rejected by 25–4, and AV by 20–5. The Liberals needed PR more than ever, but there was no support from Labour. In 1939, the Labour politician Richard Crossman wrote that PR would be a 'national disaster', lead to weaker governments and 'ensure the survival of the third party and encourage the formation of a fourth and fifth'.

With the war in Europe over, Churchill called the first general election for a decade, for July 1945. At one stage, he had hoped that this might be a rerun of 1918 – giving him a landslide victory as head of a coalition government in a 'coupon election'. But Labour wasn't interested, and neither was the official Liberal Party.

The Liberal manifesto was more detailed than earlier efforts, offering a twenty-point plan. It was much influenced by the work of Beveridge – arguing for a 'radical programme of practical reform', including tackling 'poverty and want' through policies for social security and full employment. There was a marked shift to the left on economic policy. On agriculture, it proposed that the state should 'have the right to take over all land which is badly managed or badly farmed'. The policies on 'Industry' suggested the work of multiple hands with clashing philosophies; there was a traditionalist restatement of the importance of private enterprise, followed by a declaration that

> where public ownership is more economic, Liberals will demand it without hesitation … Liberals believe in the need for both private enterprise and large-scale organisation under government control, and their tests for deciding which form is necessary are the service of the public, the efficiency of production, and the well-being of those concerned in the industry in question.

It sounded like a huge fudge. The manifesto went on to make the case that both railways and electricity should be treated as public utilities and that the coal industry should be a 'public service'. This was all a dramatic departure for a Liberal manifesto. But the commitments to electoral reform and free trade remained.

Labour's manifesto was much more left-wing. It was 'a Socialist Party, and proud of it'. It sought 'the establishment of a Socialist

Commonwealth of Great Britain', including nationalisation of coal, gas, electricity, rail, air, canals, iron and steel, land and the Bank of England. The operation of other banks would be 'harmonised with industrial needs'. The manifesto argued that 'the effective choice ... will be between the Conservative Party, standing for protection of the rights of private economic interest, and the Labour Party ... standing for the wise organisation and use of the economic assets of the nation for the public good...' The manifesto called on 'progressive Liberals' to vote Labour.

Many assumed that the Liberals would now recover – gaining from Conservative decline. In June, several newspapers forecast a hung parliament. But with the public prioritising post-war recovery and social improvement, and the Liberals no longer credible as a national party, Labour now recorded its highest ever vote share – 49 per cent, with 393 MPs. It was a landslide triumph for Attlee and the first ever Labour majority government. Attlee did not need the support of Liberal MPs and had never been an advocate of Lib–Lab co-operation: 'There were a number of core tenets from Liberalism which Attlee thought valuable, but he entirely rejected the economic system that came with it.'[3]

The Conservatives slumped from 47.8 per cent to 36.2 per cent, losing 189 seats and being reduced to just 197 MPs. Despite an increase in vote share from 6.7 per cent to 9 per cent, the number of Liberal MPs fell from twenty-one to just twelve – another disastrous result. Sinclair himself was defeated – the second time in two elections that Liberal leaders had lost their seats. Beveridge was also out. The National Liberals, under Ernest Brown, fared even worse. Only eleven of their forty-nine candidates were elected – they were well on the way to oblivion, or rather being folded completely into the Conservative Party.

The tiny band of twelve Liberal MPs vividly highlighted the problem that the party now faced. They were 'a disparate group of largely amiable, intelligent people who had very little in common in terms of a clear political agenda, outlook or set of values'.[4] Some had strong Labour sympathies, and three would later defect to Labour. Douglas notes: 'There were some … who held opinions so close to the Labour Party's that it is extremely difficult to understand why they did not join the larger body in preference to the smaller.'[5] It was somewhat embarrassing that one of those people was the Chief Whip, T. L. Horabin. Other Liberal MPs were far more sympathetic to the Conservatives. And arguably only four of the twelve were what Megan Lloyd George described as 'effectives'.

As Sinclair had been defeated, the twelve now had to elect a new leader. Their choice was rather limited. One MP, Gwilym Lloyd George, never attended group meetings and would soon be a Conservative. His sister, Megan, who in contrast stood on the radical left of the party, would soon defect to Labour. She was also 'famous for being disorganised and sometimes lazy', which are not the characteristics parties usually look for when selecting leaders.[6] The Chief Whip, Tom Horabin, we have already considered. It was unclear why he was a Liberal, and by 1947 he wasn't – he joined Labour.

Of the other nine MPs, four had only just been elected. And of those five remaining, Professor Gruffydd refused to follow the Liberal whip and wanted to focus on his academic work; Edgar Granville had only just rejoined the Liberals from the Liberal Nationals and was unknown and unreliable; and Rhys Hopkins Morris wasn't interested. That left two flyweights of the political world: Wilfrid Roberts, who was well to the left of the party, and had a slim majority of 198, and Clement Davies, MP for Montgomeryshire.

Out of this wafer-thin field, Clement Davies emerged as the

chosen one. As well as the complete absence of any remotely credible opponent, his nationality also helped – seven of the twelve MPs represented Welsh seats. In any case, the choice was fortunate, as Wilfrid Roberts would lose his seat in 1950 and join Labour in 1956.

Clement Davies had begun his career as a Lloyd George-supporting Liberal before switching his support to the Liberal Nationals, and then back. He was an alcoholic and his private life was blighted by the tragic death of three of his four children – all, extraordinarily, at the age of twenty-four.

Even his biographer, Alun Wyburn-Powell, noted his limited qualifications for the job:

> Clem came to the role with no preparation. He had devised no personal manifesto, no policies and no plan for allocating responsibilities ... He had held no ministerial or party office and he had had no experience of party fundraising ... He had spent many years away from the Liberal Party and was not fully trusted by some of his parliamentary colleagues. Even some of his closest supporters considered that his judgement was erratic ... His highly strung nature and inability to relax made him prone to nervous exhaustion and had led to his problems with alcohol.

That he was chosen despite these deficiencies causes one to reflect on the attributes of the eleven who were passed over.

At a low ebb, the Liberals needed a dynamic, energetic leader, with capability for strategic thinking and policy clarity. What they ended up with was the least dynamic and lowest-profile leader in their history. Davies's value lay only in the things he did not do.[7] He did not lose his seat. He did not take any strong policy positions that split his already-divided party. He did not go into a coalition that threatened the party's identity and existence. He didn't become involved in high-profile scandals. He wasn't involved in selling peerages or dodgy share dealing. And he didn't give up his job in the face of personal tragedy and sickness. For these things, his party had to be grateful.

Davies now needed to hold together a disunited party and position it carefully in the face of the new Labour government. He commissioned a review of Liberal Party weaknesses, under the unpromising title *Coats Off for the Future*. Initially, he welcomed the new Labour government and sought to claim credit for many of its policies. He even seemed to be pursuing a strategy of attacking Labour from the left, and in 1945 the Liberal Assembly sent Wilfrid Roberts to Moscow, to communicate best wishes to Stalin. They should have left him there. The 1945 Liberal manifesto had of course advocated nationalisation of railways, electricity and coal. But all this was not a plausible approach for a Liberal Party and deepened divisions. And the longer the Labour government was in office, the more the tendency was for those on the opposition benches to oppose – not least against a background of the difficult post-war times.

Archibald Sinclair had initially worried that Davies might seek to find distinctive territory to the left of Labour. He had traditionally backed left-wing causes and in 1945 Labour did not put up a candidate against him. But although Davies did support the early nationalisations, by 1949 he was opposing Labour's policy on steel.

This was a difficult parliament for Davies, as the party was again dividing between those whose instincts were to support Labour and others who favoured a deal with the Conservatives. Davies decided he had to steer an independent course.

Violet Bonham Carter, a leading Liberal, had other ideas. She regarded the party now as a 'splinter of a splinter'. She was a close friend of Winston Churchill and favoured a pact with the Conservatives. There were many, too, in the Conservative Party who saw the Liberals as natural allies. In September 1945, the young Conservative MP, Quintin Hogg, wrote to *The Spectator* highlighting the existence of a 'Tory Reform Group' of thirty to forty moderate Conservative MPs, whose policy views had in his opinion 'no striking difference from the Liberals'. Hogg suggested that 'if only the Liberals would come and help … we would, together, capture the Conservative Party'.[8]

In February 1946, a significant number of Conservatives MPs and Liberal parliamentary candidates jointly published a pamphlet entitled *Design for Freedom*, which set out their policy views. But both parties became highly nervous about the initiative, and in February 1947, Clement Davies condemned those involved. One Liberal MP described it as 'the greatest act of sabotage to the Liberal Party since 1931'.[9] Had these developments continued, they might have led to the disappearance of the Liberal Party into the Conservatives.

But Churchill and his party chairman, Lord Woolton, were not giving up. They wanted to attract Liberal voters to their cause. The Liberal Nationals started fresh talks in 1946 for a reunion with the Liberals, to be based on a pact with the Conservatives. This was declined, and in 1947, the 'Woolton–Teviot Agreement' – between Lord Woolton and Lord Teviot of the Liberal Nationals – absorbed the Liberal Nationals into the Conservative Party. Several of the merged local associations even adopted the title 'Conservative and Liberal'. And in many seats now there were no real Liberal candidates. The Liberal Nationals were now to re-emerge as the 'National Liberals'. They were again to be spared Conservative competition in their seats, in exchange for their sell-out. Some candidates now also stood as 'Liberal-Conservative' or 'Liberal-Unionist', prompting an angry Clement Davies to write to Churchill in 1950 asking him to desist from seeking to steal away the 'Liberal' label. Churchill replied, publicly and rather brutally, pointing out that:

> As you were yourself for eleven years a National Liberal, and in that capacity supported the governments of Mr. Baldwin and Mr. Neville Chamberlain, I should not presume to correct your knowledge of the moral, intellectual and legal aspects of adding a prefix or suffix to the honoured name of Liberal.[10]

Mischievously, he pointed out that he was not aware of any 'Liberal-Socialist' candidates – 'the reason, no doubt, that the two terms are fundamentally incompatible'. He had a point.

While all this was going on, Churchill continued to scheme for a deal with the official Liberals too. In March 1947, he told Violet Bonham Carter that he was willing to give her party an uncontested run in thirty-five constituencies, and electoral reform, if they fought the 1950 election as part of an anti-Labour alliance. Lady Violet met Churchill on 22 April 1947 to discuss the offer.[11] She was sympathetic but emphasised that her party would insist on electoral reform. Churchill was forced to admit that he could not promise this.

Churchill also met Clement Davies in both 1946 and 1950. He was contemplating offering the Liberals a more generous unopposed run in sixty parliamentary seats. Davies was not biting, but in January 1950, Churchill invited Violet Bonham Carter to his home at Chartwell for a champagne lunch. Extraordinarily, he tried to persuade her to accept use of one of his party's five election broadcasts, but she declined – recognising that Liberal MPs would be furious.

At the 1950 election on 23 February, there would ultimately only be one Conservative–Liberal pact – in Huddersfield. Here, the two local seats were divided between the Liberals and Conservatives, giving each a straight fight against Labour.

As the Labour government struggled with all the challenges of a post-war economy, the Liberals were starting to get their act together – raising funds, selecting more candidates and increasingly positioning themselves to benefit from disillusion with the government. The party went into the 1950 election with high expectations.

Unsurprisingly, after five years of Labour, the Liberal manifesto of 1950 saw a sharp move to the right. It promised 'enormous savings on government expenditure', a bonfire of controls and bureaucracy, opposition to nationalisation, 'government out of business which can be more efficiently and economically operated by private traders' and reversing the nationalisation of iron and steel. Free trade and voting reform (by 'single transferable vote') were still trusty staples.

Liberal pre-election optimism soon hit the usual buffers of reality. The election did produce a huge swing, but it went to the Conservatives. Labour lost seventy-eight seats, while the Conservatives gained ninety. Labour's majority was slashed from 146 to just five. Fifty-five candidates had also stood separately under a 'National Liberal and Conservative' banner, and sixteen of these were elected.

The Liberals held their vote share steady at around 9 per cent, but this was because of an increase in candidates. With their average vote per seat going down, they managed to lose more seats, returning with only nine MPs. Fortunately, the party had paid Lloyds of London a premium of £5,000 to cover any lost deposits. It turned out to be one of the insurers' less profitable enterprises.

Clement Davies was despairing of the result, complaining that 'there is no Party today, but a number of individuals who … come together to express completely divergent views'.[12] He said that the only thing his colleagues could agree on was that the party should remain independent, but 'having made that statement they then differ not only about how that independence is to be achieved or maintained, but almost upon everything else'. It was impossible for him to give a clear lead without dividing the party and 'any further division now would, I fear, just give the final death blow'.[13]

Davies could see that the party's only hope would be if they could achieve electoral reform, but he wasn't optimistic, noting in a letter in May 1950 that: 'Churchill is struggling manfully to get his party to grant at least AV [Alternative Vote].' But even if this was conceded, Davies appreciated that there would likely be a price to be paid in agreeing not to oppose the Conservatives in certain seats, and this would split the party.

Churchill persisted, though, with his attempts to win over the Liberals. The February 1950 election had served up a photo finish, with only seventeen more Labour MPs than Conservatives. The Conservatives ended up only 730,000 votes behind Labour, with the Liberals securing 2.6 million. Churchill knew that if only he could get the Liberals and their voters onside, he could be back in Downing Street.

In March 1950, Churchill hinted in Parliament at the case for voting reform, noting that the 2.6 million Liberal voters had secured only nine MPs. He implied that if the Liberals had secured more MPs, then a Liberal–Conservative pact would have kept Labour out of office – noting that this matter could not be 'brushed aside or allowed to lie unheeded'.

As Wyburn-Powell has noted: 'Churchill's motives for making overtures to the Liberals were a mixture of hard-headed electoral advantage and sentimentality.'[14] He had a great liking for several

Liberals, including Violet Bonham Carter, Archie Sinclair and Clem Davies, who had helped remove Chamberlain in favour of Churchill in 1940. On 18 April 1950, Churchill had lunch with Jo Grimond, the newly elected Liberal MP, and Lady Violet and told them that he had asked Rab Butler to draw up secret plans for a partnership with the Liberals to help remove Labour from power. Butler would look at the case for electoral reform and make his work public. But Butler warned that the mood amongst Conservative MPs was very opposed to voting reform – as Churchill had discovered at a recent meeting of the backbench 1922 Committee.

While Churchill was carrying on his discussions with senior Liberals, Megan Lloyd George was talking to Labour's Herbert Morrison about a possible Lib–Lab pact. It was all a horrible mess, and there was a real risk that the party would – once again – split in two.

By May 1950, Sinclair was writing to Davies to state that electoral reform was the only way of 'preserving the life and securing the independence of the Liberal Party'.[15] He felt that if the Conservatives would grant electoral reform, then more pacts such as that at Huddersfield would make sense. Davies wanted electoral reform but didn't like the idea of having to stand down Liberal candidates. He had decided he should also explore the possibility of electoral reform with Clem Attlee, and in mid and late March he and the Labour leader had exchanged several letters on the subject – with Davies pressing the idea of holding a 'Speaker's Conference'. Attlee eventually rejected the proposal – pointing out that Labour had no manifesto commitments on reform and that the last Speaker's Conference, in 1944, had rejected the idea. His party was in office. It had displaced the Liberals as the main alternative to the Conservatives. Why should he give oxygen to the Liberals in their current parlous state?

If the prospect of a deal with Labour was dead, there were still many senior Liberals who were keen to push for a Conservative arrangement. Between March 1950 and January 1951, Davies was bombarded by at least twenty-five letters from Archibald Sinclair, Violet Bonham Carter and others, all making the case for some type of pact.[16] But it was difficult to overcome the tribal suspicions and interests in all parties. Many Conservatives felt that Churchill should be trying to eliminate the Liberal Party, not breathe new life into them. And most Liberals suspected that Churchill wanted to emasculate their party, so they would lose their identity and eventually end up as part of the Conservatives.

Davies met with Churchill and Conservative chairman Lord Woolton and made clear that there would be no national deal over seats, and he would certainly not support any candidate who stood under a 'Liberal–Conservative' label. But what happened in individual seats was a matter for each local association. Davies later confided to David Butler that he was personally willing to contemplate local deals in up to sixty seats.[17] Violet Bonham Carter was still pressing this sort of arrangement – writing to Davies in September 1950 and suggesting it should cover up to thirty seats, where the Conservative or Liberal candidate was best placed to beat Labour. She argued that such a deal was 'the only way to save the party from virtual extinction'. But at the September 1950 Liberal Assembly a motion was passed opposing electoral pacts with either of the other parties.

If this hinted at a greater degree of party unity, this was not to last. On 6 November, the Conservatives tabled a motion criticising government housing policy. Three Liberal MPs voted with the government, four with the opposition, and two were absent. Liberal incoherence was leading to ridicule. Three months into the new parliament, one paper claimed that the Liberal MPs had only voted in the same lobby four times in twelve divisions.

Attlee decided to seek a new working majority after just twenty months. In the election of October 1951, the Labour vote surged from 46.1 per cent in 1950 to 48.8 per cent – even higher than in 1945. Labour had secured the largest number of votes in any election in British political history. It looked like Attlee's strategy had paid off. But the Conservatives were rescued from a third defeat by a disastrous decline in the Liberal vote, which fell from 9.1 per cent to a mere 2.6 per cent. In February 1950, the Liberals had polled 2.6 million votes. This time they were down to just 730,000. It was the worst result in Liberal history, by a considerable margin. Only 109 Liberal candidates were fielded for 625 seats. The insurers who had covered the cost of Liberal deposits in the last election had refused to be bitten twice.

Only six Liberals were now successful, and a mere eleven even finished second. Of the six who won, at least three benefited from local pacts in which the Conservatives didn't field a candidate. In Bolton West, the Conservatives stood down and in Bolton East the Liberals gave the Conservative a free run. Bolton West was the only Liberal gain of the election. In Huddersfield, an arrangement made in 1950 to give the Liberals a free run against Labour in West Huddersfield, while the Conservatives faced no Liberal opponent in East Huddersfield, was continued. The situation in Colne Valley was rather more extraordinary. The Liberal candidate was Lady Violet Bonham Carter. Not only did the Conservatives give her a free run, but Winston Churchill himself visited her constituency and urged voters to back her. It was not, however, enough to secure a Liberal win.

All three of the most left-wing Liberal MPs lost their seats

– Megan Lloyd George, Emrys Roberts and Edgar Granville. This would at least make the parliamentary party more manageable but was hardly a price worth paying for just six MPs.

The Conservative vote was boosted by the Liberal disaster, rising to 48 per cent. With fewer votes than Labour, Churchill emerged with more MPs – 321 to Labour's 295. David Butler's election analysis suggests that the decline in Liberal candidates had been more help to the Conservatives than Labour – with 60 per cent of former Liberal voters switching to the Conservatives where there was no Liberal. In seventeen of the twenty-two seats lost by Labour, the most decisive factor was the lack of a Liberal candidate. Liberal weakness and complicity had helped eject Labour from power.

First Past the Post had this time helped the Conservatives and not Labour. Just over 13,700,000 Conservative votes had delivered 321 MPs. But Labour's 13,948,000 votes resulted in just 295 seats. The country had ended up with a Conservative government with a working majority, even though more electors had voted for Labour. This was not going to help convert the Conservatives to electoral reform.

But Churchill was still committed to his project of bringing the Liberals and Conservatives together. Having tried and failed in both 1946 and 1950, he now set out again to achieve his ambition. And this time, as Prime Minister, he had much more to offer. Most Conservatives wondered why Churchill was bothering to court a party that was on life support. But with a modest majority of seventeen, Churchill now invited Clement Davies to his London home at Hyde Park, on the night of Saturday 27 October – the day after the election outcome was clear. The new PM offered the Liberal leader a deal: a coalition government along with the post of Education Minister in the Cabinet. Davies promised to consider the offer.

The next day, Sunday 28 October, Davies travelled down to Churchill's Kent home, Chartwell. He arrived at 1 p.m. and held discussions for two hours over lunch. As well as the Education post, Churchill promised Davies that he would be consulted on all major government policies. He seems also to have offered the Liberals two junior ministerial roles – one of which would have gone to Violet Bonham Carter. It must have been a tempting offer for a leader of a party with six MPs, which was in the political equivalent of Outer Mongolia. But it was an offer with huge potential consequences. It could easily mean the end of the Liberal Party and its eventual complete absorption into the Conservative Party.

Davies returned to London and recounted the discussion to the party's executive. With exemplary courtesy, he then left the room to allow them to debate the matter freely. His own inclination was to reject the offer, but he felt it should be properly considered.[18] Violet Bonham Carter was the only one in favour, with the vote being 11–1 against. Davies contacted the PM to reject his offer. Had he accepted, he would have secured his first ministerial office, but he might also have finished off the Liberal Party. He made the right choice.

The party was now microscopically small, but it remained independent. It had rejected a tempting offer from the Conservative PM and had lost its most passionately pro-Labour MPs.

But it was on its knees, and morale was low. It largely owed its survival to the Conservatives, who had calculated that it was better for Liberals to win seats than Labour; in the longer run, this was to prove a strategic blunder. The Liberals would re-emerge as a third force in British politics, and they would do so with a distinctly anti-Conservative ideology.

But in 1951, the paltry number of MPs were all on the right on economic policy. *The Economist* even argued that the Liberals should now outflank the Conservatives to mop up middle-class votes. In 1955, the Institute of Economic Affairs was established to promote free-market thinking. It was strongly associated with the Liberal Party and one of its two original founders was Arthur Seldon, a Liberal member. At the 1953 party conference, the economic liberals carried a motion in favour of unilateral free trade and an end to agricultural subsidies (which was unpopular with many Liberals fighting in rural constituencies).

From 1953, the party's decline appeared to have been arrested, and there were some modest local government gains. Contacts with Churchill continued, and in February Lady Violet, Jo Grimond and other senior Liberals visited him. Lady Violet again made the case for voting reform, arguing that the local pacts in Huddersfield and Bolton might be working to deny a couple of seats to Labour but were not easy to sell to party supporters. Churchill promised to review the results of the earlier inquiry that he had commissioned into alternative voting systems. But he was realistic about the prospects – he faced strong opposition from both his party and Labour.

In April 1955, Churchill finally stood down as PM and was replaced by Anthony Eden, who immediately called a general election for 26 May. Liberal chances of converting the Conservative Party to electoral reform were dead and buried.

The party, still led by Davies, struck a traditionalist note in its manifesto. On public spending, 'value for money must be the keynote', and 'this country will never be prosperous so long as some 40 per cent of the national income is taken from the earner by the Government and Local Authorities'. On industrial policy, there was criticism of both main parties: 'Conservatives want to protect employers who are economically inefficient against bankruptcy; Socialists want to protect workers against the loss of the particular jobs in which they happen to be working.' The overall pitch was very much along the lines suggested by *The Economist*, portraying the Labour and Conservative parties as the 'two class parties' and the Liberals as representing 'the hardest working and least vocal people … the vast middle class who seek an opportunity to support a common-sense progressive policy'. As well as the usual commitment to electoral reform, the manifesto included a robust defence of personal liberty: 'We exist as a Party to defend the rights of the individual … to be subject to no penalty or discrimination by reason of his colour, race or creed.' This was the strongest commitment to personal liberty that had so far been included in a party manifesto and the first mention of fighting racial prejudice.

The manifesto also struck a new note on foreign policy and defence. It was more enthusiastic about Europe than any yet produced by a UK political party. It argued for greater European unity and criticised the two big parties for their 'timidity and hesitation'. It was to be the beginning of a new theme – passionate support for a bigger UK role in Europe.

In many respects, this was a radical and distinctly liberal manifesto. But the commitment to social liberalism – the improvement of the lot of the least advantaged in society – was glaringly absent. None of the sub-sections covered housing, education, social security or even health. The progressive traditions of 1906 and 1910 were absent. The contrast with the Labour manifesto was striking. These were two parties still on diverging paths.

Labour's rather thin manifesto included extensive sections on housing, 'health and old age', and education. The emphasis was on 'social justice' and not the Liberal pledge to 'defend the rights of the individual'. Its economic policy was the opposite of the Liberal offering. It promised to renationalise the steel and road transport industries and bring parts of the chemical and machine tool sectors into public ownership. It also planned 'new public enterprises.' There was no mention at all of Europe. Instead, the development of the Commonwealth was the foreign policy priority. Labour was struggling with the emerging splits between its right and left wings. This was the last general election to be fought with Clement Attlee as leader. Nye Bevan and Hugh Gaitskell were now offering very different Labour visions of the future.

And it was the Conservative Party rather than the opposition that was the beneficiary of the better economic times being experienced. Food rationing had been scrapped. Trade was improving. The Conservatives had accepted the 'mixed economy' and the new 'welfare state' and were out-building Labour on housing. The Conservative Chancellor, Rab Butler, delivered a pre-election tax-cutting Budget. When the results were in on 27 May, the Conservatives had polled a mighty 49.7 per cent – the largest vote share for any single party since the National Government of 1931. This was only a modest increase from the 48 per cent of 1951, but it was the first time an incumbent government had increased its majority since 1867.

The Conservatives gained twenty-three seats, to end on 345 in the 630-seat Commons. Labour delivered a very respectable 46.4 per cent but lost eighteen seats to finish with 277. These years were undoubtedly the high point of two-party politics. The Liberal vote stabilised at its miserably low level, rising from 2.5 per cent to 2.7 per cent and delivering the same number of seats – the grand total of six. Five of these six MPs hadn't faced Conservative opposition. If they had, it is likely that the number of Liberal seats would have fallen to a mere three. The Liberals were no longer part of a Lib–Lab progressive alliance. They were a tiny party on a Conservative-sponsored life support machine.

The election of 1955 was not only to be the last with Clem Attlee as leader. The other Clem – Davies – stood down in 1956. He had kept the Liberal Party alive – just. But he had achieved little more than this. His political positioning had been inconsistent and errat- ic – as he moved from left-wing radical to leader of a party standing on a more centre-right platform. His alcoholism undermined his health, and for two of the three general elections during which he had served as leader, he had spent time in hospital.

The Liberals desperately needed a leader who could inspire, mo- tivate and find a clear purpose for the party. Clement Davies was not that man. From the six MPs in the parliament of 1955, could the Liberals now discover such a leader?

CHAPTER 4

'A-WHORING AFTER FOREIGN WOMEN' 1956-74

For twenty-five long years, from November 1931, when Lloyd George had resigned, the Liberal Party had suffered from solid but uninspiring leadership. Exceptional leadership and dynamism were needed but not on offer. Could this be found in a party of six?

In fact, six rather overstates the real choice. One of their number, Sir Rhys Hopkin Morris, was Commons Deputy Chairman of Ways and Means, which ruled him out. Another was Davies himself. Two – Arthur Holt and Donald Wade – would lose their seats if the Conservatives decided to stand against them in Bolton and Huddersfield. The fifth, Roderic Bowen, a right-wing Liberal who would back the Conservatives over Suez, was far too busy with his legal practice. That left a choice of one – Jo Grimond, Chief Whip and MP for Orkney and Shetland. He was elected unopposed. The fragile position of the party can be seen by the fact that of the six MPs, five had no Conservative challenger at the 1955 election. Grimond was the exception.

Grimond was of good Liberal pedigree – married to Laura Bonham Carter, the granddaughter of Asquith. He presented a reassuring image to traditional Liberal voters, with his Eton and Balliol background. But he was a highly effective and motivating speaker, and his views were more radical and progressive than those of his colleagues. Grimond's election ushered in a new Liberal era in which its leaders, from Grimond to Ashdown, would be energetic, risk-taking and inspiring – helping the party to punch well above its parliamentary weight.

When the Suez crisis arose in July 1956, Grimond initially seemed to support the Conservatives. But as the government's dishonesty and incompetence emerged, he led his party in opposition to Eden, taking a strongly internationalist line. The party was being noticed again. With the Conservatives in office, the Liberals were now also on a natural, oppositional course away from proximity to them. Opposition parties generally define themselves against the party in power. And Grimond's political instincts were anti-Conservative and led back to the political space that had been filled by the Liberals before 1916. But the move leftwards took time. Lib–Con deals in Bolton and Huddersfield would survive the 1959 general election but were terminated by 1964.

Grimond was passionate about policy. Under him, devolution to Scotland and Wales was championed more energetically. He was strongly internationalist and committed to Britain's role in Europe. The EEC was created in 1957, and by the 1959 general election the party was backing membership.

The gradual stirrings of life in the party were confirmed when Mark Bonham Carter secured an astonishing by-election win in the constituency of Torrington in Devon, in March 1958. It was their first Liberal by-election victory since 1929 and was to usher in a long era in which the party would benefit from by-election 'surges'. The Liberals had been buoyed by disillusion with the Conservatives, as inflation spiked and the number of industrial disputes rose. But by 1959, the Conservatives had chosen a new leader – Harold Macmillan – who called an election for 8 October, on the back of a better economy and opinion poll ratings that touched 50 per cent. All three parties had new leaders – Hugh Gaitskell had replaced Attlee in 1955. The Conservatives had now been in power for eight years, and according to the usual rhythm of the electoral cycle, they should be seeing a marked swing against them. Could they retain power?

The first Liberal manifesto under Grimond made an appeal to 'progressively minded people', an echo of earlier times. It presented its prospectus as that of the 'New Liberal Party'. Compared with 1955, there was much more on social policy. On relations with Labour, it claimed: 'A big Liberal vote would show that there are people who share Labour's concern about poverty but who are opposed to nationalisation.' It was offering a non-Socialist alternative to the possibility of 'Tory government for ever'. The economic sections were notably less free market than in 1955. This was now the era of the mixed economy, and party thinking evolved towards an odd mix of the old commitment to economic liberalism, married to a new and fashionable focus on 'planning'. There was also talk of 'co-ownership and co-partnership encouraged through tax-relief' – an attempt to find an economic third way. On nationalisation, the manifesto promised to 'cut out waste in nationalised industries' rather than privatise them.

On constitutional reform, there was a pledge to establish Scottish and Welsh Parliaments – the first such clear commitment. Oddly, relations with Europe hardly merited a line. And at the end was a short list of twelve key policies – a more populist mix than 1955, with pledges to 'end hospital queues', 'slash taxes on goods in the family shopping basket', reduce pension means-testing and 'free the police to do their job'.

Overall, it was a broader policy offering than 1955, but it was not one of high quality, with eccentric elements including the claim that 'Russia spends seven times as much per head on education as we do', and a pledge that new H-bombs should be 'held in trust for all the free peoples'. By whom was not made clear.

Labour, meanwhile, was aware of the risk that better economic times would help the government. Its manifesto warned of 'the mood of complacency and self-deception'.

It began with long sections on social policies, claiming that improvements in public services would be paid for by higher growth and not by tax rises. Gaitskell had already publicly ruled out raising income tax. Tax rises were to be limited to a few areas – 'the businessman's expense account', 'capital gains' and 'loopholes … which lead to the avoidance of death duties and surtax'.

Modest new commitments were made to renationalise steel and, oddly, long-distance road haulage. Beyond this 'we have no plans for further nationalisation', though the party 'reserved the right' to take industries 'failing the nation' into public ownership. Gaitskell feared that the Clause IV Labour Party commitment to nationalisation was out of date and politically damaging. In 1956, he had published *Socialism and Nationalisation*, which had made the case against further public ownership.

Gaitskell inspired loyal support amongst Labour moderates such as Roy Jenkins, Anthony Crosland and Douglas Jay. But as he was trying to shift to the right, the unions were moving leftwards – by 1957 even calling for the state purchase of shares in small businesses. Neither the unions nor the Labour left were willing to see nationalisation dropped completely. Of importance for the future, the

Labour manifesto pledged to limit inflation by negotiating with the unions to limit pay rises, rather than by constraining growth and increasing unemployment. On constitutional matters, caution was in evidence – offering Wales a new Secretary of State but promising devolution to neither Scotland nor Wales. On foreign policy, the focus was again on disengagement from Empire. Europe barely merited a mention. Gaitskell fought off pledges to unilaterally renounce nuclear weapons.

After eight years of Conservative government, Labour hoped that a moderate manifesto would now help sweep it back into power. But better economic times were a gift to the Conservatives, who fought on the slogan: 'Life is better with the Conservatives; don't let Labour ruin it.' And there were questions about whether Labour could really pay for its plans without raising the main tax rates.

On 8 October 1959, the electorate gave its verdict. It was another strong Conservative performance, with a 49.4 per cent vote – only marginally lower than the 49.7 per cent of 1955. Labour had fallen back 2.6 per cent to 43.8 per cent and shed nineteen seats. With twenty Conservative gains, the government had been returned with a majority of 100. It was a huge blow for Labour – three Conservative election wins in a row, each time with a bigger majority. The Liberals had fielded 216 candidates, twice the figure of 1955. Their vote share rose from 2.7 per cent to 5.9 per cent – still disappointing. And they were stuck on six seats – two of them (Bolton West and Huddersfield West) held because of Conservative pacts.

Labour responded to the election loss with a period of bitter internal strife and introspection. Gaitskell blamed the Labour left, including the 'albatross' of Clause IV. On the weekend after the election, he met key allies. He realised that unless Labour won the next election, the party would be in crisis, and the risk of splits would dramatically increase. Douglas Jay suggested that Labour needed to consider a deal with the Liberals, to bind together the 'progressive vote'. Jay was prepared to consider any alternative, right up to merging the two parties.[1] Others suggested a new Lib–Lab deal to stand down candidates in particular seats. Gaitskell was unenthusiastic about both options. He felt that while such arrangements might help the Liberals to recover, they would be of limited value to Labour. He was unconvinced that Liberal voters would back Labour in preference to the Conservatives. But he was worried about the rising Liberal vote and feared that for once this might be coming at the expense of Labour. Gaitskell liked Grimond and saw him as a potential ally. But short of hoovering up Liberal support, he could not see a pathway to a more constructive inter-party relationship.

The election raised questions about whether a socialist party, with an agenda of public ownership, could win again. Some argued that Labour's ideology and policies were out of date and unattractive to a changing country. At its 1959 conference, Labour splits over public ownership and wider policy were on full display. In 1960, Gaitskell attempted to water down Clause IV, but the change was vetoed by the larger unions.

Grimond, meanwhile, had now repositioned the Liberals away from the Conservatives. He sought not a close relationship with Labour but a 'realignment of the left', a phrase borrowed from Mark Bonham Carter, and a position he set out as early as 1958. He advocated a new, non-socialist alternative made up of Liberals, Labour's social democrats and perhaps even some moderate Conservatives. At a rally in November 1958 at the Royal Albert Hall, he claimed: 'The long-term objective is clear: to replace the Labour Party as the progressive wing of politics in this country.'

But it was always unclear how Grimond proposed to achieve this.

In his memoirs, he explained how it was unrealistic to go from a small number of MPs to a majority government: 'It would have to go through a period of coalition.'[2] He knew this was a difficult sell to many in his party – 'the prospect of coalition in those days scared Liberals out of their wits ... they were frightened it would flatten them.' He went on to explain that: 'By the 1960s, our strategy depended upon the Labour Party or some part of it being convinced that, as a socialist party ... it had a poor future ... there was a hope that the full-blooded socialists would split off to the Left leaving a radical party ... free of socialist dogma.' Unfortunately, that meant precisely that Liberal strategy was dependent on 'hope' and decisions made by another party. Grimond and his party were left waiting for something to turn up.

In October 1959, Grimond gave an interview to *The Observer* stating that he could contemplate some sort of alliance between Labour and the Liberals to remove the Conservatives.[3] On some issues, Labour and the Liberals 'can and must combine'. This was a big break from the Liberal positioning of recent decades. But Grimond didn't seem to have thought out sufficiently clearly what it was that he wished to communicate, and – having second thoughts after the interview – he telephoned *The Observer's* editor to express his worries. In the face of a predictable backlash from some in the party, Grimond also spoke to *The Times* that same evening of 11 October to make clear that 'I am not talking about any immediate coalition, and I am merely speaking for myself'.[4] But Grimond was not some stray backbench MP; he was party leader. And over the next few weeks, he had to publicly backpedal from notions of deals, pacts or coalitions, telling the *Daily Telegraph* instead that he wanted a 'growing together of radical opinion ... as part of a longer-term process of realignment'.

Meanwhile, by 1960, Labour left-wingers were once again pressing the cause of unilateral disarmament, and they successfully carried a unilateralist amendment at the October 1960 conference. It took Gaitskell a year to reverse the decision, and Labour was looking increasingly like a divided party that was unfit to govern. Although Gaitskell was generally seen as a 'moderniser', he disappointed many allies by opposing British membership of the European Economic Community, which from July 1961 was supported by Harold Macmillan. In an emotive speech in October 1962, in which he referred to British and Commonwealth troops fighting together on the battlefields of the First World War, Gaitskell argued that European membership could lead to 'the end of Britain as an independent European state, the end of a thousand years of history!' The Labour left loved it, but not the moderate right. 'All the wrong people are cheering,' noted Gaitskell's wife. Three months later, Gaitskell was dead, aged just fifty-six.

With Labour in-fighting and the Conservatives grappling with economic problems, Liberal support began to rise. From 5 per cent in October 1959, by late 1961 it was hitting 17 per cent. And in November 1960, the Liberals scrapped their local pact with the Conservatives and fought them in Bolton East. They came in third but took a quarter of the vote. There was a price to pay, as Conservatives stood in Bolton West and Huddersfield West in the 1964 general election, with Labour winning both seats. But ending these local pacts played a big part in restoring Liberal independence and self-confidence. And in March 1962, the party scored a famous by-election victory at Orpington, on a mighty 29 per cent swing. With the positive publicity, Grimond's charismatic leadership and Labour still divided, the party polled at around 25 per cent from April to June 1962. Conservative support had dropped markedly to

35 per cent, and for once it was a united and forward-looking Liberal Party that was the beneficiary. Liberal membership surged, and the party gained seats in local elections.

Grimond now toyed publicly again with the issue of Lib–Lab co-operation. On 18 May 1962, questioned on how Liberals might deal with the prospect of a hung parliament, he stated that he was 'nearer the aims of the Labour Party', but that a coalition was unlikely. Instead, he could envisage supporting a Labour government on a range of policy issues 'to make a government possible for a limited time until the country can pronounce again.' But the very next day, he was expressing two completely different views – implying to Liberal activists that he was not interested in pacts while letting one newspaper know that he wasn't ruling out a coalition, provided 'Labour were in the political lead ... and there was genuine agreement on major heads of immediate policy'. It was unclear what his political strategy was, but it was at last an exciting time to be a Liberal. And at the Liberal Assembly in September 1963, Grimond fired up his activists by famously promising to 'march my troops towards the sound of gunfire'. The party was finally back in the political fight.

Grimond hoped the emergence of 'Orpington man' was signalling that middle-class voters would turn away from Conservatives and Labour to support his party. But what looked like a new political era soon came to a juddering halt. There were no more scintillating by-election wins. Harold Wilson was elected as the new Labour leader, in February 1963. He was from Labour's left wing, and therefore more suspicious than Gaitskell of the Liberals. He was also, at age forty-six, the youngest of the three leaders (three years younger than Grimond and twenty-two years younger than Harold Macmillan). And he managed to portray himself as a unifying and modernising force, challenging a Conservative Party that was look-ing tired and out of date. Alec Douglas-Home replaced Macmillan in October 1963. By then, the Liberals were back down to 14 per cent. Their support continued to drift lower in 1964, while Labour surged to 50 per cent.

The Conservatives eventually called an election for almost the last possible date – 15 October 1964. Could they secure a fourth term? They were badly damaged by the Profumo affair of March 1963, and they looked tired. Labour, by contrast, fought the election on a modernising agenda – promising a 'New Britain', 'fresh and virile leadership' and a policy of 'mobilising the resources of technolo-gy under a national plan'. On policy, their manifesto condemned the Conservatives' 'economic free for all' and 'stop-go' policies and advocated an era of planning. A new 'Ministry of Economic Af-fairs' would draw up a national economic plan to create a 'modern economy'. A 'Ministry for Technology' would 'guide and stimulate' efforts to bring technology into industry, and 'if production falls short of the plan … then it is up to Government and industry to take whatever measures are required'. No longer would inflation be controlled by altering the growth rate of the economy. Instead, there would be a 'planned growth of incomes so that they are broadly related to the annual growth of production' – a 'National Incomes Policy'.

It was all presented in modern terms, but economically liberal it was not. Under the plan, 'each industry will know both what is expected of it and what help it can expect'. Public ownership would play a 'vital contribution'. The steel industry would be nationalised, as would road haulage. Water would come under 'full public own-ership'. The government would 'establish new industries', either in the public sector or in a private sector partnership. But beyond this, there was no long list of nationalisation targets – Labour feared that this might put off voters. It was socialism with a glossy new coat of paint.

On taxation, the manifesto promised a lower burden of rates on those on low incomes, paid for by 'fair' taxation, which meant taxing capital gains and closing 'notorious avoidance and evasion devices'. Labour would ensure 'value for money' in public spending and would deliver better education, housing, health and social security. This would all be paid for from higher growth. For the first time, Labour promised a policy of 'integrating the public schools into the state system'.

On international policy, the party would 'seek closer links with our European neighbours [but] ... the first responsibility ... is still to the Commonwealth'. The manifesto shied away from specific commitments to unilateral disarmament, but the argument and tone was clearly unilateralist. Wilson played down the nuclear issue – he recognised the independent UK deterrent was popular with electorate, if not with Labour activists. On constitutional reform, there was barely a word – and no commitment to devolve power to Scotland and Wales. Immigration was becoming a controversial issue and here Labour trod carefully – proposing immigration quotas alongside equal rights for those who had already arrived.

The Liberal manifesto was more detailed than the 1959 offering. It started with a blunt and clear statement: 'The Liberal Party offers the electorate a radical, non-Socialist, alternative.' The long-term goal was a Liberal government, but 'in the short run, we seek sufficient support to send back a force of Liberal MPs which will hold a decisive position'.

The robust economic liberalism of earlier times had been seriously infected by the new craze for planning. The manifesto proposed a 'Ministry of Expansion … and a national plan for growth'. The plan would be drafted by the 'Minister of Expansion in consultation with industry and the unions and then submitted to Parliament for debate and approval. Parliament would weigh up the implications and decide on a 4, 5 or 6 per cent rate of growth.' It was utter twaddle – the least liberal and least credible economic strategy the party had ever proposed. The manifesto also promised an incomes policy but preferred employee participation in industry to nationalisation. On nationalisation, it proposed a 'truce'. On taxation, there was a pledge to lower income tax, paid for by 'spreading the indirect tax net', 'taxing capital gains over a longer period' and 'stopping tax dodges'.

On constitutional reform, the commitments to a Scottish Parliament and a 'Council for Wales' were restated, along with backing for new regional government in England. For once, electoral reform did not merit a mention. In his memoirs, Grimond admitted that PR was 'perhaps not given enough emphasis. I myself was attracted by the single-member constituency and the simplicity of the British system.'[5]

In a low-profile section, the manifesto committed to seeking to join the 'European Political and Economic Community'. By now, Macmillan's attempts to join had been vetoed by the French. The party position on Europe had evolved significantly over the past decade. The traditional Liberal support for free trade meant that many members had been suspicious of the development of the 'Common Market' – seeing it as likely to lead to cartels and trade barriers. Initially, the party had moved towards supporting membership of the European Free Trade Association but not the European Economic Community. But in 1960, the Liberal conference agreed a motion urging the government to start negotiations to join the Common Market, if the right deal could be done. Many members now saw the EEC as a way to build links between nations and expand trade. By 1962, the party position on Europe had hardened to unambiguous support for the Common Market – causing the resignation of several senior members. A Gallup poll in late 1962 showed that Liberal voters were split on the issue.

Those were the opposition programmes. The fight was on. After thirteen years in power, could the Conservatives finally be ejected? On 15 October, the public decided. It was, indeed, 'time for a change'. But only just. Conservative support fell by 6 per cent to 43.4 per cent. Labour was just ahead on 44.1 per cent, up just 0.3 per cent – a narrow margin over a party that had been in power for so long. The Liberal vote increased by a healthy 5.3 per cent to 11.2 per cent, with 365 candidates, up from 191 in 1959.

The electoral system delivered a small majority for Labour of just four seats – they had secured 317 seats (up fifty-nine), while the Conservatives had fallen sixty-one, from 365 to 304. Had just 900 voters in eight seats changed their vote from Labour to Conservative, Harold Wilson would have been denied his majority. Indeed, had the Conservative–Liberal pacts in Huddersfield and Bolton continued, Labour would probably have failed to secure these seats and their majority.

The Liberals had increased their seat number from six to nine. They were still fringe players, though, and after the excitement of 'Orpington man', the result was a huge disappointment for Grimond. So much of his strategy had been riding on the election outcome. But if they could not break through under these circumstances, could they ever? Grimond had seen the 1964 election as crucial – if Labour lost, 'I believe that it might have split.' He was 'baffled … we had to pretend that we could influence events … It put paid for the time being to any realignment on the Left.' He concluded that 1964 was 'the beginning of the end for the social democrats or Gaitskellites upon whom rested the main hope of Liberals for a realignment'.

There was no major Liberal breakthrough. No Labour split. No hung parliament. And Grimond lacked the number and quality of MPs to realistically be part of a government. He could also see that if his party got too close to Labour, they would lose the Tory-inclined vote that they had picked up. The Conservatives would be able to claim that a 'vote for the Liberals is a vote for Labour'. That had been fatal in 1924 and 1931.

Harold Wilson was Prime Minister – the youngest since Lord Rosebery in 1894. Labour's small majority provided the only opportunity for Grimond. But there was a gulf between the parties on both policy and strategy. Labour was still a socialist party, committed to nationalisation and planning. Despite the greater enthusiasm for planning in the Liberal manifesto, it was still essentially a liberal party, opposed to state intervention in industry. The Liberals were also committed to joining the European Community, devolving power to Scotland, Wales and the English regions and changing the electoral system. Labour favoured none of these things. Only on social policy was there an obvious overlap.

And if Grimond favoured a realignment of the left and a fracturing within the Labour Party, this was most definitely not Harold Wilson's strategy. Unsurprisingly, given the Liberal history since 1931, Wilson did not see Grimond's party as natural allies. Indeed, the left of Labour saw any co-operation with other parties as representing a dilution of their socialist faith and a return to the days of their discredited former leader, Ramsay MacDonald. So, there was no call from Wilson to Grimond and no attempt by the Liberal leader to court the new Prime Minister.

On the weekend after the election, Grimond made his position clear. He anticipated another contest soon but stated that in the meantime his MPs would not 'harry' the new government. They would remain on the opposition benches but try to demonstrate that Liberals could have an impact on government policy and behave in a constructive manner. He wanted 'stable government ... for a reasonable period of time' but made clear that his party would fight the planned nationalisation of the steel industry. Eventually, Grimond would come to see electoral reform as the only prize that could justify the risks involved in cross-party co-operation.

It was two right-wing Labour MPs – Woodrow Wyatt and Desmond Donnelly – who now stirred press interest in the idea of a pact. Both were opposed to steel nationalisation and stated publicly that they saw Liberal influence on the government as likely to strengthen their position. Wyatt argued publicly for a full coalition, with Grimond in the Cabinet. Grimond responded cautiously, telling the party council on 31 October 1964 that he was opposed to pacts and didn't want to prop up a socialist government. In any case, he knew that Wyatt did not speak for Harold Wilson. Grimond did, however, ask his assistant Christopher Layton to contact Roy Jenkins, to see how seriously Labour viewed these possibilities. But nothing came of this.

In Parliament, the Liberals sought to maintain their difficult balancing act – a similar approach to that which Paddy Ashdown would take in 1997–99 – the oxymoron of 'constructive opposition'. In November, Liberal MP Emlyn Hooson led for the party in the debates on Labour plans for steel. Hooson made clear he would oppose full nationalisation but then set out a hare-brained scheme that would involve the government taking a 51 per cent stake in a limited number of steel producers, with state and private firms competing. It pleased nobody, and all nine Liberals voted with the Conservatives against the government.

Meanwhile, Wilson was keen to keep the Liberals sweet and buy time. With his usual cunning, he announced in the Commons on 10 November 1964 that the government was 'considering various proposals for electoral reform', including cross-party talks. He was borrowing from MacDonald's 1920s strategy of stringing the Liberals along.

Privately, Wilson gave the impression that he was keen to progress electoral reform but would need to keep his sceptical party on board. He had no intention of delivering anything substantive but did give the Liberals three life peerages – the first since this innovation had been introduced. Grimond was grateful. But it was a trivial concession.

For Grimond, the political balancing act was tough to maintain. Even though his MPs more often voted against the government than supporting it, his activists were complaining that they were doing too much to prop Labour up. On 21 January 1965, there was a by-election in the Labour seat of Leyton. But it was the Conservatives, not Liberals, who won, and the Liberal vote fell.

In February, Liberal MPs refused to back a Conservative censure motion against the government. It again left the Liberals in the uncomfortable no man's land of politics. By March 1965, Grimond was telling *The Times*: 'Either we must have some reasonably long ranging agreement with the Government or a general election ... I should be very much opposed to going back to the 1929 system, in which the Labour Government and the Liberal Party made practically daily ad-hoc decisions.'[6]

And in April 1965, Grimond once again talked loosely about a 'radical coming together of the two non-Conservative parties ...

The Liberal Party have to be the kernel of this new coalition.' The Liberal and Labour Chief Whips were now meeting informally every month, but this was more focused on discussing parliamentary business than any formal co-operation.

Two months later, in June, Grimond gave an interview to *The Guardian* that appeared under the breathless headline: 'Coalition Offer to Labour by Mr Grimond.' Again, he was speculating about a 'serious agreement on long term policies'. He seemed to be suggesting that he was still committed to his long-term realignment plan but could contemplate a near-term deal with Labour to keep the government in power in exchange for Liberal policies. In a later interview, he made clear that he didn't want to enable the return of a 'Tory Government'.

Some Liberal supporters were excited and sympathetic. Others were furious. A new Liberal 'Independence Committee' was established by four former parliamentary candidates, all of whom were sympathetic to the realignment strategy but not to deals and pacts with a Labour government. They posed a very important question: if the Liberals wished to replace Labour as the non-socialist alternative, why would they want to prop them up?

Others have argued that if Grimond 'sought to bring Party advantage to the Liberals by inclining to Labour in a balance of power situation, it is difficult to see why he thought he would succeed with ten MPs, when Lloyd George had failed with fifty-eight'.[7] And there was not much support amongst the majority in both parties to allow any organised form of co-operation.

In June 1965, just before the summer recess, Grimond held private talks with Wilson. These came at the initiative of the editor of *The Guardian*, Alastair Hetherington – a strong advocate of closer Lib–Lab relations. The aim was to discuss their respective attitudes to 'co-operation.' Grimond told Hetherington after the meeting that while it was friendly and constructive, it seemed unlikely to lead anywhere. Wilson had talked optimistically about the economic outlook, assured Grimond that Labour's legislative agenda would be moderate and uncontroversial, and said that Labour ministers would always be happy to meet Liberal MPs. Unsurprisingly, Grimond was unimpressed. He concluded that Wilson was simply trying to understand more about the Liberals' political strategy. Grimond was cautious about being seen as 'throwing a lifebelt to a sinking government' but remained unwilling to rule out deals.

Wilson's own conclusion was that Grimond would struggle to deliver his party into any longer-term deal with Labour. But in August, he took the precaution of asking his adviser, Gerald Kaufman, to sound out Labour MPs about their attitude to a Lib–Lab pact. Kaufman reported back that they were opposed to any deal in a ratio of around 3–2. Wilson concluded that even if he wanted a deal, his party wouldn't support it.

In any case, Wilson wanted an easy parliamentary ride more than a deal. He talked of 'parallel courses' not pacts. But he was forced to drop steel nationalisation from the 1965 Queen's Speech in recognition of the lack of parliamentary majority.

Up to May 1965, the Liberals had voted against the government on eighty-five occasions but with it forty times. This type of balanced attitude was relatively easy to manage with a small Labour majority. The question was, what would happen if the majority disappeared? Then there would be nowhere for Liberals to hide.

Wilson had taken out a 'hedging strategy' in case he later needed Liberal support. In May 1965, he had promised a Speaker's Conference on electoral reform, which held its first meeting in June. The conference lasted until February 1968 and was asked to look at a variety of issues including 'methods of election, with particular reference to preferential voting'. Labour was still cautious, however, of adopting the Alternative Vote, as a Gallup poll in September 1964 seemed to suggest it would have lost them that year's election. For Labour, voting reform was only something to keep in play as a possibility if the alternative was losing power. And by the time the Speaker's Conference reported, in 1968, Labour no longer needed Liberal support. The gathering of twenty-nine MPs had also rejected PR. The experience of this Speaker's Conference would make Liberals wary of similar such offers in 1974 (from Heath) and 1977 (from Callaghan).

In July 1965, the Conservatives had elected a new leader, Edward Heath, who immediately tabled a motion of censure against the government. Grimond and his Chief Whip would have liked to oppose it, but at a meeting of all their MPs it was decided that they would abstain instead. They were stuck in political no man's land.

Meanwhile, all the talk of pacts was leading nowhere. On Sunday 12 September, Harold Wilson held an all-day Cabinet meeting at Chequers. According to Crossman, Wilson assured his ministers that he had not held talks with the Liberals about a pact.[8] He had seen Grimond but on 'quite a different subject'. He reported Grimond as saying that there was 'no question of a Lib–Lab pact' and stated that even if he (Wilson) wanted a pact, he knew he could not persuade his party. Wilson also said that he felt that the Liberals would be happy to delay an election, as their opinion poll rating was low, at around 8 per cent.

While some in the Liberal Party welcomed continuing talk of a progressive realignment, others were much more dubious. At the 1965 Liberal Assembly in Scarborough, the party president Nancy Seear warned her leader in striking terms: 'We have not spent these years isolated but undefiled in the wilderness to choose this moment ... to go, in the biblical phrase, "a'whoring after foreign women".

Grimond sought to defend his strategy but only ended up affirming the uncomfortable position that his party was now in:

> British politics have been bedevilled all my lifetime by the love-hate relationship of the Liberal and Labour parties ... it would have been utterly wrong not to have raised the question at least of a working partnership ... If the Government loses its majority, we cannot escape our share of the decision as to whether an election should be held or not. It is no good trying to find a halfway house, half keeping the government in, and half putting them out.

But this halfway house was not a bad description of where the party found itself located.

By Labour's own autumn conference, it was differentiation and not realignment that was firmly back in vogue. Wilson's speech included several attacks on the tiny Liberal contingent in Parliament. He noted that they had now voted with Labour on just sixty-eight occasions, compared with 157 with the Conservatives, dismissing Grimond's claim that his party were 'the Radical Left'.

The truth was that Grimond had a sensible aspiration over realignment, but not the vehicle to pursue it. Labour in 1964 was neither a willing nor a compatible ally of the Liberals, and it would take fifteen years before a portion of the Labour Party would break with its left wing. Grimond could wish for realignment, but he could not deliver it. He knew this, felt demoralised and would now have stood down as leader, but for the imminent election.

Wilson wanted a solid majority of his own, not dependence on the whims of nine Liberal MPs. The lost by-election in Leyton in

January 1965 had seen his majority cut to just two. Economic conditions were improving and by early 1966, Labour had opened an opinion poll lead of between 6 and 8 per cent. Wilson seized his chance and called an election for 31 March.

Labour fought under the slogan: 'You know Labour government works.' The manifesto was even longer than the lengthy 1964 effort. On economic policy, it promised a 'mixed economy' and played down nationalisation. On the sensitive issue of immigration, it offered both 'realistic controls, flexibly administered', combined with 'racial equality'. European policy was now notably bolder: 'Labour believes that Britain ... should be ready to enter the European Economic Community, provided essential ... interests are safeguarded'. This was probably the most modern and moderate of Labour's policy offerings to date and a clear pitch for the centre ground.

The Liberal manifesto sought to take credit for having 'acted as a powerful brake and a positive influence on the policies of the Labour Government', citing the 'shelving' of steel nationalisation and (less convincingly) a new 'Highland Development Board'. It still argued for an incomes policy but had backed away from the jarring emphasis on planning in the 1964 manifesto. In a nod to economic liberalism, it argued for new motorways, funded by road user charging. On defence, it was unilateralist. The commitment to join the EEC 'at the earliest opportunity' remained. Backing for electoral reform 'through the Speaker's Conference' was now renewed.

The election result was a big success for Wilson – Labour's vote rose from 44.1 per cent to 48 per cent, with a gain of forty-seven seats, to secure 364 in total and a very healthy majority of ninety-eight. The Conservatives had fallen back from 43.4 per cent to 41.9 per cent and lost fifty-one seats. The Liberals gained three seats, but their vote share declined markedly from 11.2 per cent to 8.5 per cent. For Grimond, it was another blow. The prospect of a political realignment had given him the motivation to carry on. But now any hope of Liberal influence was gone. Wilson had offered a moderate version of Labour, and most of the 'progressive' vote had rowed in behind him.

Grimond's strategy had failed and left his party with a headache: it seemed that a moderate Labour Party would always crowd out the Liberals and steal away their potential voters, while any move by Labour to the left would scare voters and make it dangerous and difficult for Liberals to co-operate with them. Without a deep split in Labour and a completely new alignment of politics, they were likely to remain fringe players.

Wilson was a ruthless political operator, who played Grimond along but never planned to offer anything of substance in return. He wanted power for himself and his party, not dependence on a small number of maverick supporters of a party that had flipped and flopped across the political spectrum for the best part of forty years.

For Grimond, ten years of exhausting leadership had achieved little. He was shattered by the death by suicide of his eldest son in the middle of the 1966 election campaign. In January 1967, he stepped down as leader. Grimond had failed to deliver the realignment he sought. But in three respects his leadership had been of real value. Firstly, he had restored Liberal independence and ended the Conservative pacts. Secondly, he had repositioned his party in policy terms as a non-socialist alternative to Labour – generally economically liberal but with a clear commitment to social reform, devolution and Europe. Finally, he had inspired new members who would carry the torch in the future, including a new MP, David Steel, elected aged just twenty-six, in a by-election in March 1965.

Steel, and later Paddy Ashdown, whom Grimond also inspired, were part of a new generation who would take forward the policy of realignment into the 1970s, 1980s and beyond.

Liberal MPs would now choose their next leader. Excluding Grimond, there were eleven potential contenders, and three now put their names forward – Jeremy Thorpe, Eric Lubbock and Emlyn Hooson. Thorpe was the clear favourite. He was known to be energetic, charismatic and dynamic. But some regarded him as superficial, risky (both in relation to his private life and approaches to party fundraising) and with an outdated image. He knew little about economics at a time when the challenges of the economy dominated political debate. And he was better at tactics than strategy.

On 18 January 1967, Thorpe secured six votes, while his rivals managed three each. The second preference votes of the two rivals both went to each other, rather than Thorpe, suggesting an absurd three-way draw in a twelve-person party. Fortunately, the two rivals gave way to Thorpe, who was declared winner. In future, ballots of party members would be used to help determine the leader.

After Labour's election win, the economic environment was more challenging. And in an embarrassing U-turn, the government had to devalue the pound in 1967. Inflation rose above 6 per cent in 1970. The trade unions were becoming more militant as they sought to protect and improve their members' pay.

But from a low point of 28 per cent in the polls in mid 1968, by early 1970 Labour had recovered to above 40 per cent, and in May and June it was at 49 per cent. It was the first time for over three years that Labour had been ahead of the Conservatives. Harold Wilson now decided to pounce and called an election for 18 June – according to the polls, a comfortable victory was in store. Labour produced another long manifesto, along the lines of its 1966 offering. This time, however, it signalled a clearer willingness to join the EEC, noting that 'we have applied for membership'.

The Liberal manifesto was thin and notably feeble. Someone had presumably concluded that a short manifesto would be sharper edged and more effective. It wasn't. It looked as if it had been cobbled together by someone on work experience, with only a passing knowledge of liberal ideology, tradition and policy.

All was looking good for Wilson, and then just before election day, economic data revealed that unemployment was at the highest level for thirty years. The trade data – closely watched in those days – also showed a large deficit. And on 14 June, England was beaten by West Germany in the World Cup. It was hardly the 'feel-good factor' that Wilson had banked on.

In a surprise result, Heath defeated Wilson, polling 46.4 per cent and securing seventy-seven extra MPs to deliver a secure-enough Conservative majority of thirty. Labour fell almost 5 per cent to 43.1 per cent and lost seventy-five seats.

The Liberals, as a self-declared anti-Conservative force, often did badly when the Conservatives returned to power, and that was now the case. Their performance was shockingly bad – they lost six of their existing thirteen seats, and their vote share fell to 7.5 per cent. After twenty-five years of work to rebuild the party, they were worse off than in 1945.

Edward Heath would now negotiate for the UK to join the EEC on 1 January 1973, with Liberal MPs offering at times crucial support. Labour was badly divided on the issue and sixty-nine Labour MPs, led by Roy Jenkins, rebelled against a three-line whip and supported the government. The cracks within Labour were beginning to show again.

Since the 1930s, Conservative governments had always managed more than one term in office. But Heath's government was operating in the toughest economic times for forty years. And in 1973, the Arab members of OPEC (Organization of Petroleum Exporting Countries) proclaimed an oil embargo on the US, which sent world prices surging. By 1974, the oil price 'shock' had driven UK inflation above 16 per cent. Recession followed, with UK output falling by 4 per cent. Unemployment rose above 1 million and continued to climb.

Unions responded to sky high inflation by raising wage demands, backed by industrial action. Heath was forced to U-turn on his free-market policies and seek to control wages. It didn't work. Instead, coal miners went on strike, there was a three-day working week to save power, and at certain times of the day the electricity was cut off and families had to make do with candles. Voters were not impressed.

But, for once, it wasn't Labour who benefited from Conservative weakness. Voters had experienced thirty years of unbroken single party Conservative/Labour government. It had ended in economic shambles and a Labour Party that now appeared to be turning left again. Thorpe was a showman and an opportunist and exploited his opportunity to the full. The Liberal vote soared from 6 per cent in late 1970 to 12 per cent in late 1972, and then on to a peak of 28 per cent in August 1973, before settling back to around 20 per cent into 1974. Huge by-election swings now occurred, delivering Liberal gains at Rochdale, Sutton, Isle of Ely, Ripon and Berwick. The swings of up to 33 per cent were some of the largest in UK political history. Thorpe was suddenly the Liberal in the right place at the right time.

Meanwhile, Labour MP Dick Taverne was de-selected by his local party for his pro-European views, but he successfully retained his seat as a 'Democratic Labour' candidate, with discreet Liberal support. This was another small sign that the tectonic plates of politics might be moving, as Labour became more divided between its left and right wings, which were bitterly split over Europe, economic policy, and management of the unions.

In early 1974, the Conservative poll rating recovered to 40 per cent, just ahead of Labour. It was the first Conservative poll lead for two years, and on 7 February Heath struck. Even though the Queen was abroad in New Zealand, he requested an election, requiring the dissolution to be promulgated in her place by the Queen Mother and Princess Margaret. Polling day was to be 28 February. Heath was determined to make the issue: 'who governs Britain' – the elected government, or the militant unions.

The miners went on strike again on 10 February, and the three-day week continued. Governments don't usually win elections in times of economic crisis, but Heath felt this time it would be different – he expected the public to back him rather than the unions. However, late in the campaign, government statistics showed inflation running at 20 per cent, and a Pay Board report made the case for a better deal for miners. Some voters now backed Labour, feeling the party might have more success in ending the strikes. Just before the election, the curse of bad trade figures hit again.

Finally, in a speech in Birmingham on 23 February, the Conservative MP Enoch Powell urged people to vote against Heath because of his European policies and to ensure Britain 'remained a democratic nation [and not] one province in a new Europe super-state'. He explicitly backed what was Wilson's carefully crafted fudge to hold Labour together – a renegotiation of UK membership, with a national referendum on the result. The divisive issue of Europe had now entered the British political bloodstream.

Wilson fought the campaign as an experienced Prime Minister promising to bring the unions and employers together. It was a moderate message, but it was not backed by a moderate manifesto. Left-wingers such as Tony Benn had a major role in writing it, and it marked a significant turn away from the more centrist programmes of previous years. The narrative on Europe was distinctly negative, whatever was said about renegotiation and a referendum. On economic policy, there was to be a 'drastic redistribution of wealth and income'. The position of the National Union of Mineworkers was asserted to be 'in the national interest', and the Conservatives' Industrial Relations Act would be repealed. There would be price controls. And an annual wealth tax. The oil industry would be nationalised along with mineral rights, shipbuilding, marine engineering, ports and the manufacture of airframes and aeroengines. This would also be the fate of profitable business where there was a national interest in controlling prices – including road haulage, pharmaceuticals, construction, machine tools and possibly banking, insurance and even building societies. Private schools would lose all forms of tax relief and charitable status. NATO would eventually be 'phased out'. It was a dramatic and explicit lurch to the left.

The Liberal manifesto was about three times the length of the miserable 1970 effort. But if 1970 was a short dog's breakfast, February 1974 was just a longer version of the same lightweight offering. The price and wage proposals were eccentric and illiberal. The section on Europe faced both ways, deploring the delay in joining the Common Market but criticising its structure as 'not what we voted for'. This was the moment for a clear, distinctive, principled and easily communicable set of policies to exploit the problems that both Labour and Conservatives were grappling with. But the party and its leader failed to deliver.

So great were the government's economic difficulties, however, and so left-wing was Labour's manifesto, that when the election was held on 28 February, the two big parties received less than a combined 80 per cent of the vote – for the first time since 1929.

The Conservative vote plummeted by 8.5 per cent, to 37.9 per cent, while Labour was just behind on 37.2 per cent, down by almost 6 per cent. The Liberals were for once the big winners, with 19.3 per cent – over 6 million votes. This was the best Liberal result since 1929, but it delivered only eight more MPs – fourteen in total. The First Past the Post electoral system protected the two big parties – the Conservatives shed only twenty-eight MPs, while Labour managed to gain fourteen, despite losing 5.9 per cent of the vote.

For the first time since 1929, there was a hung parliament. Edward Heath had most votes. Harold Wilson had more seats – but was still seventeen short of an overall majority.

Had the Liberals' big chance finally arrived?

CHAPTER 5

'TURKEYS VOTING FOR CHRISTMAS'
1974–79

Edward Heath fought the February 1974 election on the question 'Who Governs Britain?' On 28 February, the public gave their answer: no one.

Heath was not yet ready to give up power. He hoped that a deal with the Liberals and Northern Ireland's Unionists might still deliver a majority. On the night of Friday 1 March, Heath's Downing Street staff were charged with urgently tracking down Jeremy Thorpe. They found the number for his home – Higher Chuggaton – in North Devon – but the Liberal leader was not in. 'I'm afraid he's in Barnstaple – leading a torchlight victory procession. Could you perhaps call back at 10.30 p.m.?' The somewhat baffled staff at No. 10 agreed, but the local telephone exchange, at Chittlehamholt, was notoriously unreliable, and they failed to get through. Eventually, sometime after midnight, an intrigued Thorpe phoned Downing Street.

Heath now made a strong pitch for Liberal support – pointing to similarities in their positions on Europe and incomes policies. Thorpe agreed to visit Downing Street the following day – Saturday

2 March. It did not seem to have occurred to him that he might want to consult first with his senior colleagues. Forty years of political irrelevance had entrenched a high degree of amateurishness in the once-great party of Gladstone.

The next morning, Thorpe caught the express train from Taunton to London. He had still not bothered to update his colleagues. But by the time he reached Paddington, the news had leaked out. David Steel, Liberal Chief Whip, found out from his car radio, as he was driving in his constituency. He was astonished and concerned.

Thorpe now met Heath in 10 Downing Street. Heath's pitch was that since his party had secured the largest vote share, he had first rights to form a government. He was offering the Liberals a full coalition and a seat for Thorpe in the Cabinet. Thorpe later denied making a request for the post of Home Secretary, as claimed in Heath's memoirs. In his autobiography, Thorpe recounts that he was later told that the PM was thinking of 'a Foreign Office job with specific responsibility for Europe'.[1]

Thorpe pointed out that his party had secured almost one in five votes but only one in forty-five MPs. His price for coalition was electoral reform. 'We have no set policy on this,' said Heath. 'Perhaps it is time you had,' replied Thorpe.[2] It was a rerun of the Davies/Churchill liaisons of 1946–51. Thorpe raised other challenges in forming a coalition – firstly, it would seem to many voters that Heath had lost the election, so it would look odd for him to return as PM. Secondly, even adding the 297 Conservative MPs to the fourteen Liberals would not give a majority in the Commons. Such a coalition would therefore be very weak, if it could govern at all. Both these arguments were to be replayed in May 2010, in the post-election talks between Nick Clegg and Gordon Brown.

The leaders agreed to consult their senior colleagues and meet again the next day. Thorpe finally spoke to David Steel, who insisted they should clarify if the PM was willing to offer electoral reform. That same night, Steel drove Thorpe back to Downing Street and waited outside in the dark. After half an hour, Thorpe was back out. All Heath was offering was a Speaker's Conference on PR, a seat at the Cabinet table and one or two junior ministerial roles. Steel was clear with Thorpe that this was hopelessly insufficient. Meanwhile, Liberal MPs and party officials were fielding an unending series of angry phone calls from activists and voters who were furious and fearful of being bounced into a coalition with their Conservative enemies.

On Sunday, Steel, Jo Grimond and Lord Byers (Liberal leader in the Lords) met Thorpe at his London home. Over a roast beef lunch, they told Thorpe of their doubts about any deal. Steel argued strongly against a coalition, pointing out that Heath had lost the election and that the large Liberal vote should be seen as a rejection of his policies. Steel's view was that it would be disastrous to contemplate propping up a defeated Prime Minister. In addition, he underlined that a Liberal–Conservative pact would not command a Commons majority. The only concession that would make a difference was a 'cast iron commitment to change the electoral system'.[3] But that was not on offer.

Late that night Thorpe headed back to Downing Street. Heath claimed that his colleagues were adamant that he should stay as PM. He would still only offer a 'Speaker's Conference' on electoral reform, with a free vote on the outcome. It was very thin gruel indeed. Thorpe made clear that he could only proceed if the Cabinet backed electoral reform and made it an issue of confidence for Conservative MPs.

The next day, 4 March, Liberal MPs met. They were unanimously against any deal, unless there was a bankable offer of proportional representation. Steel drove Thorpe to Downing Street to relay the news – again, waiting in his car while Thorpe went in to end Heath's career. Thorpe later wrote formally to Heath to reject the coalition offer but mentioned instead the possibility of support from the opposition benches for a minority government, with an agreed programme. But Heath had already rejected this possibility. The short-lived negotiation was over. Heath resigned. Harold Wilson was now back in No. 10.

In this episode, there were some lessons for the future but also some fundamental questions. One obvious lesson was that talks with a Prime Minister over a potential coalition required at least some degree of cross-party consultation. Never again would the Liberal Party allow its leader to behave in such a cavalier way.

But there were three decisions that the party and its leader did get right: firstly, that it would be difficult and dangerous to prop up a PM who had lost his majority and was regarded as having lost the election. Secondly, it would be highly risky to enter a coalition in a situation where the combined coalition parties would still not have a majority in the House of Commons. And thirdly, it would be unwise to enter a coalition or pact without ensuring a change in the electoral system, which might help compensate for the lost support of those voters who would oppose an arrangement to put into power a party they had not voted for.

This much looked like common ground, but the discussions on Monday 4 March had highlighted some serious differences of attitude in the Parliamentary Liberal Party, which were important over the years ahead. Some MPs were strongly of the opinion that joining a coalition or giving support to a minority government would be electorally disastrous and should be avoided at all costs. Others took a different view. While they agreed with rejecting Heath's offer, they did not want to close off the possibility that the party might in the future be part of a government. David Steel, Jo Grimond and Russell Johnston all took this more pragmatic stance. This in part reflected a difference between those who believed that 'one more heave' might deliver a major Liberal breakthrough and those who thought that Liberal influence was more likely to come through playing a part in a National Government in partnership with another party.

Steel's views were to be particularly important in this regard. He believed that the country was moving away from single-party governments and that tackling the economic problems of the time would require cross-party co-operation. He was already thinking of the opportunities for co-operation that might arise with Labour. On the weekend after the election, without consulting his own leader, Steel had telephoned Roy Jenkins, formerly Labour deputy leader (who had resigned from this post in 1972 over Labour's decision to oppose entry to the European Community) and asked him whether Labour would be open to the type of deal that the Liberals were discussing with Heath. Jenkins was keen, and within six weeks of becoming Home Secretary, he tabled a paper to the Cabinet on 4 April 1974, suggesting that a Speaker's Conference on electoral reform should be established to consider STV. Michael Foot spoke strongly against. Wilson summed up saying that it was better to 'let sleeping dogs lie as long as possible' and Jenkins later admitted 'it did not get much of a reception'. Barbara Castle recorded: 'We sent Roy away with a flea in his coalition ear.'

Jenkins had already predicted correctly to Steel that Wilson would reject any Lib–Lab deal and simply form a minority government, while looking for an early opportunity to win a decisive mandate of his own. That is exactly what Wilson did, rerunning the strategy of 1964–66. Jenkins returned to the issue of a pact or coalition in another Cabinet meeting on 18 November 1974 but with the same result as in April. Denis Healey, now Chancellor, described the idea as 'absolute madness', with only Shirley Williams, Harold Lever and Reg Prentice speaking in support. Barbara Castle again noted that it was 'pleasant to have Roy Jenkins slapped down' and confided to her diary that 'those rightists will go on beavering away, with Harold and Jim [Callaghan] as their instruments, until they have finally destroyed the Labour Party's independence and power to govern single-handedly'.

This was a Labour Party increasingly at war with itself. The left wing saw co-operation with the Liberals and talk of electoral reform as an attempt to marginalise them and block a truly socialist government. In 1976, Ron Hayward, former general secretary of the Labour Party, wrote that PR would mean coalition and 'it is goodbye then to any dreams or aspirations for a Democratic Socialist Britain'. But others saw a relationship with the Liberals as a way of strengthening and moderating their party and keeping it in touch with the electorate.

Over the next few decades, resistance to PR united a number of different groupings in Labour: the left, worried that it would dilute their influence; the hard-nosed pragmatists like Jack Straw who would note in 1985 that PR was all about 'giving parties who get the least number of votes the most power'; and some on the right who were dubious that Labour would necessarily benefit from PR. Healey summed this latter position up in his memoirs, where he wrote: 'Labour cannot escape from its problems through alliance with the Centre parties, or through PR. The non-Labour majority is probably as large as the non-Conservative majority; there is no guarantee that members of the Centre parties would vote Labour if their own candidates stood down...'

But Steel was not to be deterred. He considered that a strategy of independence at all costs favoured by some of his colleagues 'left us looking like an alternative embryo government in permanent exile'.[4] In June 1974, the Liberals had one of their rare, televised, party-political broadcasts. As Chief Whip, Steel oversaw this. He decided to make the broadcast himself. More surprisingly, and without consulting any of his colleagues (this was clearly becoming a Liberal habit), he delivered an address which argued: 'In our crisis, we surely need a much more broadly based government backed by a real majority of public opinion, and that means that all parties must be willing to come together on an agreed programme...' He went on: 'Naturally ... we would prefer you to give us an overall majority ... but if you don't, we remain ready to contribute towards the kind of government based on partnership which you ... might be seeking.'

Four days after the speech, the Liberal Party's National Executive Committee put out a statement appearing to reject the Steel approach. They did not rule out participation in a National Government but lobbed a bucket of very cold water over the broadcast. And Thorpe, taking his lead from his party, argued that the Liberals would be fighting the next election aiming for an overall majority. Total twaddle, but the sort of twaddle much favoured by party tribalists. But the Steel approach was more popular amongst voters, who seemed to yearn for a less divisive politics. And in July 1974, the Labour MP Christopher Mayhew defected to the Liberals. This was mainly down to his disillusionment with Harold Wilson, but Steel argued that it was an endorsement of his attempts to make the Liberals more relevant.

These arguments on party strategy mattered. They mattered because 1974 was to be the first year since 1910 in which there would be two general elections. And, like 1910, they would both lead to photo finishes. A failure to secure solid, working, majorities had plagued Labour since the foundation of the party. In 1923, 1929 and (February) 1974, Labour governed as a minority. In 1950, their majority was just ten. In 1964 it was four. Only in 1945 and 1966 had Labour come to power with a clear margin over its opponents.

A second election was therefore always likely. It came rapidly. Wilson announced polling day for 10 October 1974. Not much had changed since the February election, but the miners' strike was over. As with 1910, two elections held close together unsurprisingly delivered very similar results. Labour achieved a small swing in its favour, with its vote rising from 37.2 per cent to 39.2 per cent. The Conservatives fell by roughly the same amount, and the Liberal vote dropped back slightly to 18.3 per cent. 'One more heave' had failed again.

Labour had secured eighteen more seats, with 319 MPs versus 277 Conservative and thirteen Liberal. In a Parliament of 635 seats, they now had their majority – but a tiny one of just three. It was just enough to govern, but for how long?

Steel was frustrated by the result and felt that the Liberals were in danger again of being 'cast into irrelevance'. In summer 1975, he authored a pamphlet on Liberal strategy. It concluded with a call which would in time be of huge significance:

Many of the self-styled social democrats would be happier company in combination with Liberals than with Socialists. Should such an opportunity for an effective regrouping of the left come about it is important that the Liberal Party should not behave like a more rigid sect of the exclusive brethren but be ready to join with others in the more effective promotion of liberalism.[5]

It was an astute assessment of the challenges and opportunities for his party. It was also of particular significance because within the year, Steel would take over as the new leader.

Within four months of the October 1974 election, Margaret Thatcher replaced Ted Heath as Conservative leader. The leadership change, and the economic crisis that was by now overwhelming the Labour government, saw the Conservatives soar in the polls. Within eighteen months, Wilson had resigned as PM. A month later, in May 1976, Jeremy Thorpe was forced to stand down as Liberal leader, after extraordinary allegations about his private life had become public, in January. The Thorpe news received huge publicity, and the Liberal Party became the subject of widespread ridicule. By February 1976, the Liberal bubble had burst, and the party was back down into single figures in the polls – half the level of October 1974.

In July 1976, David Steel was elected as the new leader – he was to be the longest-serving since Asquith. He was not a particularly original policy thinker, but he spoke clearly and effectively for the moderate majority at a time of polarising politics. He also offered 'direction, a purpose and an ambition'.[6] Steel continued to challenge his party: 'We should combine our long-term programme with a readiness to work with others wherever we see what Jo Grimond has called the break in the clouds – the chance to implement any of our Liberal policies.' His party couldn't say that it hadn't been warned. He went even further at the 1976 conference in Llandudno in September, telling activists: 'I want the Liberal Party to be the fulcrum and centre of the next election ... we must not give the impression of being afraid to soil our hands with the responsibilities of power. We must be bold enough to deploy our coalition case positively.'[7] This was the most decisive and ambitious leadership since Lloyd George.

By 1977, the Labour government, now led by Jim Callaghan, was in serious trouble. Propelled higher by the oil price 'shocks' and a wage–prices spiral, UK inflation had soared from 16 per cent in 1974 to over 24 per cent in 1975 – the highest since the First World War. Inflation remained over 16 per cent in 1976 and was just under this level in 1977. Over a period of just five years, prices more than doubled. The economy had suffered a severe contraction, and this drove up unemployment and wrecked the public finances. In 1976, the pound plunged, and the UK was forced to go cap in hand to the International Monetary Fund for a $3.9 billion loan. A condition of the loan was public spending cuts, which were deeply divisive within the Labour Party. High inflation. Higher unemployment. Real incomes falling. Surging government debt. Strikes. There could hardly have been a worse economic environment.

The Labour Party was also increasingly divided on both economic policy and Europe. Labour left-wingers were emboldened by the economic crisis to press for more radical, left-wing policies and were angered by the tough economic medicine enforced by both the IMF and their own Chancellor, Denis Healey.

In November 1976, after two by-elections, Callaghan lost the slim majority that Wilson had bequeathed. By March 1977, it was becoming clear that Labour could no longer 'muddle through'. It had lost the support of Scottish and Welsh nationalist MPs over its handling of devolution. If there was an election, Labour would be decisively defeated – they were over 15 per cent behind in the polls.

It was at this point that discussions between Liberals and Labour over some sort of 'deal' began. The unlikely initial contact was the Liberal MP Cyril Smith, who on 7 March 1977 sought a meeting with the Prime Minister. As a backbench opposition MP, with a limited reputation for discretion, he was unsurprisingly referred instead to the chair of the Parliamentary Labour Party, Cledwyn Hughes. He took some offence at this. However, after discussing the matter with Callaghan, Hughes contacted David Steel, and they met in Steel's pokey Commons office on Thursday 17 March.

The pressure on Callaghan increased that evening when the government lost a key vote on public spending cuts. The next morning, Mrs Thatcher rose in the Commons and announced she was tabling a vote of confidence. It would be held the following Wednesday – 23 March 1977. The PM now needed extra votes, urgently. Callaghan initially focused on doing a deal with the Ulster Unionists. According to his adviser Bernard Donoughue, he preferred the Unionists to the Liberals as they were, like him, 'tough, old-fashioned conservative people'.[8] In addition, Callaghan knew that the Unionists were focused only on issues affecting their own constituencies and would make few wider demands.

But Steel sensed that the opportunity he had long sought had arrived. On Friday 18 March, he made a public statement saying that there should either be a general election or a government that the Liberals might support 'on the basis of agreed measures in the national interest for the next two years'. Before long, Steel had received further calls from both Cledwyn Hughes and the Labour Transport Secretary, William Rodgers. They reported that the Prime Minister wished to meet urgently. Learning lessons from Jeremy Thorpe's failure to consult in February 1974, Steel spent the weekend phoning his MPs. They were all willing for him to see Callaghan. But Jo Grimond and David Penhaligon sounded strong notes of caution.

The first meeting between Steel and Callaghan took place on Monday 21 March at 6 p.m., in the PM's offices in Parliament – out of view of the news media. Although Steel was the leader of a party with just thirteen MPs, he was in a potentially powerful position. Callaghan was in talks with the seven Ulster Unionists but had no guarantee of their support. He was at high risk of losing the confidence motion, now scheduled for debate from 3.30 p.m. on 23 March. If this was lost, Labour faced a landslide defeat. Meanwhile, the Liberals were polling at around 14 per cent – down on their October 1974 result but a decent election launchpad and enough to hold their existing seats.

What would Steel now demand as his price for keeping an unpopular Labour Party in office? A full coalition, with Liberals in the Cabinet? A solid and bankable commitment on electoral reform for the Commons? Or perhaps a laundry list of Liberal policies or additional spending targeted at their constituencies?

Callaghan's own opening offer was understandably modest. In exchange for Liberal support, he favoured an informal agreement, with discussions on some policy areas that would 'take account of Liberal thinking'. He suggested his government could muddle through, sometimes with Liberal support and sometimes with Unionist or SNP backing. He was clear that neither he nor his party favoured electoral reform.

With any Liberal leader other than Steel, this might have been the end of the matter. But for years Steel had wanted the Liberals to take some share in government. He was not put off by the thin gruel on offer. He said that he was uninterested in the Callaghan approach but instead favoured a 'framework agreement'. Both parties would co-operate over the economic strategy and consult over other policy areas. Callaghan was expecting a list of Liberal policy demands. Instead, Steel was pushing for a Consultative Committee that would embed Liberal involvement in the government.

This would have seemed to most people a gobsmackingly small request, but Callaghan was concerned about how such a consultative arrangement might look to the trade unions and the left of his party, and there was a good deal of discussion on how an arrangement would work. Steel also raised the issue of moving forward on Scottish and Welsh devolution, where agreement was not difficult to reach. Finally, Steel raised the issue of direct elections to the European Parliament.* Callaghan indicated his personal support for direct election but would not agree to the Liberal proposal of this being based on a proportional voting system. Europe, direct elections to the European Parliament, and electoral reform were all deeply divisive issues within the Labour Party.

As Michie and Hoggart noted: 'The central dilemma was that the things the Liberals really wanted, such as proportional representation for the Scottish and Welsh assemblies and the European elections, could not be promised, because too few Labour MPs would vote for them.'[9] And the Liberals lacked a deliverable list of more voter-friendly policies. The party was pushing for a shift away from direct taxation, but this could not be afforded without economic recovery. The other Liberal 'asks' – including that the Labour Party should drop left-wing policies on nationalisation – would have occurred anyway, thanks to the loss of Labour's majority.

The Steel/Callaghan meeting lasted an hour and ten minutes. Both men agreed to consult further. But neither was satisfied. Callaghan did not really understand what the Liberals wanted, and Steel had expected a much more positive reception. Later that night, there

---

* Prior to 1979, the members of the European Parliament were 'indirectly elected' from existing national parliaments, rather than in separate elections.

was a further Lib–Lab meeting, this time between John Pardoe, the Liberal economics spokesperson and effectively Steel's deputy, and the Labour Leader of the House, Michael Foot. Pardoe was as vague as Steel over how a Consultative Committee might work. There was also discussion about a new voting system for European elections. Foot wasn't encouraging, noting: 'Just as the Liberals had a permanent interest in PR, so the Labour Party had a permanent non-interest.' Foot himself was a strong opponent of electoral reform.

Later that evening, at 10.30 p.m., Liberal MPs met. Steel emphasised that he was seeking policy changes conducive to the Liberals through an established process of consultation, rather than in an upfront agreement. MPs generally objected to a long-term deal. Most favoured a renegotiation in the summer of 1977 – just a few months away. They wanted Steel, and Labour, on a short leash. Steel's colleagues were also clear that they gave top priority to the issue of direct elections to Europe by PR. This was an obsession of Liberal activists but a fourth-order issue for the public. Meanwhile, Grimond and Penhaligon remained dubious about the benefits of any arrangement.

After the meeting, Steel drew up a short paper, setting out his key requirements. As Michie and Hoggart noted: 'It was … a document to please the Liberal Party rather than the Liberal voter.'[10] Nevertheless, Steel's paper was sent over to Downing Street. It arrived on the PM's desk on the morning of 22 March. By then, the chance of a deal with the Ulster Unionists was low. However, Callaghan had still not reconciled himself to the concessions he would need to make to secure Liberal support. After reading Steel's letter, he threw it down, exclaiming: 'Well, I cannot take that.' Callaghan's advisers urged him to think again. Even if he could persuade some of the nationalist MPs to abstain in the confidence debate, this would buy him only limited time. A longer-term arrangement was needed to allow time for the economy to recover.

That afternoon, at 12.30 p.m., Steel met the PM for the second time, again in his Commons office. Callaghan played hardball: 'This letter cannot be published. It is wholly unacceptable.' He was having difficulty accepting that he now had to dance to the tune of a party that in his political lifetime had been an irrelevance. Fortunately for Callaghan, Steel was a patient man, and a determined one. He now even agreed to pass the drafting of a possible Liberal–Labour agreement to Tom McNally, the PM's own political adviser. The Labour Party was now holding the pen.

A few second order issues were covered in the talks, but eventually the two men came to the key issue – what voting systems would be used for the proposed devolved assemblies and direct European elections. Steel made clear that this was the 'only sticking point', and that he could not sell an agreement to his party without progress. Foot, who was attending the meeting, suggested a free vote of Labour MPs. Callaghan seemed more persuadable, talking of growing support for the 'list system' of PR. But he was conscious that the issue would divide Labour and stated that he was not able to make any commitments. He had always opposed PR, and it seems likely that this was still his view.

Steel made clear that a free vote was not enough, and the talks broke up after just thirty minutes without agreement. After the meeting, the discussion between Callaghan and Foot continued. The PM was finally realising that if he could not strike a deal, his party might be out of power. The minutes, now released under the thirty-year rule, record Callaghan concluding that 'the Cabinet would, in return for an agreement, settle for proportional representation on the list system for 1978 [for European elections] because the outcome would be one of total obscurity in relation to the prospective outcome of a general election'. Callaghan was beginning to see PR for European elections as a price worth paying. Foot was still sceptical and wanted to push back: 'Yes, perhaps, but this was not a gnat to swallow…'[11]

Foot was still determined to see off PR for any major elections and told his private secretary that he doubted that the Liberals would break off talks on the issue: 'They would look very silly if it were known that the Government had offered a free vote and they had rejected it.'[12] Meanwhile, Liberal Party executives took soundings. The view from local constituency parties was clear – nineteen of the twenty-one contacted were opposed to any deal without guarantees on PR.

Callaghan asked his advisers to draw up a document setting out a potential way forward, and a third meeting was arranged for 5 p.m. The clock was now ticking. The confidence debate would start in less than twenty-four hours. Steel's paper had now morphed into McNally's. The Labour draft completely deleted a reference in the original Steel letter to a planned 'reduction in the burden of taxation on personal income'. This was a key Liberal economic policy and one of the few commitments likely to chime well with the ordinary voter. The document still contained a pledge that 'no measures of nationalisation should be introduced', but this would also later be deleted.

Crucially, the Labour draft also removed any clear commitment to PR for European elections, and replaced this with a weak undertaking that the government would 'take account of the Liberal Party position but no [government] recommendation would be made'. Callaghan showed Steel a proposed draft White Paper on direct elections to Europe. This set out a choice of electoral systems but did not indicate a preference.

Ramsay MacDonald: negotiated the 1903 pact and became Labour's first Prime Minister.

Herbert Gladstone: Liberal Chief Whip who 'nursed into life' the Labour 'serpent'.

David Lloyd George: 'the Goat' – the Liberal who could have saved his party but sunk it.
© Scherl / Süddeutsche Zeitung Photo / Alamy Stock Photo

Herbert Asquith: would never come to terms with Lloyd George's betrayal.
© IanDagnall Computing / Alamy Stock Photo

Winston Churchill: advocate of a Liberal–Conservative alliance.
© Keystone Pictures USA / Alamy Stock Photo

Clement Attlee: Labour's first majority Prime Minister. The nationalisation agenda created a deep ditch between liberalism and Labour.

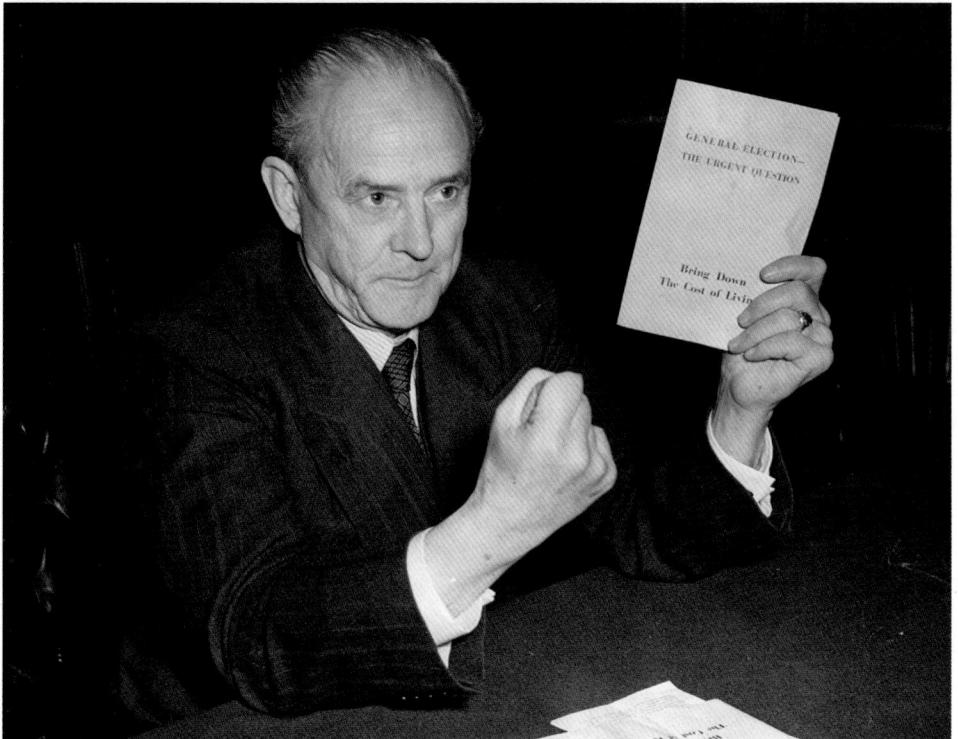

Clement Davies: the Liberal leader whose value to his party was to lie only in the things he didn't do.

Jo Grimond: wanted to realign politics.
© Keystone Pictures USA / Alamy Stock Photo

Harold Wilson: …didn't. © Mirrorpix / Alamy Stock Photo

David Steel: persuaded Liberal turkeys to vote for Christmas. © PA / Alamy Stock Photo

Jim Callaghan: lukewarm
beneficiary of Liberal
turkeys' support.
© David Bagnall /
Alamy Stock Photo

Tony Benn: left-wing
bogeyman of '70s Britain.
© Mirrorpix / Alamy Stock Photo

Michael Foot: his 1983
manifesto was dubbed
the 'longest suicide
note in history'.
© Mike Goldwater /
Alamy Stock Photo

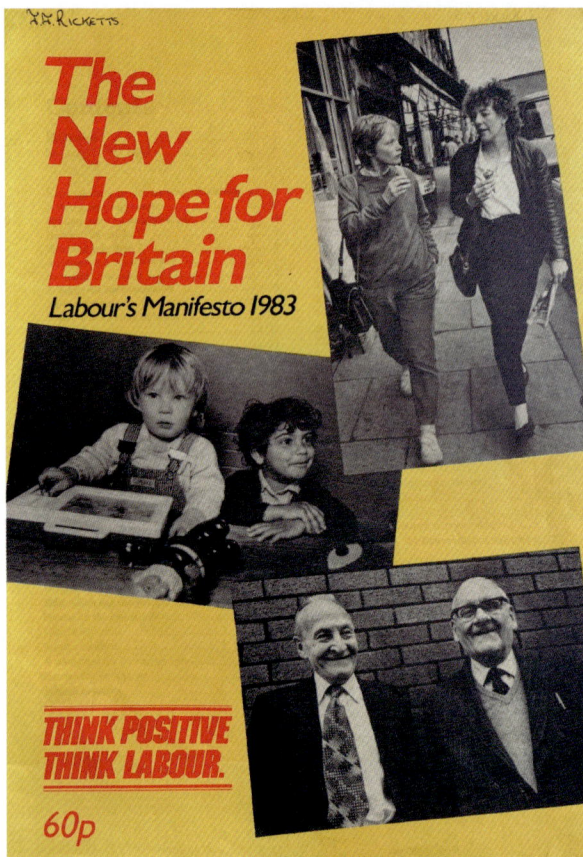

The suicide note itself: 'New Hope' was provided mainly for Labour's Conservative and Alliance competitors.

Author's collection

Roy Jenkins: failed to 'break the mould' or persuade Tony Blair on electoral reform.

© Brian Harris / Alamy Stock Photo

Paddy Ashdown: Labour's 1997 landslide ruined his hoped-for 'Full Monty'.

© Allstar Picture Library / Alamy Stock Photo

Tony Blair: preferred hegemony to partnership. © Jeff Morgan 16 / Alamy Stock Photo

ABOVE Gordon Brown: too little, much too late. © David Levenson / Alamy Stock Photo

LIBERAL DEMOCRAT - LABOUR PARTY DISCUSSIONS

9 May 2010, 1945

The new government will be founded on a core commitment to fairness. It will pursue the key objectives of economic growth, democratic and political reform, social justice and environmental sustainability. It will be pro-European and internationalist, offering engagement and leadership to its international partners.

LEFT Labour's proposed draft coalition agreement, 9 May 2010, in the distinct bold lettering that Brown favoured.

Author's collection

Nick Clegg: faced a 2010 'Zugzwang' and delivered 'an unfortunate but necessary coalition with the wrong party'.
© Mark Thomas / Alamy Stock Photo

Jeremy Corbyn: serial rebel who became Labour leader in 2015.
© Russell Hart / Alamy Stock Photo

Despite the significant changes made by Labour, Steel raised no major concerns. Instead, he focused on the single issue of the electoral system for European elections. Callaghan said that the Labour Party could give no guarantees on PR 'at this stage'. Steel countered that the government should give a 'lead' on the PR issue when the debate arose in the Commons. Callaghan now agreed to this vague demand. Even this was not to make it into the final agreement. Steel now concluded that what was proposed was 'acceptable'. The meeting was short, and by 6.45 p.m. the Liberal leader was again huddled with his parliamentary party. Some MPs pressed him for a firmer undertaking on PR. But by now, Steel was personally committed to a deal. He played down the importance of PR for Europe, to the frustration of some MPs. He accepted a few minor amendments to the proposed draft agreement but then insisted his colleagues should decide. They could not delay their decision any longer.

The fourth and final Lib–Lab meeting took place that evening at 9.45 p.m. Steel was this time joined by Pardoe, and Callaghan by Foot. When the PM started the meeting, he set out the agreements reached so far. Pardoe immediately interrupted, arguing that a solid pledge on PR for Europe was required. But before the issue could be resolved, just after 10 p.m., Pardoe left to do a live BBC *Tonight* interview, in which he played down the chances of any deal.

In his absence, Steel signed off on the agreement. Labour committed on paper to no more than a free vote on PR for Europe. But in the meeting, Callaghan made an additional promise: a personal and private undertaking that when the Commons vote on PR came, he would vote for the list system of PR and would make public his support. This was a verbal commitment, with nothing in writing. Nor was the PM pledging to deliver his party. It was therefore a concession of little real value. And it was a concession that Callaghan would decline to reveal to his own Cabinet when the proposed pact was discussed. No matter; Steel had finally got what he wanted. 'It was the first stage towards his dream of a Liberal Party first in coalition, and then in power ... Steel had placed himself right on the spot he had aimed for.'[13]

It was now late at night, but Steel had promised to update his MPs. One, Richard Wainwright, had gone home – claiming his Methodist principles forbade him from working beyond midnight. Steel briefed the others, including on Callaghan's private commitment, which he insisted must remain secret. Pardoe was appalled, but the deal was done. Jo Grimond and David Penhaligon said they were opposed, while others expressed significant reservations. But no formal vote was taken, and those objecting agreed to accept the collective decision. At 1.20 a.m., Steel phoned Downing Street and spoke to the PM's private secretary, Kenneth Stowe. The deal was on.

Jo Grimond's concerns might have been considered particularly significant, as a former party leader and one who favoured 'progressive realignment'. Grimond felt that most of his colleagues were now 'too indulgent to the Labour government and too oblivious to the need for a restatement of liberalism.'[14] Labour had been moving leftwards in the 1970s, and their manifestos now pledged a policy of large-scale nationalisation, which was in direct opposition to Liberal policy and ideology. On the crucial issue of Europe, Labour was deeply split. Its manifesto offered a renegotiation of British membership of the EEC and a referendum – a strategy also adopted (unsuccessfully) by David Cameron to manage his own party divisions, forty years later. Grimond believed that Labour was still a fundamentally socialist party. He considered that in the early 1960s, there had been a real chance of the social democrats within the Labour Party taking control – people the Liberals could do business with.

But that was not the case in the 1970s. Grimond therefore felt that electoral reform was the minimum requirement to make any deal with Labour worthwhile – it was 'the prize, the only prize, which could have justified the pact'.[15]

Grimond judged that some Liberal MPs were agreeing to the pact out of fear of an election. But his view was that if there was one, the Liberals would perform well, and that if Labour lost, this would lead to a party split, which could only be beneficial:

> A general election seemed to me to offer not disaster … but the chance of the century: a chance that there would be a shake up on the Left from which [we] could gain lasting advantage. Therefore, we were, so far from being weak, in a strong position. Either Callaghan delivered electoral reform or electoral disaster might split the Labour Party.[16]

Grimond also cites Christopher Mayhew as suggesting that if the Liberals had insisted on PR for the European elections, they would have forced Labour into accepting it. We cannot now know whether this was the case, or whether Labour MPs would have been willing to vote in sufficient numbers to make good this pledge – indeed, this seems unlikely. What we do know is that Steel was determined to have his pact and was not prepared to make a firm pledge on PR a requirement.

The Cabinet met the next day at 12.30 p.m., just three hours before the confidence debate. On the table were copies of the draft agreement with Steel. Most present knew of the talks with the Liberals but were unaware of the outcome. Callaghan, according to Tony Benn, looked 'red-faced'. Michael Foot he described as 'white and drawn'. After a discussion lasting an hour and a quarter, in which various small amendments were suggested, relayed to David Steel and agreed, a vote was taken. The leading left-wingers, Tony Benn and Peter Shore, voted against. Benn confided to his diary that he would rather face an election, and potentially lose office, than give the Liberals any influence: 'If we lost, it would be the end of the Government, but by God at least things would be clarified a bit … it will open the way for the party to go left…'[17] Benn and Shore were joined by two other lower-profile Cabinet ministers. Given the modest concessions that had been made and Labour's dire predicament, it says much for the state of the Labour Party that any should have voted against the agreement. But this was a divided Labour Party, often contemptuous of their Liberal competitors, in the middle of a national crisis, at a time of deep-seated ideological differences.

Callaghan's adviser, Donoughue, also concluded: 'The Benn faction … prefer an election – if we lose then Jim will resign, and they will go for the leadership again'.[18] The attitude of Labour's left wing is important, because even if the pact could be pushed through without their support, there was no guarantee that they would be willing to vote in the Commons for concessions to the Liberals on issues such as PR. The leverage on Labour MPs would only work for those who wanted the pact to succeed. It was an ominous signal of what was to come and a warning about doing deals with other parties when a leader cannot deliver the support of his or her MPs. During the pact, Callaghan had to be alert to the risk of losing the support of the thirteen Liberal MPs. But 'I sometimes had to remind [Steel] that there was a net loss to the Government if we won the support of the thirteen Liberals but lost the votes of forty [left-wing] Tribunites…'

Even the moderates in Labour embraced the pact with limited

enthusiasm. Roy Hattersley wrote that 'retaining power by kind permission of the Liberals was a humiliation … we thought of the obligation to discuss our plans with inexperienced "shadows" … as a daily indignity. And we were on principle opposed to anything which resembled a coalition.'[19]

At 10 p.m. that night, the confidence debate concluded. By then, the 'Lib–Lab Pact' was public. The government secured a majority of twenty-four. Without Liberal votes, it would have lost by two – assuming that the nationalists would still have voted against the government, rather than abstaining. It is possible that without the Lib–Lab deal, the government might just have survived. But what Labour secured from the deal was stability and longevity. Their position was, for now, safe, and they could wait for better economic times before calling an election. For Labour, the deal was therefore of immense value.

The pact was unusual and important – the first and only formal, national, cross-party agreement between 1945 and 2010. The UK had become used to single party government over a period of thirty-two years – the longest period of this type since the years of Liberal dominance in the nineteenth century. But what had Steel and his party secured? The 'deal' was set out in a 'Joint Statement' from Callaghan and Steel, which was published that day.[20] In exchange for propping up a divided Labour government at a time of national economic crisis, when it would certainly have lost any general election held, the Liberal leader had secured five concessions.

The first was a 'Joint Consultative Committee' under the chairmanship of the Leader of the House. This would discuss upcoming government policy and Liberal proposals. There would also be 'regular' meetings between Steel and Callaghan, as well as Pardoe and Healey. The second pledge was for direct elections to the European

Parliament. But there was no promise on PR. Instead, the Labour Party, in deciding the government's position, would 'take account' of the Liberal Party's views, and MPs would then have a free vote. Steel hoped that he might win the support of many Conservative MPs for PR. But, with a Lib–Lab pact, this was now much less likely.

The third pledge was on Scottish and Welsh devolution, where Labour had planned to legislate anyway. Voting systems for the devolved assemblies would again be decided by 'a free vote'. The fourth pledge was that the government would make time for a Private Members Bill on homelessness, sponsored by Stephen Ross, a Liberal MP. This measure was suggested by Callaghan, rather than Steel. Indeed, the Cabinet had already decided to support the Bill as far back as 10 February, before the talks. Finally, the government pledged to amend the Local Authorities (Works) Bill, to deal with a minor issue relating to direct labour activities of local authorities.

What had been requested by the Liberals in exchange for their support had been extraordinarily modest, and what had been secured had been strikingly feeble. The Conservative leader, Margaret Thatcher, was demoralised by discovering that her opportunity to defeat an unpopular government had been snatched away. It is therefore not surprising that she took a cynical view of Liberal motivations: 'Although the Lib–Lab Pact did the Liberals a good deal of harm, while doing Jim Callaghan no end of good, it did allow Liberal Party spokesmen the thrilling illusion that they were important.'[21] But she was right to conclude: 'I was astonished that they had signed up to such a bad deal,' with policy concessions that essentially constituted 'a lacklustre shopping list'.

However, Steel had got what he wanted – a Consultative Agreement that gave the Liberals a foot in the door and a whiff of power. Pardoe was later to reflect: 'David was determined to do a deal at all costs.' Michie and Hoggart conclude: 'To Steel, the pact was an end in itself, or rather a stage leading towards wonderful new super-pacts in the future.'[22]

But would the electorate give credit to the Liberals for moderating a Labour government and bringing a measure of political stability? Or would they be blamed for keeping an unpopular administration in power? It did not take long to find out. While voters professed to like cross-party co-operation, in practice they seemed less sure. And the Tory-leaning press trashed the Liberals for 'selling out'. Steel's claim that it was an 'agreement' rather than a 'pact' made no difference. For the media and many voters, the Liberals were prop-ping up a discredited government. Steel was portrayed as weak; his MPs, as motivated by fear of another election. And for voters, the Liberals had extracted no policy concessions of any value. Centrist voters who might have previously professed support for the Liberals but who loathed the Labour Party now deserted them.

In October 1974, almost 20 per cent of voters had supported the Liberals. Between January and May of 1977, Liberal support in the polls sank by 40 per cent, from 14.5 per cent to 8.5 per cent. The first big test came in the local elections in early May. The Conservatives gained almost 1,300 councillors, and Labour lost some 1,100. Lib-eral losses were 163 seats – two thirds of Liberal councillors up for re-election and a truly disastrous result. Liberal support had been declining in the year before the pact, when they were typically ex-periencing by-election swings against them of around 4 per cent. But a week after the pact was signed, the Conservatives won the Birmingham Stechford by-election (in Roy Jenkins's old seat), with the Liberals experiencing a larger 6.6 per cent swing against them and finishing in a humiliating fourth place, behind the National Front. And in April 1977, there were further by-elections at Ashfield and Great Grimsby, with swings against the Liberals averaging over 9 per cent. By the announcement of the end of the pact, in May 1978, by-election swings against the Liberals were averaging 10 per cent – over double those in the year before the pact.

There was an early test of Liberal–Labour co-operation in the 1977 Budget, just a week after the pact had been agreed. Labour's Chancellor, Healey, had decided to cut direct taxation, financed by an increase in indirect taxes, including the tax on petrol. Extra taxes on motorists were very unpopular in the predominantly rural seats that Liberals represented. Steel did not want his precious pact to fall to pieces after just days. But other Liberal MPs were immovable. No compromise could be found, and after a month of painful disagreements, Healey was forced to withdraw the extra motoring taxes. There were further difficulties in June. Michael Foot announced that the Devolution Bill would be delayed, and the PM made clear that the Cabinet would be free to vote as they wished on the European Elections Bill. These were ominous signals of what was to come.

But for most of the rest of 1977, there was a degree of harmony. Meetings between Labour ministers and their Liberal 'shadows' got underway. The economic environment was gradually improving, with inflation falling. Meetings were scheduled with Labour for July to discuss the renewal of the pact. Steel wanted this resolved in advance of his party conference in September. In late June, he held a two-day meeting of his MPs to consider their 'asks' for the renewed deal. David Penhaligon and Jo Grimond both argued that they needed to secure prizes of more relevance to voters – for example, lower income tax or higher family allowances. They remained highly dubious of the pact's value.

Fortunately for Steel, Grimond and Penhaligon were still in a minority. But Steel wanted to renew the pact for another eighteen months, while the consensus was that it should be limited to a year. MPs felt this gave them another chance to push for policy concessions in summer 1978, before a general election. On the second day of the meetings, a list of policy demands was drawn up. Inevitably, devolution to Scotland and Wales and direct elections for the European Parliament were the top priorities. But Pardoe argued that the pact had to make voters better off: 'Money in the pocket of the electorate means votes in the ballot box,' he claimed.[23] He wanted income tax cuts.

Ten policy priorities of varying degrees of importance were agreed. There was also a laundry list of another twenty-one minor proposals, including a suggestion from Clement Freud that they should veto any ban on hare-coursing. The list of top ten asks was to be privately put to Callaghan, but within twenty-four hours it had been leaked – probably by an opponent of the pact. According to the *Daily Express*, these were 'Steel's Ten Commandments'. The publicity was rather useful, for once giving the impression that the Liberals might negotiate toughly. Mrs Thatcher even complained that some of her own policies were being pinched.

However, as at the beginning of the pact, Steel chose not to press Labour too hard. He prepared a draft letter of the policy asks, but these were generally written in a loose and flexible style and highlighted just six of the ten proposed new priorities. Callaghan's adviser, Bernard Donoughue, recorded in his diary on Friday 8 July:

Yesterday the PM had a meeting with David Steel ... apparently it went very easily. They agreed renewal of the pact for next year will be decided this month. It would be just an 'understanding' that Labour would take full account of the Liberal point of view in the ten chosen areas of policy.[24]

Steel had further meetings with the PM on 25 and 26 July and again met his MPs to update them. Grimond could not attend the meeting but had written a letter to his colleagues setting out why they should end the pact – this soon leaked to the press.

The next day, 27 July, Liberal MPs met again. This time, Steel informed them of the draft policy letter he had already sent to Callaghan, and his meeting with the PM. Penhaligon was furious about being presented with a *fait accompli*, but Steel retained the support he needed. Later that day, the PM and Steel met again. They agreed minor changes to the draft letter alongside renewal of the pact, for an unspecified period. On 28 July, Liberal MPs met to sign off on the deal. Only Grimond and Penhaligon recorded their disagreement. Afterwards, Steel privately thanked Callaghan for his 'patience and understanding'. The PM's equally private reply noted: 'It has been a pleasure to work with you … I hope it won't do you any harm!'[25]

The next day there was a public exchange of letters between the two leaders. The letter from Steel to the Prime Minister outlined their new agreement. It gave priority to the need to deliver economic recovery and reduce inflation and unemployment. There was a commitment to consider the Liberal policy of encouraging profit-sharing schemes in industry and a vague commitment to shift taxes away from incomes. The pledge on the European Assembly Bill was renewed but with only a weak obligation on the government to use its 'best endeavours' to secure passage of the Bill. Liberal attempts to deliver additional policy impact amounted to three paragraphs, promising help for first-time home buyers, more 'effective' competition policy, additional legal assistance at public inquiries (hardly a major issue in the Dog and Duck), a worthless commitment to ensure 'greater scrutiny of public expenditure' and reform of the Official Secrets Act.

Over the months to come, there was co-operation in government on other issues, but this delivered a similarly modest and obscure list of policy prizes.[26] These included: the decision not to sell arms to El Salvador; an inquiry into the impact of tourists on the NHS in Cornwall; a Pricing Commission to control charges at caravan sites; and a separate National Farmers Union for Wales. These measures all had two things in common: they were of no interest whatsoever to most voters and – in the diplomatic language of Kirkup – 'did not constitute a coherent collection of policy concessions'.

Despite this, Steel won his party's support at its September conference, arguing that pulling out of the agreement would leave them looking like 'purposeless incompetents'. He saw off an amendment to renegotiate the pact by 716–385, but he had to concede another, insisting that a crucial indicator of the pact's success would be that a 'substantial majority' of Labour MPs should back PR for Europe. But Steel still declined publicly to play hard ball on the issue. In early November, a BBC interviewer asked him if a failure to deliver PR for Europe would be a pact-ending issue. His reply was that, while disappointing, 'there would be no question of our pulling out on a vote of that kind'. It hardly sent a strong message to wavering Labour MPs. Steel still thought he had a 50–50 prospect of getting PR for Europe through. Most Westminster watchers could tell him he had no chance.

The next session of Parliament would be an important one for the Liberals – dominated by Bills on Scottish and Welsh Devolution and direct elections to Europe. There was also to be action on a Liberal hobby-horse – tax incentives for profit-sharing. This seemingly rather dull and obscure policy was regarded by Liberals as highly important in an era dominated by industrial strife.

The Liberals did secure some other useful concessions on

various issues, including preventing government action that would have impeded cut-price air fares. The party had hoped for a good public row on this, resulting in a Liberal 'win' on a populist issue. But Labour conceded the point in private, and the Liberals secured no credit. It highlighted how tough it can be for a smaller party to benefit from its achievements in pacts and coalitions, as the Liberal Democrats were to discover during the 2010–15 coalition.

From November 1977 onwards, the limited value of the pact to the Liberals soon became apparent. On 24 November, the party was pushed into a miserable third place in a by-election in Bournemouth – which should have been a promising seat. In late November, the Commons voted down PR for the Scottish Assembly by a huge 183-vote margin. Under the pact, there was meant to be a free vote for Labour MPs, but John Smith (leading for Labour) spoke against PR, and ministers were whipped to vote against. Liberal activists were furious and by 11 December, Steel was having to warn them that he might resign as leader if they insisted on ending the pact.

Then, on 13 December, there was the critically important vote on the issue that Liberal MPs and activists regarded as the most precious prize of their pact – Clause III of the Direct Elections Bill, for PR for elections to the European Parliament. Steel had always known that some Labour MPs would vote against this, but he thought that an overwhelming majority of them would support the measure. In addition, he was banking on as many as 100 Conservative MPs supporting change, as they had previously done in votes on PR for the proposed Scottish Assembly. At this time, there was sympathy for electoral reform under certain circumstances in the Conservative Party – some Tory MPs considered that if there was to be Scottish devolution, PR would be likely to deny the nationalist SNP an outright majority in the new Assembly. But the Conservatives now imposed a three-line whip against PR, and most Conservative MPs were not going to support a measure that was so crucial to the 'Lib–Lab Pact'. Only sixty-one Conservatives (including Heath) backed PR, not the 100 Steel had hoped for. And Labour MPs were not universally going to support a measure that they considered against their long-term interests. Meanwhile, the government continued to make support for electoral reform only a 'free vote' issue.

The result can hardly have been a surprise. The Commons decided by a big majority – 321 to 224 – to stick with First Past the Post. Only 147 Labour MPs – fewer than half – supported PR, with 122 voting against and another forty-six abstaining. Twenty-five government ministers either voted against PR or abstained, and of those voting against, four were Cabinet ministers.

Steel took the charitable view that Labour had done all they had promised him. But Liberal MPs were livid. For many, the possibility of achieving a measure of voting reform was the only good reason for the pact. John Pardoe went on television to warn: 'If the Labour Party is incapable of continuing the pact like this, it is incapable of running the country and should be turned out immediately.'

Angry Liberal MPs met Steel in their Whips' Office straight after the vote, and later that night Steel visited Callaghan in his Commons office. When he returned to brief his MPs, he announced: 'He's going to see the Queen in the morning.' Someone said, 'Oh, Christ, he's not!' There was silence as the MPs contemplated a general election, with Liberal support at just 8 per cent. Then Steel revealed that he had been joking. But he wanted to focus minds. Were they prepared to bring down the government on this issue?

Next morning Liberal MPs held another lengthy meeting. Still furious, they voted to terminate the pact – with only Russell Johnston and Geraint Howells backing continuation. David Penhaligon argued that carrying on would be like 'turkeys voting for Christmas' – the first known use of the phrase. But Jo Grimond – always a sceptic of the pact – warned that the public would not understand the party triggering an election over what they would consider a 'non-issue'. Grumpily, the MPs agreed that Steel should meet Callaghan later in the day to hear what he might offer.

Steel was determined to proceed with the pact. He took the view that it was always likely that many Labour MPs would vote against PR. A large number disliked the EU, were opposed to direct elections for Europe and were bitterly opposed to electoral reform. Steel did not consider that the PM had done anything against either the letter or spirit of the agreement. The pledges given by Labour had, in other words, always been weak and conditional. He did, however, regret that he had not at least insisted on the loyalty of Labour's 'payroll vote' of ministers and whips.[27]

When Steel saw Callaghan that afternoon, the PM was unsympathetic and offered no concessions. He argued that getting 147 of his MPs to back PR was quite an achievement. He maintained that he had demonstrated 'best endeavours', as required by the pact, and said that Liberal MPs 'must grow up'. At 6 p.m., Steel met his MPs again, and claimed that if they broke off the pact, there would be an election, which would be disastrous. When the pact had been formed, Labour had been on just 33 per cent in the polls, way behind the Tories on almost 50 per cent, with the Liberals on 13 per cent. But the improving economy had raised the Labour poll rating in December 1977 to 44.5 per cent – just ahead of the Conservatives on 44 per cent. Meanwhile, the Liberals were languishing on 8 per cent. The Callaghan threat was therefore a plausible one. The Liberal bluff had been called. The allegations about Jeremy Thorpe appeared extensively in the media, putting even more pressure on Steel and his party.

Liberal MPs now realised that if they voted to end the pact, they would lose their leader and face an electoral wipeout. But many felt that continuing would lead to political oblivion too. Penhaligon's warning was ignored, and the 'turkeys' decide to vote for Christmas after all – by a majority of 5–4 (6–4, including Steel himself). Smith, Penhaligon, Wainwright and Hooson all voted to end the agreement. But Beith, Howells, Johnston, Ross and Grimond all voted with their leader. Pardoe and Thorpe abstained, and Clement Freud was absent. For Steel, it was a very close-run thing.

Within the party there was now bitterness and division. But Grimond continued to warn that this was not the issue to break over: 'The public were not likely to be impressed by a party which claimed to have conferred great benefits on the country, but which then announced it would throw all this to the winds because we could not get the List system in the European elections.'[28]

The party now decided to hold a Special Conference. Steel made clear that this was an issue of confidence. He informed Callaghan that if he lost, he would resign. Callaghan suggested that in the event of this, Steel might join the Cabinet – an offer he instantly rejected.

The Special Conference took place in Blackpool on 21 January 1978. Around 2,500 Liberal activists turned up – the largest attendance for many decades. The position of Pardoe – Steel's effective deputy – was crucial. But he stayed loyal, and most MPs fell in behind their leader. With few wanting to lose Steel, his opponents pulled their punches – Penhaligon suggesting that the pact should end in the spring, with future support for Labour being on an issue-by-issue basis. The motions before the activists gave them a choice of immediate termination or a more nuanced position that hinted that the pact would only continue until the Budget – just a few months away, by when it would have 'successfully achieved

its immediate purpose for the good of the country'. Richard Wainwright was persuaded to move the compromise position, and eventually the conference backed this by 1,727 to 520. Steel saw this as a
victory, but in truth his party was sending him a clear message that
it wanted out.

By April, even Callaghan was telling Steel that the Liberals
would be wise to break off the pact in July. He had decided that
his economic priority now needed to be lower inflation. He wanted
to keep wage rises in the year ahead below 5 per cent, even if this
meant taking on the unions. It was a decision that was to break his
government.

Later that month, the two parties again fell out over the Budget.
Ever since the start of the pact, Healey and Pardoe had clashed.
Before Christmas 1977, there was an angry meeting on pay policy,
which ended with Pardoe storming out and describing Healey on
radio as 'the second worst Chancellor since the war'. Now Pardoe
was insisting on a reduction in the basic rate of tax. He had developed plans for what he called 'incentive taxation'. These were hugely
ambitious and envisaged the standard rate of income tax being cut
from 34 per cent to 20 per cent. Pardoe argued that this could in
part be funded by increasing VAT and hiking payroll taxes.

He wanted progress in the spring 1978 Budget, delivered on 11
April. Healey was refusing to give way – concerned both about
affordability and that higher VAT would drive up inflation. The
two stubborn men now had some further difficult meetings. In his
memoirs, Healey was to refer to Pardoe as 'Denis Healey with no
redeeming features'.[29]

Eventually, the Liberals voted with the Conservatives to force the
government into cutting the basic rate of tax by 1p – less than the
2p Pardoe had been pressing for. They also stopped Healey from

introducing a 2.5 per cent surcharge on employers' National Insurance contributions to pay for the basic rate cut. Instead, after defeating Labour in a Commons vote, they forced Healey to settle for 1.5 per cent: 'The Liberals perhaps too late had learned to … use persistent bloody-mindedness to win popular concessions.'[30] The party also achieved several of its other Budget objectives by agreement – including profit-sharing incentives and a new, lower, tax rate of 25 per cent on the first £750 of taxable income. But they got little benefit from these 'wins', either in the press or with voters.

On 25 May, Steel finally announced an end to the pact in the summer. He was under pressure from his party but also favoured a 'quarantine period' between the pact and the election. Donoughue recorded in his diaries:

> This suits us both. It leaves us free to call an autumn election … And the Liberals can fight an independent campaign from now on. It has been a fruitful and civilised relationship … A great credit to Steel, though sadly he has not got any political benefits from it – yet. He is hoping that in an election campaign he can sell the Liberals as the party that will tame the extremists of either side. And if we get another 'hung parliament', he will be able to negotiate tougher terms – possibly proportional representation, or a coalition with seats in the Cabinet.[31]

By June, Callaghan was even considering what policy 'concessions' he might throw to the Liberals. He had concluded that he needed a Liberal recovery to syphon off Conservative votes. On 12 July, Bernard Donoughue met Steel's adviser, Archy Kirkwood, whom he described as a 'nice lad'. They discussed how Labour might help the Liberals in the coming election – including trying to get the *Daily*

Mirror to campaign for tactical voting in Liberal seats. Donoughue also agreed a secret dinner with Steel and Pardoe in September 'to help plan their election campaign'.

By July, when the pact ended, Liberal poll ratings were around 6–8 per cent. The party had lost every single by-election during the pact. The Liberals remained around the 6 per cent level through the winter. By-election swings after the pact, meanwhile, were around 6 per cent against the party – a little worse than pre-pact but slightly better than experienced during the pact itself. The big beneficiaries of the pact were the Labour Party. From 33 per cent in March 1977, they had risen to 45 per cent by October 1977 and peaked at 48 per cent in November 1978.

Callaghan's minority government now limped on alone. And to Steel's astonishment and the despair of many of his advisers, the Prime Minister ducked an autumn election. Callaghan had received contradictory advice on the best timing. One weekend in September, he returned home to his farm and immersed himself in the latest opinion polling, and with the help of the latest 'Times Guides' to the 1970 and 1974 elections, went through seat by seat and finally concluded that the turnout was too close to be sure of a majority.

In his memoirs, perhaps with an eye to how history would judge his decision, he claimed that his calculations showed that Labour might end up on around 303 seats, with the Conservatives on 304. But in January 1979, he admitted to Bernard Donoughue a slightly different calculation: 'He came to the conclusion that the best we could achieve was 325 seats, and we might be as low as 305.' Since Labour had 310 seats, Callaghan felt that the outlook was not yet clear enough to take the plunge.

The PM thought that the prospects for carrying on into 1979 were better. He was wrong. The 'Winter of Discontent', with unburied dead and uncollected rubbish, finished his government off. In early 1979, the devolution referendums were held in Wales and Scotland. In Wales, devolution was defeated and in Scotland the majority for devolution failed to clear a bar of 40 per cent of the registered electorate, which had been added following a Labour rebellion. There was anger amongst the nationalist parties and the Liberals.

Steel told Callaghan in a private meeting on 6 March that he did not want the parliament to run on much longer. The trial of Jeremy Thorpe was expected in May (serious allegations of conspiracy to murder an alleged male lover had been made against him), and in June were the European elections, which Steel expected to go badly for his party. They would therefore vote against the government on confidence motions and the Budget. And on 28 March, Labour lost a confidence motion by just one vote. All Liberal MPs voted against them. The election outlook was good for the Conservatives, but for the Liberals and Labour, it was gloomy.

But now, just when they needed it most, a by-election came to the rescue of Steel's party.

The Labour MP for Liverpool Edge Hill, Sir Arthur Irvine, had died in December 1978. This was a seat where the Liberals had in David Alton an energetic local candidate. A by-election had been expected for two years, so the seat was already a major focus of party efforts. The Liberal Chief Whip, Alan Beith, had a good relationship with the Labour whips, and he managed to persuade them that if they called the by-election early in 1979, they could hold their seat. He assured them Labour would win, and the Liberals would push the Conservatives into third position – giving both parties a boost.[32]

The Liberals now ran a formidable local campaign. Labour began to realise the mess they were in, but it was too late. The day before the by-election, 28 March, was the day of the confidence vote, and desperate Labour whips tried to persuade Liberal MPs to miss this, to enable the government to cling on. The Liberal MP Clement Freud, who was campaigning in Liverpool, was told that if he 'accidentally missed his train back to London' and couldn't attend the vote, the government would concede to him a Bill on Freedom of Information, which he was trying to secure. Freud ignored the message, sneaked back into the Palace of Westminster and popped out to vote at the last minute, to help defeat the government.[33]

The next day, 29 March, the voters of Edgehill had their say, and at last, there was some better news for Steel – a stunning by-election victory, on a mammoth swing of 36.8 per cent. David Alton took 64.1 per cent of the vote, to Labour's 23.8 per cent. The Conservatives were third on 9.4 per cent – humiliated as Beith had predicted. But it was Labour who had lost and the Liberals who had the best possible start to their election campaign. It was just the boost the Liberals needed and, together with a strong manifesto and effective campaign by David Steel, helped lift their poll ratings.

The May general election saw the Conservatives sweep back into power, with 44 per cent of the vote, versus 37 per cent for Labour. The Conservative majority was a workable forty-four seats. The Liberals secured 14 per cent, after a late recovery and an election in which they were able to present themselves as a moderate centre party in a world of increasing division. The party still lost two of its thirteen MPs, but after the difficulties of the Lib–Lab pact and the dreadful publicity relating to Thorpe, most Liberals were hugely relieved.

However, at a time of such political polarisation, the Liberals had a strong pitch and might have been expected to do much better. The pact had been a godsend to Labour, giving it two more years in office. But the Liberals had gained nothing. One of Callaghan's closest aides was later to comment on the pact: 'We took them to the cleaners! Yes, we took them to the bloody cleaners!'[34]

The longer-term consequences of the pact for British politics were less clear cut. The Labour left initially feared that it might strengthen the social democrats in the Cabinet. But Benn was soon claiming that the pact was a 'pyrrhic victory for the right. They think it is the big rebirth of a social democratic party, but it isn't.'[35] For once, Benn was at least half right.

Mrs Thatcher later argued that the pact had been of some help to her:

The pact ... hardened our support ... I can see now that in March 1977 we were not yet ready to form the kind of government which would have achieved a long-term shift away from the policies which had led to Britain's decline. Neither the shadow Cabinet, nor the parliamentary party, nor in all probability the electorate would have been prepared to take the necessary but unpalatable medicine, because they had not witnessed how far the disease had spread. It took the strikes of the winter of 1978–79 to change all that.[36]

Pardoe remained critical of the pact: 'I believe we would have done better [in a 1977 election] than we did two years later in 1979.'[37] He argued that Steel 'was absolutely determined to make the pact work at the expense of actually achieving anything about which the Liberals could say; "look what we have done". Many years later he reflected: 'I have always taken the view that unless it becomes very, very large – probably number two in terms of seats – the party cannot enter into any arrangement with another party safely without the absolute certainty that the next general election will be fought under PR. Otherwise you are opting for total disaster.'

But Steel was unapologetic, arguing that his pact brought economic stability, moderated Labour extremism and showed that the Liberals were not just a party of protest. Tom McNally agreed that the achievement of the pact was in 'loosening the cement of the old two-party system and improving the prospects for cross party co-operation. It gave the social democrat wing of the Labour Party a place to go when this was later needed.'[38]

Steel reflected that one lesson of the pact had been how difficult it had been to persuade Labour MPs to vote 'loyally' on issues such as PR, when they had had no share in shaping, approving or 'owning' the agreement. He vowed to avoid that in any future arrangement. Reflecting on whether a full coalition might have been better than a pact, he saw some advantages in 'operating on the inside of a future government rather than on the fringes' but concluded that this would only be possible if the Liberal Parliamentary Party was much bigger, to allow an 'effective presence' in government. He had struggled even with the looser arrangement of the pact, with the limited human resources available. But he was opposed to an electoral 'deal' with another party, with one party standing down in favour of another in certain constituencies. He regarded that as both anti-democratic and difficult to impose.

Steel had put the Liberals at the centre of political debate and ended their long era of irrelevance. He had shown ambition for the party and that he was willing to take risks to realign politics. But it is difficult to avoid the conclusion that the pact was a mistake and a failure for the Liberals. While it showed that they could accept some responsibility for government and helped build relations with more moderate figures in the Labour Party, it came at a high electoral cost and secured no policy concessions of any lasting value. And the big prize of voting reform was as far away as ever. It also highlighted that too much of the Liberal policy agenda was of second or third order importance to voters, who were typically more focused on issues such as the economy, crime, health services, prices and taxes, rather than constitutional reform. A more successful Liberal Party would need a more exciting and relevant policy prospectus.

But whatever the lessons of the pact, Steel was now looking to the future. In 1980, he declared:

> As long as the interests of the rich and powerful demand political protection there will be a Conservative Party. The question is what the main opposition to it should be ... During this [new] parliament I shall demonstrate that the only genuine alternative to the narrow policies of Tory dogma is the modern Liberal Party ... I want to form a great alliance of progressives, radicals and social democrats with Liberal leadership, to change a rotten political system.

The era of Margaret Thatcher had begun. The short period of Lib–Lab co-operation was over. The two parties were now about to embark on a bitter contest to emerge as the progressive alternative to the new and right-leaning Conservative government.

Could Steel deliver on his vision of a great progressive alliance?

CHAPTER 6

'BREAKING THE MOULD?' 1979-92

This was now a time of deep political division in which the two major parties were increasingly under the control of their more extreme elements. So, despite the electoral damage done by the Lib–Lab pact, there was still a market for the centrist and moderate politics that the Liberals stood for. Without the pact, perhaps there would have been a significant rise in the Liberal vote in 1979, but in any case, the election out-turn gave the party 13.5 per cent – well below the 19 per cent of October 1974 but around the level of March 1977 when the pact began.

Up until 1979, there was a pattern to politics, and the fates of Labour and the Liberals were loosely tied together. The Liberal vote tended to fall when Labour was ejected from office but rise when the Conservatives were. The year 1979 changed all that. An era of bitter competition to be the principal opposition to the Conservatives began.

After the 1979 defeat, Labour was divided and moving sharply leftwards. Callaghan stepped down as leader on 10 November 1980. In the Labour leadership contest, Michael Foot and Denis Healey emerged as the strongest candidates. Healey, champion of Labour's right wing, secured most votes in the first round. But Foot emerged as the narrow winner in the second and final ballot – securing 139 votes (amongst MPs) to 129 for Healey.

Some of the Labour MPs who voted for Foot saw him as a moderate, compromise candidate. But many regarded the new leader as a weak left-winger who would be pushed further left by the more radical forces in his party. After his election, Foot declared himself 'as strong in my socialist convictions as I have ever been'. It was not what moderates wanted to hear. Nor were they reassured by the January 1981 Labour Wembley conference, which committed the party to unilateral nuclear disarmament, withdrawal from the European Economic Community and a radical, left-wing economic policy. Meanwhile, in many Labour constituency parties, the 'Militant tendency' had started working to move the party further left.

For many years, Labour moderates had worried about the future of their party. As far back as 1959, the Labour MP Roy Jenkins had advocated dropping nationalisation, reconsidering Labour's trade union links, and doing a deal with the Liberals.[1] And in 1962, Jenkins was worrying about whether Labour could win the next general election by itself and speculating that in a hung parliament, the Liberals were more likely to support Labour than the Conservatives, provided Labour had a positive line on joining the Common Market. In October 1971, Jenkins had led sixty-nine Labour MPs in voting against a party three-line whip on Europe. From this moment onwards, the divisions in Labour between right and left, pro- and anti-European, flared up. They would divide the Labour family for almost two decades. In April 1972, Jenkins resigned from the deputy leadership of the party over Europe. The Labour conference was set on rejecting the 'Tory terms' for EEC membership, and Labour's left were determined to stay out of the EEC, seeing it as a 'capitalist club' that would prevent them from developing their own socialist economic strategy.

In 1979, Jenkins had delivered the Dimbleby Lecture – 'Home Thoughts from Abroad'. This argued for a 'strengthening of the radical centre'. It noted that the division between the Liberals and Labour had produced a period of twenty-one years between 1918 and 1939 when the Conservatives were in power almost continuously. Jenkins now openly advocated PR.

The result of this thinking and Labour's leftward lurch was that on 26 March 1981, the UK saw its first significant new national political party since Labour's birth, some eighty years previously. The Social Democratic Party was launched, led by four defectors from Labour – Roy Jenkins, David Owen, Bill Rodgers and Shirley Williams. These were senior, much-respected politicians of the centre who had all held major posts in government. They were to lead a new party that rejected socialism but would fight the new 'Thatcherism', which was tearing the nation in half and whose economic policies were demolishing large swathes of British industry and driving unemployment up beyond 3 million.

The new SDP would be pro-European, in favour of strong defence (including a nuclear deterrent) and the market economy (generally), but it would work to deliver a society of greater equality and social protection. Unlike Labour, they would not be tied to the trade unions, who were deeply unpopular with many voters after the Winter of Discontent. Over time, twenty-eight Labour MPs and nine Labour peers would leave their party and declare their support for the SDP. They were joined by one Conservative MP. Jenkins and Williams were not MPs at the time of the SDP launch, but they were soon elected in high-profile by-elections at Crosby (Williams, on 26 November 1981) and Glasgow Hillhead (Jenkins, on 25 March 1982).

Jenkins became the new party's first leader, beating off a challenge from David Owen in July 1982.

The party secured huge publicity at a time when the Thatcher government was deeply unpopular and during which Labour seemed extreme and unelectable. SDP membership rose rapidly – many joiners had never been engaged by politics before, and others came from Labour (25 per cent), the Conservatives (10 per cent) and even the Liberals (5 per cent).

David Steel, still Liberal leader, warmly welcomed the new party. Jenkins was a friend and political ally, and the two men had agreed that it would be better for Jenkins to form a new party rather than join the Liberals. A new party might reach out to new centrist voters and help attract many of those alienated by Labour. The political mould was being broken, and in June 1981 the two parties formed the SDP–Liberal Alliance, with Steel and Jenkins as the joint leaders. They could see that it made no sense to have two moderate, liberal, internationalist parties trying to compete in the centre ground of politics.

And Jenkins proved a great unifier. In September 1982, he became the first UK party leader to address the conference of another party, overcoming tribal tendencies to tell Liberal activists:

> Our areas of agreement are vast. Our islands of disagreement are tiny. Just as there is an unhealthy hypocrisy in politicians who fundamentally disagree clinging together on the raft of a bankrupt old party because of the coldness of the sea around them, so there would be an equal hypocrisy in politicians who agree as much as we do … pretending that we must keep apart and stress our differences.[2]

Since the 1960s, many Liberals had dreamt of a progressive movement that would reunite the centre and moderate left of politics while driving the socialist left off to the fringes. This new party could then take on the Conservatives and ensure that their dominant position as the 'natural party of government' would finally be broken. For a magical moment in British politics, in 1981–82, it really did seem as if the mould was broken. In late 1981, the Alliance was polling at over 50 per cent. At the Liberals' autumn conference, David Steel famously finished his leader's speech by telling his party: 'Go back to your constituencies and prepare for government!' It was the most exciting moment to be a Liberal since 1906 – though the bar, admittedly, was low.

But three factors now conspired to kill off the dream of a new politics. Firstly, on 2 April 1982, Argentina invaded the Falklands Islands, a British dependent territory in the south Atlantic. Mrs Thatcher sent a naval taskforce, and by 14 June the UK had retaken the islands. This led to a huge surge in patriotism and a restoration of national self-confidence after what had seemed to many people to be decades of post-imperial decline. In April, the Conservatives were at 31 per cent in opinion polls. By July, they were on 46 per cent. Alliance support fell from 33 per cent to 24 per cent over this period.

Secondly, there were signs that Mrs Thatcher's tough economic medicine was working, or at least that the corner had been decisively turned. Unemployment had doubled from 1.5 million to 3 million by 1982, but the rate of increase was slowing. Inflation surged above 20 per cent in 1980 but was now falling steeply and in 1983 fell below 5 per cent. Interest rates had peaked at 17 per cent in 1979 and were down to 10 per cent in late 1982. And while the economy was in a deep recession in 1980 and 1981, by 1982–83, growth was back. Meanwhile, a populist policy of selling off council houses, with discounts of up to 70 per cent, was winning new converts to Conservatism.

Finally, while Labour had fallen back sharply in the opinion polls, after the birth of the SDP, and with its lurch to the left, it was still much larger and better resourced than either Alliance party. It had well over 200 MPs, funding and support from the trade union movement and a membership galvanised by the fight against 'Thatcherism'. And Labour still had the protection of First Past the Post, which meant that the Alliance had not just to poll well but convert national support into seats.

With her opponents seriously split, the economy turning around and the Falklands factor, Mrs Thatcher decided to hold an election one year earlier than she had to. Polling day would be 9 June 1983. This was one of the most polarised UK elections ever. Labour's leader, Michael Foot, widely regarded by voters as not up to the job of PM, launched a 39-page manifesto that was later described by Labour MP Gerald Kaufman as 'the longest suicide note in history'. The leader's introduction was two dense pages of A4 text, with no photos or charts or boxes, that even a political obsessive would find indigestible. But the presentation was not the real problem.

The real problem was that it was the most left-wing manifesto that Labour would ever present to the electorate. The UK's nuclear deterrent would be scrapped and US cruise missiles sent home. The country would exit the European Economic Community. The House of Lords would be abolished. There would, 'if these prove necessary', be import controls, tariffs and quotas. Privatised industries would be renationalised. North Sea oil and BP would be placed in public ownership. There would be 'significant public stakes' in new sectors

– electronics, pharmaceuticals, health equipment, road haulage and building materials. The major banks might be taken into public ownership. There would be a new annual tax on personal wealth and a lower starting point at which the higher tax rates would begin to be paid. Money would be sprayed over all the public services, and benefits and pensions would rise. Private schools would be phased out. Ireland would eventually be reunited 'with the introduction of socialist policies', and the United Nations would be asked to find a solution to the 'intolerable burden' of the Falklands Islands. This was socialism unbound.

The SDP–Liberal Alliance manifesto, entitled 'Working Together for Britain', was an altogether different prospectus. This attacked both the Conservatives and Labour for making the country an 'industrial wasteland' and offered centrist economics, including a jobs plan, an incomes strategy and 'partnership in industry'. It rejected nationalisation, import controls, leaving the EEC and unilateralism.

It was sensible and moderate stuff, but the Alliance bubble had now burst, and Steel and Jenkins were being squeezed by the bigger parties and by the polarised debates between right and left. Seeing the Alliance as an unlikely government in waiting, some voters backed Mrs Thatcher to block a left-wing Labour administration. In the Darlington by-election, in March 1983 on the eve of the campaign, the SDP candidate was relegated to third place. The Alliance needed momentum, but they had lost it.

In the election, Jenkins was the Alliance's 'Prime Minister designate', a rather silly title. While an impressive and experienced politician, his views could come over as rather 'flabby' and his style old fashioned, to the extent that during the campaign, there was a botched Liberal attempt to have him replaced by Steel as campaign leader. It was not a good omen. Even his official biographer has concluded that 'he turned out not to be a very good leader ... his moderate, sensible policies suddenly seemed platitudinous and his prime ministerial pretensions merely pompous.'[3]

When the results came in on Thursday 9 June, Mrs Thatcher had notably improved her grip on power. The Conservatives' vote share had dropped 1.5 per cent to 42.4 per cent, but they had gained fifty-eight seats and now had a mighty total of 397. Labour's vote had plunged 9.3 per cent, to 27.6 per cent. It was a dreadful result, but despite its left-wing manifesto and the breakaway SDP, it had clung on to second place – just. And it still had 209 MPs. The Alliance parties had polled a mere 2 per cent behind Labour, at 25.4 per cent. But this was half their peak support, and it gave them a risible twenty-three MPs. The Alliance had aspired initially to be the government. When that was no longer possible, they hoped to elbow Labour aside. They had failed in both objectives. But worse, much worse, the First Past the Post system had ensured that for all their 7.8 million votes, they were still a parliamentary irrelevance.

It had taken 32,777 votes to elect each Conservative MP. Each Labour MP was backed by a similar total of 40,464 voters. But each Alliance MP had taken a mighty 338,302 voters to elect. The Liberals and SDP were paying a high price for the failure to deliver electoral reform. Outside Scotland, Wales and parts of the south-west, the Liberals and SDP had only a modest presence.

The election saw the loss of the left-wing Labour pin-up, Tony Benn, in Bristol. And by October 1983, Michael Foot had stood down as leader. He was succeeded by Neil Kinnock. It turned out to be a shrewd choice. Kinnock, at forty-one, was much younger than Foot. He was on the 'soft left' of Labour – acceptable to most party activists but increasingly aware that Labour would need to move back to the centre ground to have a chance of winning. Kinnock distanced himself from the left-wing miners' leader, Arthur Scargill, during the 1984–85 strike. Next, he moved against the Militant tendency, pledging to drive them out of the party. By early 1984, Labour was doing better in the polls. It looked like the Alliance might have missed its chance.

David Owen took over the SDP leadership from Roy Jenkins in June 1983. He promised to offer a sharper and better-defined critique of the other two parties. The problem was that he had a low opinion of most Liberals and was committed to the SDP as a permanently separate party. Compared with the Liberals, he wanted a stronger pro-nuclear defence policy and a greater focus on the economy and other mainstream policy areas. He did not seem to realise that there was barely room for three major parties in British politics, let alone four. And while to him and some of his allies, there were important policy differences between the Liberals and the SDP, this was neither understood nor interesting to most voters.

The Liberals and SDP now needed to come together as one party under one leader, but with Owen, this was never going to happen. Jenkins would later write that he saw the Alliance as a 'union of hearts as well as a partnership of principle', but that Owen viewed it as 'a marriage of convenience … not to be confused with affection'.[4]

Labour was back from the dead but still distrusted by a large section of the electorate, who thought Kinnock too left-wing and Labour too reliant on the unions. The Alliance were too focused on their differences and were incapable of punching at their full weight due to their miserably small number of MPs. In these circumstances, the Conservatives were going to do well. And they did. While unemployment was still very high, the economy was doing better, and the government was cutting income tax and selling off state-owned industries, generally at knock-down prices.

Mrs Thatcher was again confident enough to go to the polls a year early – this time on 11 June 1987. In a third election victory in a row, the Conservatives polled 42.2 per cent, almost exactly the same as in 1983. They lost twenty-one seats, but still held 376 – and had a majority of 102.

Labour's result was poor. They had polled just 30.8 per cent. Most of their small rise came at the expense of the Alliance – which dropped from 25.4 per cent to 22.6 per cent. Critically, Labour had been returned with 229 MPs – and the Alliance only twenty-two. Labour had survived the disaster of 1983 and were slowly clawing their way back at Alliance expense.

The Alliance still suffered in 1987 from a double-headed leadership – Steel and Owen. They were popular and effective politicians, but it was becoming more difficult to patch up in public some of the rows going on behind the scenes. Chris Rennard, Liberal campaigns director, describes how on one day of the 1987 campaign, Steel was ruling out working with Mrs Thatcher, while Owen was dismissing a deal with Labour because of their policies on nuclear weapons.[5] Nor was the campaign as professional as it needed to be. On one occasion, the media team found out too late that one of its television election broadcasts was due to be ten minutes in length rather than the expected five. 'This resulted in lots of footage, not originally intended for broadcast, of Rosie Barnes [SDP MP] stroking her pet rabbit.'[6] It did not win over many voters.

1987 was Mrs Thatcher's last election as leader. She was finally ousted in a Cabinet coup in November 1990, after she had lost her Chancellor and sacked her deputy. In her place, the Conservatives chose the low-key, moderate figure of John Major. They had been in power for thirteen years when Major called an election for 9 April 1992. The economy had been doing badly and opinion polls in the election run-up pointed to a small Labour majority or hung parliament. Labour was still led by Kinnock, who had continued to nudge his party back towards more centrist ground, and who had appointed in John Smith a reassuringly boring and moderate shadow Chancellor.

By now, the SDP had packed up, and a large portion of the party (though not David Owen) had combined with the Liberals to form a newly named party which, after much tedious discussion and many rows, emerged finally as the Liberal Democrats. In 1988, the party was in such a parlous financial state that while its new leader, Paddy Ashdown, was being proclaimed outside party headquarters, staff from the Inland Revenue were in the Liberal Democrat HQ considering if the party could still be considered a going concern. Ashdown feared that the great party of Gladstone might finally fold on his watch. As ever, a by-election helped save the day. The Lib Dems secured a stunning gain from the Conservatives in Eastbourne, in 1990, after considering not standing a candidate.

Ashdown was an energetic, dynamic and ambitious leader. A former Royal Marine, Special Boat Service officer and spy, he was not about to sit around waiting for an opportunity to fall into his lap. He could see that the post-1980 dream of replacing Labour was now dead, and in the run-up to the 1992 election he started to devise a strategy for what he thought might well be a hung parliament.

As early as 1989, the Lib Dems were receiving informal contacts from Labour MPs who wanted to explore the possibility of pacts to defeat the Conservatives. One MP, John Evans, even argued in 1988 for an election deal between the Lib Dems and Labour in up to sixty marginal seats – thirty where the Labour candidate would stand down, and a similar number where the 'Liberal' candidate would give way. It was a modernised version of the 1903 pact that had served Labour so well. But neither party leader was attracted to it.

In any case, many Labour figures thought they needed just 'one more heave'. On 11 May 1989, Ashdown had late-night drinks with Labour's John Smith, while at a conference in Spain. Smith was cautious about co-operation and opposed to pacts. He thought Labour could win by themselves.[7]

Lib Dem planning continued, and on 18 July 1989, Andrew Adonis, then a Liberal Democrat member, came to brief the Lib Dem Parliamentary Party on hung parliament scenarios. This made Ashdown worry that a Labour minority government might deliver a Queen's Speech without PR but with items that would be difficult to vote against – such as a Scottish Parliament, elected by PR. Ashdown concluded: 'A hung parliament would not be a dream. It would be a nightmare.'[8]

By January 1991, Smith was less confident about Labour winning outright – suggesting to Ashdown on the way to a media engagement that the coming election might lead to a hung parliament, and a possible Lib–Lab deal.[9] During February, Ashdown embarked on a programme of work to prepare for a hung parliament, including asking the Lib Dem MP Robert Maclennan to consider their options. Maclennan swiftly concluded that to extract a PR commitment from Smith, Labour needed to believe that the Lib Dems might go into coalition with the Conservatives. After thirteen years of Conservative government, Ashdown rightly thought it would be 'God's own job to sell it to the Party'.[10]

In April 1992, an election could no longer be much delayed. The Conservatives had been in power for thirteen years. Labour and the Liberal Democrats were optimistic that they would now see a repeat of 1964 – when the Conservatives lost power while trying to pull off a fourth consecutive win.

When the election was called for 9 April, Ashdown felt that it could result in a hung parliament. Alternatively, another Labour defeat could be an opportunity for the Lib Dems. As far back as August 1988, Ashdown had confided to his diary that 'there could be a real chance for realignment if the Conservatives win for a fourth time', and when he met Neil Kinnock on Remembrance Sunday that year he found him 'curiously unimpressive ... difficult to imagine him as a future Prime Minister'.[11]

But the polls suggested either a modest Labour win or a hung parliament, and Ashdown and his team of advisers now prepared for a scenario in which he would offer Labour a full coalition in exchange for four Cabinet places – and PR for Westminster elections. Towards the end of the 1992 campaign, Ashdown and his team were content to feed public speculation about a hung parliament – hoping it would persuade voters that the Liberal Democrats were not a wasted vote. Others in the party, including the campaigns chief, Chris Rennard, felt this was a risky strategy, given voter worries about political instability and Kinnock's suitability to be Prime Minister.

Ashdown was in his Yeovil constituency on election day, 9 April, when the BBC exit poll was released. It was a shock. Against expectations, the Conservatives had won. Their vote share had fallen only 0.3 per cent since 1987, to 41.9 per cent. Indeed, at 14,094,000, John Major had banked the largest number of votes for any political party in British history, smashing Labour's 1951 record. Labour had recorded a feeble 34.4 per cent, up 3.6 per cent, and the Liberal Democrats had dropped 4.8 per cent to 17.8 per cent. Ashdown was demoralised and saw Kinnock on television looking 'broken'. This was a grim outcome for both opposition parties after such a long period of Conservative government.

The new House of Commons would consist of 336 Conservative

MPs (down forty), 271 Labour (up forty-two), and just twenty Liberal Democrats (down two). The Conservatives had a majority of twenty-one. The Lib Dems had avoided the annihilation that the shambles of 1988 had risked but otherwise experienced the usual Liberal combination of great hopes and miserable reality.

For Labour, the result was much more serious. After thirteen years of Conservative government, they had barely secured a third of the national vote. Kinnock would soon resign and was replaced in July 1992 by the solid, if unexciting, John Smith. It is unclear whether even limited electoral reform – such as AV – would have rescued Labour in 1992. One analysis suggests that Lib Dem voters favoured the Tories over Labour by 45 per cent to 41 per cent.[12]

Ashdown was now determined to convert apparent disaster into opportunity. On the day after the election, he told his colleagues that 'despite the disappointment, this is the result I always said I wanted … we must make use of this'.[13]

Ashdown did not yet know it, but what might still offer him the opportunity he craved was the election, in 1983, of a Labour MP – Anthony Charles Lynton Blair. Blair had started off on the soft left of London politics in the early 1980s. In July 1982, he had written a rather sycophantic 22-page letter to the then Labour leader, Michael Foot. In this, he praised Foot's books, distanced himself from Labour pragmatists and explained that he 'came to socialism through Marxism'. He might not have seemed an obvious potential ally of Liberalism, but in the decade to come, Blair would breathe more life into Lib–Labbery than any other Labour politician in history.

At last, the Liberal Party had found a Labour partner that it might do business with.

CHAPTER 7

'FROM BURNT OFFERING TO BLAIR'
1992–99

On Saturday 9 May 1992, one month after polling day, Ashdown headed for the market town of Chard, in the west of his constituency. After a short advice centre, he walked to the Guildhall to deliver a speech to a small group of loyal party members. He noted that they had 'come from as far away as Honiton, West Dorset and Bridgwater', confiding to his diary that this was 'very gratifying'. It was not quite on the scale of the crowds of 20,000 that Gladstone had addressed in his Midlothian campaign, but this was a different era, and Liberal leaders had needed to lower their sights over the past 100 years.

The speech opened cautiously, noting that 'sensible politicians' take time to reflect on election results and their implications. But after this nod to caution, Ashdown launched into the main purpose of his speech. Labour could no longer hope to win by itself. If Britain was to avoid permanent Conservative rule, there was a need to 'draw together the forces in Britain which will bring change and reform'. Out was any sense that the Liberal Democrats could hope to win power by themselves or replace Labour. The fevered competition of 1979–88 was dead and buried. It was back to Grimond and Steel.

The new task was 'to work with others to assemble the ideas around which a non-socialist alternative to the Conservatives can be constructed, with the Liberal Democrats at the centre of the process and a reform of the voting system as the starting point'. This would require a more respectful relationship between Labour and the Liberal Democrats. He was not prepared for the 'new politics' to be 'delivered in a specially constructed bungalow annex in the grounds of Transport House'.

Here, set out in black and white, was the Ashdown strategy of the next seven years. Most Lib Dem MPs thought the Chard speech a mistake – dubbing it the 'Burnt Offering'. They wanted to keep their distance from Labour. Even many of Ashdown's allies were sceptical. Rennard noted: 'I did not see how appearing to line up with another party would help us in a first-past-the-post system.'[1]

Meanwhile, John Smith still believed that Labour could win by itself. Ashdown arranged a meeting with Smith, on 19 October 1992. The two men shared a large amount of whisky but not much else. Smith made clear that he was not enthusiastic about pacts and deals. He said he was supportive of PR for Europe but that Labour was now backing away from change at Westminster.

Smith had always been cautious about electoral reform. But under Kinnock, Labour had established the 'Plant Commission', to investigate the case for a change. This was driven by two factors. Firstly, Labour was committed to devolution in Scotland and Wales and needed to consider the electoral systems that would be used. Secondly, Labour had not won a Westminster election for almost twenty years, and many were wondering if it would take a Lib–Lab arrangement to get the Conservatives out: 'Primarily, PR was a response to the electoral despair...'

The commission emerged after the 1990 Labour conference, which had, by a narrow majority of 2,766,000 to 2,557,000, decided to set up a review. Kinnock emphasised that Labour was starting a debate on PR, not committing itself to change. Plant, an academic, was chosen to chair the review. Some saw him as agnostic, others felt he was privately committed to change. Like all good people given such a difficult task, he seems to have managed to leave different impressions with different people.

The membership was deeply divided between those opposed to reform and those who backed change. PR for Scotland, Wales and Europe was the easy bit. What was more divisive was Westminster. As the commission progressed its work, Plant gradually moved to favour reform. A series of interim reports were published in 1991 and 1992. Labour's 1992 manifesto referenced the work of the commission and committed that it would be converted in government into a formal inquiry. During the election, Kinnock avoided committing himself to reform, saying he was awaiting the outcome of the review.

The Plant Commission would eventually report in March 1993. It rejected STV as too radical a change, saying that it would break the constituency link and risk permanently hung parliaments. But it did come out for a variant of the Alternative Vote – the Supplementary Vote. This was short of what Raymond Plant himself now preferred – the Additional Member 'top-up' system.

Plant had thought that there was a small majority on his commission for an Additional Member System, but before the final meeting of the group, several members appeared to switch their support from AMS to the Supplementary Vote. According to Plant, this may have been due to pressure from John Smith, who saw AMS as a bridge too far and likely to divide the party.

The commission members seem to have voted 10–6 for reforming the electoral system and 9–7 for the Supplementary Vote. Plant would later make clear: 'I did not want the Supplementary Vote … I did vote for it or else the majority would have gone for FPTP which I didn't want.'[2] It was a great missed opportunity to deliver almost exactly the system that Roy Jenkins would propose five years later.

Smith's deputy, Margaret Beckett, was strongly opposed to any change. Smith, however, was prepared to commit a future Labour government to a binding national referendum on the Commission proposal. But in May 1993, he made clear that he remained 'unconvinced of the need for a change'. 'Unconvinced' was a fudge – a way of papering over the large cracks in Labour. The formulation would suit party leaders for some years to come. So it was that a referendum on voting reform became as much a way of managing Labour Party divisions and keeping the Lib Dems sweet as it might be a constitutional imperative. Indeed, when Plant had raised the idea of a referendum at a meeting of his commission, it had received little support. 'The referendum was a device that prevented the Labour Party from splitting in the run up to the next general election … In effect … a party management device.'[3] Had Labour been able to unite around a single reform option, it could simply have included this in its manifesto and sought public endorsement through that route.

The good news for the Lib Dems was that Smith was far more pragmatic about the system to be used for a new Scottish Parliament. He was willing to concede PR for Scotland to achieve consensus amongst the parties. After negotiations in the Scottish

Constitutional Convention, Labour eventually agreed to a voting system that would include seventy-three First Past the Post constituency MPs, combined with fifty-six regional top-up 'Additional Member' seats to ensure broad proportionality.

While the Plant Commission was coming to its conclusion, other events were having a dramatic impact on British politics. In September 1992, the pound fell sharply and was forced out of the European Exchange Rate Mechanism. It was a chaotic period, with interest rates moving from 10 per cent to 12 per cent to 15 per cent, then back to 10 per cent – all within a 24-hour period. There was a complete loss of confidence in the Conservative Party's economic competence – its former electoral trump card. As the Conservatives dropped sharply in the polls, this encouraged those in Labour who felt the party was now set to defeat the Conservatives by itself. And it did not help Lib–Lab relations that in 1992 and 1993, Lib Dem MPs sided with the Conservative government to vote through the European Maastricht Treaty. On several occasions, the Major government only won key votes due to Lib Dem support.

Those Lib Dems who argued that their party should pursue an independent course were also emboldened by the collapse of the Conservative vote, which delivered huge Lib Dem gains in the 1993 and 1994 council elections. The party rose to 25 per cent in the polls. And there were dramatic Lib Dem by-election successes, with gains in Newbury and Christchurch in 1993 and in Eastleigh in 1994. In June 1994, the party won its first two seats (still under First Past the Post) in the European Parliament. It looked as if the Conservatives would be swept from power, with both opposition parties sharing the spoils.

But Ashdown was unwilling to give up on his project. By June 1993, he had concluded that co-operation with Labour could boost

Lib Dem performance in target seats, provided the Conservatives were more unpopular than Labour in those seats. And in July 1993, he and his wife, Jane, had their first dinner with Labour's new shadow Home Secretary, Tony Blair. Blair struck Ashdown as interested in realignment and he noted his ruthless focus on winning: 'The history of the Labour Party is littered with nice people who get beaten. I don't intend to be one of them.'[4] Ashdown saw in Blair another politician who, like him, was willing to take risks. The July dinner was followed by another on 1 December, this time at Ashdown's flat in Methley Street, Kennington. Blair and Ashdown found they had much more in common. Blair was clear that co-operation with the Lib Dems was possible. Ashdown agreed but emphasised that it must lead to pluralist politics, via electoral reform. At their very earliest meetings, the extent of their alignment was obvious. But so were the seeds of the future failure of their project.

Blair was clearly troubled by John Smith's strategy. He confided to Ashdown that his leader was too cautious on modernisation and against co-operation with the Lib Dems. Blair wanted to work with the Lib Dems but had always been sceptical of electoral reform – seeing it as a distraction from the key task of modernisation. In the *New Statesman* in 1987, he had written: 'The campaign for PR is just the latest excuse for avoiding decisive choices about the party's [Labour's] future'. In July 1996, he was delivering the same message: 'My worry is more … you carry on with the policies the electorate won't support, change the voting system and hope you can somehow gain power by joining forces with other political parties. It doesn't work.'[5] In September 1996, he also argued in *The Economist* that 'an electoral system must meet two democratic tests: it needs to reflect opinion, but it must also aggregate opinion without giving disproportionate influence to splinter groups. Aggregation is particularly important for a parliament whose job it is to create a single, main-stream government.'

Despite these impediments, Ashdown pressed on with his project. By April 1994, he was considering formally dropping Lib Dem 'equidistance'. This would mean working to eject the Conservatives but leaving the door open to co-operation with Labour.

And then, at 8.05 a.m. on Thursday 12 May 1994, everything changed. Ashdown was travelling into London from his Yeovil constituency and stopped at a garage on the A303. He phoned his office in Westminster. His PA answered: 'Have you heard the news? John Smith is dead.' Smith had died the night before of a heart attack. It was immediately clear that the baton would pass to a fresh, younger, more dynamic leader – Ashdown's new best buddy, Tony Blair.

Blair was determined to take his party back into government. He would present himself as a decisive break from Labour's left-wing past. All talk of 'socialism' would go. The public liked this new leader and his message. Labour surged in the polls, reaching as high as 60 per cent. The Conservatives suffered, but the Lib Dems did too. By late 1994, their poll rating had plunged from 23 per cent to 13 per cent.

Initially, Ashdown was shattered. In August 1994, he told one ally: 'I seem to have completely lost direction. I have been building the party to fill a certain gap in politics … But then along comes Blair with all the power of Labour behind him and fills exactly the space I have been aiming at.'[6]

But as Blair moved rightwards, he was leaving a vast political territory for the Lib Dems to occupy. This included targeted tax rises to improve education and health. Bold environmental policies. A stronger emphasis on civil liberties. And, of course, a commitment to devolution and constitutional change – an agenda that never enthused Blair, who was more interested in securing power than giving it away.

Many Lib Dems felt that they should differentiate their policy offering from Labour and seek to attract voters who felt 'New Labour' was timid, illiberal or still not to be trusted. Supporters of this strategy were not ruling out an eventual deal with Labour. They believed that influence would come through gaining more seats and votes. They weren't convinced that Blair was a liberal and felt that Labour could only be made to concede PR from a position of Lib Dem strength.

That was not, however, the Ashdown plan. Indeed, it was the opposite of his approach, which was now the strategy of the Chard speech with rocket boosters. Blair was the first ever Labour leader who was genuinely interested in 'reuniting' the 'progressive' parties. He shared Roy Jenkins's political perspective, and he and Jenkins now became close allies. Blair's adviser, Philip Gould, would write:

> In establishing itself as a socialist party immutably linked to trade unionism, Labour broke with liberalism and cut itself off from the other great radical movement in British politics. The separation of Labourism and Liberalism stopped dead the possibility of building one united progressive party, similar to the broader coalitions in the United States and Scandinavia. The division of the left gave the Conservatives a dominance in government which their electoral support rarely justified.[7]

Blair agreed.

Not since Churchill did the Lib Dems have another party leader who was so keen to court them. But there was a fundamental difference in strategy and destination. Blair's agenda was always about the

'Big Tent' and uniting the centre left. In Peter Mandelson's memoirs, he explains how Blair considered the Lib Dems not just as potential insurance if he fell short of an overall majority but also 'saw a governing arrangement with them as a way of diluting the power of the old-left Labour MPs and trade unions'. So, Blair wanted to make his party electable again in its own right, and as part of this he wanted to absorb the Lib Dems and their voters. He agreed with Ashdown that they were both seeking to fill the same policy space. And if they were, why not join together?

The only problem was that underneath the collegiate surface was a rather fundamental difference of view. Both men were willing to act boldly, upset and challenge their parties, break down tribal barriers and 'think the unthinkable'. But their end destinations were not the same. Blair wanted Lib Dem votes and support. He wanted Lib Dems in his government. He was prepared to contemplate constitutional reform, even voting reform, to ensure that the Lib Dems were there if he needed them. And he wanted to bring both parties together as far as possible, preferably through merger. Ashdown was not willing to rule out merger, but he saw this as a remote prospect and doubted his party would embrace this anytime soon. For Ashdown, the big prize was electoral reform, leading to a more pluralist politics. This would permit the Lib Dems to work in government with Labour, without the First Past the Post system then wiping them out. And for Ashdown, a multi-party system would mostly keep the Tories out of power, as he believed that Labour and the Lib Dems were natural allies.

Could Ashdown sell PR and pluralism to Blair? Or could Blair convert Ashdown to his vision – reuniting 'progressives' but at the risk of making the Lib Dems extinct?

By September 1994, Ashdown had regained his usual vim

and vigour. On Sunday 4, he and his wife Jane dined again with the Blairs – this time at the Blairs' home in Islington. Now party leader, Blair could be bolder. He wanted a new co-operative politics, with the most 'sensible' people in both parties working together, preferably in government. Ashdown was unsurprisingly excited by this prospect, telling Blair that while his job was to modernise his party, Ashdown's was to persuade the Lib Dems to embrace co-operative politics. Already the two party leaders were planning to liaise secretly over Prime Minister's Questions, in a pincer movement against the Conservatives.

There was still, though, one dark cloud in this sunny sky. Blair confessed that he was still 'not persuaded' of the advantages of PR. Ashdown noted that a referendum on this was of critical importance and that it would not be good enough for Blair to remain neutral.

After the meeting, Ashdown updated his closest advisers. These would meet regularly in the 'Jo Group', named after his head of office. Ashdown, a former spy well versed in the practices of concealment, would take a variety of measures to keep his liaisons with Blair a secret. The code name 'OMF' ('Our Mutual Friend') was adopted for Blair and later 'TFM' ('the Full Monty') for a full-scale Lib Dem–Labour government.

Ashdown realised that even though Labour was now well ahead in the opinion polls, Blair was a deeply cautious man. Labour had only ever once secured a decisive Commons majority – in 1945. Blair wanted a decade at least in power, and he did not want to be reliant on a block of belligerent left-wing Labour MPs.

In October, Ashdown and Blair met again. They agreed they would want to work together if there was a hung parliament, but Ashdown pressed Blair to say what his view would be if Labour secured a majority. Would he still want Lib Dems in government? After a 'three second pause', Blair replied: 'Yes.'[8] Ashdown said that he would now drop 'equidistance'.

Both leaders were in danger of getting well ahead of their parties. Blair flagged that John Prescott, Labour's deputy leader, might be a problem and that he would need to discuss his plans with the shadow Chancellor, Gordon Brown. When Ashdown briefed his inner circle, even his close adviser Richard Holme exclaimed: 'Goodness! You two have moved ahead faster on this than I would have thought wise...'

But Ashdown wasn't one to lead from the middle. He wasn't interested in consensus – he was determined to drag his party along behind him, kicking and screaming if necessary. The clandestine meetings and telephone calls continued. And the assiduous Ashdown followed each meeting with the informal Blair by sending the younger man a crisp, numbered minute setting out precisely what he thought had been agreed. For Ashdown, this new partnership was the single, biggest thing he wanted to deliver. For Blair, it was important, and he would give much precious time to it. But as PM in waiting, it was just one big issue alongside five or ten others. And in discussions with Ashdown, he was inclined to give the impression of general agreement to big decisions, which he would need more time to consider and consult on. But the ordered, military mind of Ashdown turned each Blair note of agreement into something definitive and final.

Blair and Ashdown had now agreed a direction of travel. Between 1995 and 1997, they had to see if they could overcome the impediments to the two parties working together. For Blair, that meant both parties concentrating their fire on the Conservatives and encouraging tactical voting. For Ashdown, general co-operation was not difficult to agree, though stopping attacks on Labour was much less easy to impose on his sceptical party. But the much thornier issue was still PR. For Ashdown, PR was both crucial to his long-term vision of a new, pluralist politics, and it was also the critical short-term enabler of co-operation. It was the only way his party would be persuaded to take risks.

In May 1995, Ashdown met Blair and Robin Cook at the house of Blair's friend and mentor Derry Irvine. Ashdown pushed Blair on PR, knowing Cook was supportive. Cook, though, started by saying that Labour was now committed to delivering PR across a range of elections – for the European Parliament, Scottish Parliament, Welsh Assembly and regional government. Wasn't that enough? Ashdown made clear it was not. Power in the UK is ultimately located in the Westminster government, and it was here that the Lib Dems would lose seats if they undermined their independent identity. To go into coalition without PR would be 'to invite our own destruction'.[9]

Blair repeated that he was still 'unpersuaded', though Labour was committed to a referendum – the pledge Blair had inherited. He said he was worried PR would hand power to smaller parties and that if the media detected there was a plan to permanently keep the Tories out, then they would be much more anti-Labour. He was also still concerned that 'PR will encourage my people to duck the tough decisions'.[10] The leaders did tentatively agree, however, to establish talks on constitutional reform. These would be led by Robin Cook for Labour and Robert Maclennan for the Lib Dems. The aim would be to agree a bold reform agenda for the next parliament.

It did not take long for the press to sniff out some of what was going on. Shortly after the meeting, the *Sunday Times* led on 'Ashdown and Blair prepare anti-Tory pact'. A few days later, a Lib Dem

Parliamentary Party meeting was 'the worst [Ashdown] had experienced'. Angry MPs wanted to know what their leader was up to.[11]

In November 1995, Blair proposed that Labour should give the Lib Dems a free run in seats in the south-west of England, but Ashdown rejected a deal of this type: 'It would look like a grubby plan to gain power and votes for ourselves, instead of one based around principles and what was best for the country.' Ashdown had experienced the difficulty of getting candidates to stand down in favour of those from other parties during the Alliance, and he did not want to have to go through that again. He remained concerned that Blair's dominance of politics would squeeze the Lib Dems out. But several by-election gains and defections to the Lib Dems by Conservative MPs helped keep the party in the media spotlight.

Meanwhile, Blair was making rapid progress in 'modernising' his party. In April 1995, he had persuaded Labour to drop its historic Clause IV commitment to nationalisation. The huge ideological barrier that had separated Liberalism from Labour since 1918 had been torn down. The 'longest suicide note' of 1983 was comprehensively binned. Labour was now pro-market, pro-Europe, pro-nuclear weapons and pro keeping taxes down. Indeed, Labour was moving from being left of the Liberal Democrats on many issues to being to their right – for instance, on public spending, on taxation, on civil liberties and on populist crime policies.

In 1996, Ashdown and Roy Jenkins attempted to shift Blair on PR. In January, Jenkins reported to Ashdown that he thought the Labour leader was gradually softening his position. In the same month, Jack Straw – Labour's shadow Home Secretary – told Ashdown that he personally could accept the Alternative Vote but 'no more [than that]'.

By March, crucially, Blair was telling Ashdown that he felt he could move on electoral reform. Instead of being 'unpersuaded', he might back AV. Cook suggested a two-question referendum, with the first being on the principle of reform, and the second being on the system to be used. It was progress but still a long way from Blair backing a proportional system.

Cook met Ashdown privately in April. It was a highly important meeting. Over a late-night whisky, he warned Ashdown that if Labour secured a comfortable majority in the election, the party would not allow Blair to bring the Lib Dems into government. On electoral reform, Cook's assessment was still that Blair's 'mind is moving towards AV, no further'.[12] Ashdown was insistent that AV was not a system the Lib Dems could support. Cook countered that there was one further option that they might consider – using AV to elect constituency MPs, with a modest top-up of MPs using the Alternative Member System. This was the type of system Plant would have wanted to advocate in 1993. But Cook warned: 'We have only just persuaded Tony to move towards AV. I really think the chances of getting him to move further than that are very limited…'[13] It was a shrewd assessment, but it also encouraged Ashdown.

Ashdown added that it was vital that the new system be in place at the next election (in 2001 or 2002), 'otherwise we would be signing a suicide note'.[14] Cook revealed that while he himself favoured PR, Mandelson was advocating only AV, while Straw was 'not yet fully on board'. He made clear that Gordon Brown was being difficult – apparently he was still struggling to accept that Blair had beaten him to the leadership.

Ashdown took the hint from Cook and put the 'AV Plus [AMS]' idea to Blair when they next met, on 8 May. Blair's response was that a top-up of just fifty MPs might be acceptable but if the number was

150, 'that would bring the system into disrepute'. They discussed the two-question referendum, and Ashdown pointed out that he would much prefer if both parties could agree on the preferred system. Blair finished the meeting by explaining that he was still thinking boldly. He wanted the Lib Dems in his government.

By June, Blair had spoken to Brown, who he described as broadly in favour of co-operating with the Lib Dems but 'wobbly' on PR. But Blair told Ashdown that he could now see his way to supporting electoral reform 'in my own time'. He would back change on the first referendum question and AV on the second.

In July, there was a setback for Lib–Lab co-operation when Blair came out for a two-stage referendum on the Scottish Parliament – first on the principle and second on tax raising powers. This went back on a previous agreement for one question. And in the same month, there were media reports suggesting Blair would campaign against PR in a referendum. Some of Ashdown's advisers wondered if he was trusting Blair too much. Richard Holme told him: 'You must not get carried away with the film script you have written in your head.'[15] But Blair assured Ashdown that the journalists had misrepresented his views.

At yet another meeting, on 17 July, Blair told Ashdown that he was committed to a two-stage referendum in the early stages of the next parliament. It was still likely Blair would only back AV. The other option offered would be the Lib Dem choice – quite likely AV Plus. He would still need to square Brown, but he had decided they would go ahead on this basis. The two leaders also agreed that the Cook–Maclennan Commission would be launched in October, safely after their respective party conferences. Ashdown arranged for Chris Rennard to be the Lib Dem joint secretary of the commission, to help reassure Lib Dem campaigners. Pat McFadden – Blair's adviser on constitutional reform – was to be Rennard's opposite number. Meanwhile, they would swap polling information and Ashdown said that over the summer he would work on a 'head of agreement' for a full Lib Dem–Labour joint programme, possibly announced in January–February 1997. This was bold stuff.

Blair concluded their meeting with a restatement of his driving mission: 'You need to understand where I'm coming from. In the long term, what we are talking about is rearranging the centre-left of British politics. It would … be remarkable if, a hundred years after the two parties split, they could come back together again.' Ashdown responded more cautiously: 'That may be the long-term destination. I don't exclude it. It may happen, say, in ten years from now, probably under someone else's leadership … We must arrive at it naturally, however. It can't be imposed from the top.'

They finished their discussion with Blair underlining that he was willing to support AV. He would consider going further but thought that he couldn't sell it to the Labour Party. He would announce his support for changing the electoral system publicly and before the general election.

The two men were making significant progress. Meanwhile, Robin Cook was sharing further thoughts with Richard Holme – pro-AV Plus, with a significant number of AMS elected MPs. His long-term vision was more consistent, too, with that of the Lib Dems – pluralist politics, rather than 'realignment' – which he was worried might dilute Labour radicalism. He thought a full Lib–Lab coalition was possible if there was a hung parliament or a Labour majority of between twenty and thirty, but not if the majority was bigger.

In the summer of 1996, *The Observer* ran a story citing a 'senior party strategist' suggesting that the Lib Dems wanted a ten-year partnership with Labour. Many Lib Dem MPs felt this was very damaging, as talk of hung parliaments in 1992 was perceived to have been.

But Chris Rennard was warned by Archy Kirkwood MP, a key Ashdown ally, that Ashdown might resign if MPs sought to derail his strategy.[16] Both sides were digging in. Rennard remained convinced that any suggestion of allying with Labour would damage Lib Dem prospects. He used polling evidence to show that while disillusioned Conservative voters did not want the Lib Dems to prop up the Tories, nor did they like any suggestion that the Lib Dems might form a coalition with Labour. This had some impact on Ashdown, who began to realise that any suggestion of deals with Labour during the 1997 election could be costly. By October, Ashdown was rethinking the 'big thing' of a joint Heads of Agreement. Even members of Ashdown's small 'Jo Group' were expressing doubts. Ashdown was worried that he was becoming 'increasingly isolated'. And many MPs thought that their leader was pulling his punches against Blair, when the Lib Dems ought to be maximising their distinctiveness.

The Cook–Maclennan constitutional commission was announced on 29 October. In November, Labour suggested the two parties swap a list of key seats, to avoid fighting each other where only one party could win. This took place the following month. On 3 December, Blair and Ashdown met again. Blair said he now felt the two parties should arrive at one option on voting reform, and it needed to be 'saleable' to the electorate. STV was a non-runner, while Blair felt he and his party could 'easily' accept AV. On AV Plus, there was at last a sign of positive movement. According to Ashdown, Blair recounted a recent discussion with Robin Cook:

Now I'm not promising anything, but I found his proposition, about AMS, which retains the single member system, and adapting this, very persuasive. I might just be able to get to this myself. But I don't want you to underestimate the huge row it would create in my party. I am agonising about it at the moment…[17]

This sounded like very good news. But was it creating false hope? Ashdown saw it as highly significant: 'It was clear to me that he was … outlining what their end position could be. Or maybe even what he had already agreed with Robin.'[18] He seemed to be successfully dragging Blair towards his position on PR. He hoped that the Cook–Maclennan Commission would soon make this recommendation and that Blair might back it. But Blair was candid that he would have 'God's own job' to shift some of those in his party – including on the commission. He didn't name Jack Straw, but both men knew who he meant. They also discussed Gordon Brown, who was worried that the Lib Dems might bank PR then go off into opposition.

Ashdown invited Brown to his home in Kennington on 4 December, to try to win him over. He noted: 'While Tony is all about positioning, Gordon is a man whose head is literally bulging with ideas.'[19] Brown acknowledged that on most policy issues, the two parties were closely aligned, but he said he was worried that the Lib Dems would join in Tory attacks about a potential Labour 'tax bombshell', an issue that had harmed Labour in 1992. Ashdown said he would look at that.

At the meeting's end, Brown said he was fully up for the constitutional reform agenda but had concerns about PR. He felt that it presented potentially big risks by encouraging factionalism: 'There are those in the Labour Party who push for PR because they believe it will enable them to push Labour back on to a conventional left-wing agenda.'[20] Ashdown took that as a barely coded attack on Robin Cook. It was back to pluralism versus 'strong government', or, in Ashdown language, 'control freakery'. Both Blair and Brown were instinctive control-freaks, battling to knock a difficult party into electable shape. Were they ever going to concede PR?

Meanwhile, in the Cook–Maclennan constitutional policy talks, Straw continued to be difficult – at one point suggesting that Labour could not commit to a referendum on voting reform due to the public expenditure implications. But during a 'comfort break' in the talks, Straw suggested to Rennard that he was not opposed to AV.[21]

Ashdown was now putting the final touches to the Lib Dem manifesto and establishing a 'Hung Parliament Group' of advisers. But this outcome now seemed unlikely. On 5 January, a *Times* poll put Labour on 50 per cent, with the Tories 20 per cent behind, and the Lib Dems languishing on 14 per cent – 10 per cent down on the pre-Blair days.

On 6 January 1997, Blair and Ashdown met again. It was bad news: Blair was suddenly rowing back, saying that though he was still inclined to see AV Plus as 'the way forward', he didn't want to be seen by his party as flip-flopping on policy to please the Lib Dems. By 14 January, Labour's negotiating position in the Cook–Maclennan talks was still hardening. They were now offering no more than an Electoral Commission, which would report a year into the next parliament, followed by a referendum. There was no guarantee that a reformed voting system would be in place for the following election. And at one meeting, Jack Straw had even said that he saw a referendum as a means of securing support for the existing electoral system. There was also a suggestion that Labour might not back PR for European elections, though Bob Maclennan thought this was just a bargaining ploy. That afternoon, a worried

Ashdown went to see Blair for what he considered a crisis meeting. He was deeply frustrated, pointing out that a condition of going ahead with 'Cook–Maclennan' was that Blair should come out in favour of electoral reform, and before the election. But Blair wasn't budging: 'I don't understand why you guys can't accept that a referendum is a good enough commitment. I have told you privately I am in favour of a change … provided we retain the single-member system. Can't you just accept … this … ?'[22]

Ashdown pointed out that this would mean that Blair's public position would be no different to that of John Smith – pro-referendum but 'unpersuaded'. He thought he had been patiently getting Blair to the position he wanted. And now, at the last minute, the Labour leader was slipping away.

Blair was apologetic but uncompromising:

> I have become convinced of the need for electoral reform … But it is not as important to me as it is to you. I don't see it as fundamental. In due course, no doubt, we will bring in reform. But I am only prepared to put this up the agenda because it will open the way to a relationship with you.[23]

The post-election commission would give him 'cover' to change his position – 'but that will happen after the election, not before'. Ashdown was disappointed. But he was now in too deep, and the prize seemed too great to give up. He spoke later to Roy Jenkins, who promised to give Blair a call.

Jenkins met Blair for dinner the following Sunday, 19 January. Afterwards, he confirmed to Ashdown that Blair was getting cold feet. He could only bring Lib Dems into government if his majority was either very small or huge. Would it be enough just to bring

Ashdown himself into his Cabinet? Both agreed this would be unacceptable.

On 28 January, there was another difficult meeting of the Cook–Maclennan Commission, where Labour seemed to be backing away from all their previous undertakings. On 29 January, the Jo Group discussed Ashdown's partnership document. Against the background of Blair's retreat, this was hardly good timing, and every one of Ashdown's advisers thought it unwise. Ashdown wasn't listening. Let down by Blair and opposed by his own advisers, he dug in his heels and threatened to proceed anyway. Some Lib Dems feared that Ashdown might be blocked by his party and resign. There were even talks with David Steel to see if he might step in if needed on an interim basis.

By Friday 5 February, Blair seemed to be going cold on his pledge on PR for Europe, saying he didn't want too many constitutional commitments. Ashdown pointed out that if this was what Cook–Maclennan recommended, it would be even weaker than Labour's previous position. Over the next week, Labour restored the commitment to PR for Europe in exchange for a two-question referendum in Scotland.

Ashdown now focused on the wording of the commission recommendation on electoral reform for Westminster. At 5.40 p.m. on 11 February, he and Blair spoke by phone. Blair was concerned that the Lib Dems wanted to rule out AV by itself as one of the options that the commission would look at. Ashdown, trying to be patient, explained that he felt this had been resolved weeks before – AV, he pointed out, is not a proportional system. He could consider AV Plus a top-up, but not AV only. He thought Blair had already accepted that. But Blair hadn't. He had hinted he might accept this, but he had never guaranteed it. He was even again suggesting that he couldn't guarantee PR for Europe in 1999. An exasperated Ashdown exclaimed: 'This is becoming intolerable. We are now going backwards.'[24]

The next few weeks witnessed a painful and protracted period of negotiation to get 'Cook–Maclennan' agreed. On 3 March, Ashdown and Blair met again. Blair claimed he was under huge pressure from Jack Straw, Ann Taylor and Gordon Brown, who all thought he was conceding too much. He again repeated that the 'Tory press' would 'take him to the cleaners' if he was seen to be giving priority to constitutional reform. He was going to stick with his 'not persuaded' position. Indeed, he suggested the press briefing on Cook–Maclennan would imply that he was not just unpersuaded but 'even hostile'. Ashdown was unhappy but had no cards to play. He had to settle for pushing Blair to concede a relatively clear commitment to PR for Europe. The Cook–Maclennan agreement on wide-ranging constitutional reform was finally unveiled a couple of days later. And, on 17 March, John Major went to Buckingham Palace to seek a dissolution of Parliament. Decision day would be Thursday 1 May.

The polls showed the Liberal Democrats on a miserable 9.5 per cent. Whatever Ashdown's strategy had done, it had not helped his party so far. But could he turn things around?

Labour fought the 1997 election on its most moderate ever manifesto. Gone was any reference to socialism: 'We have no intention or desire to replace one set of dogmas by another.' Instead, Labour was offering itself as 'the political arm of none other than the British people'. On economic policy, the promise was prudence: 'The level of public spending is no longer the best measure of the effectiveness of government.' There would be no increases in income tax but instead a new, lower, 10p income tax band.

This was all very different even from the relatively moderate manifesto of 1992, which had nonetheless pledged to raise the top tax rate from 40 per cent to 50 per cent, abolish the new 20 per cent income tax band, introduce a fully elected House of Lords, boost government investment spending, restore public control over National Grid and establish a 'Ministry of Women'. Only a 'sensibly set national minimum wage' and a one-off windfall levy on the 'excess profits' of the privatised utilities hinted at more radical inclinations.

Blair was offering 'leadership in Europe', albeit with a carefully constructed fudge on the possibility of joining the Single Currency, along with 'strong defence through NATO'. He was promising reform of welfare, rebuilding of the NHS, action to reduce youth unemployment and a top priority for education. In Blair's famous soundbite, he would be 'tough on crime and tough on the causes of crime'.

A lengthy section, based in part on the Cook–Maclennan agreement, promised to 'clean up politics'. This would include removing the hereditary principle from the Lords, a Freedom of Information Act and a Scottish Parliament and Welsh Assembly (subject to referendums), both to be elected using the Additional Member System. On Europe, the manifesto stated somewhat opaquely: 'We have long supported a proportional voting system for election to the European Parliament'. For Westminster, it read: 'We are committed to a referendum on the voting system for the House of Commons. An independent commission on voting systems will be appointed early to recommend a proportional alternative to the first-past-the-post system.' But there was no mention of whether Labour would support change, when the commission might report or when any change might take place. However, compared with Labour's 1992 manifesto, things had inched forward – in 1992, Labour had promised no more than a report on electoral reform.

The Liberal Democrat manifesto was entitled 'Make the Difference'. It was very much in the Ashdown mould – aiming to 'build a nation of self-reliant individuals, living in strong communities, backed by an enabling government'. It offered greater boldness and radicalism than Labour: 'Though the challenges are immense, the solutions we are offered are all too often puny.'

Like Blair, the Lib Dems were prioritising education – paid for by raising the basic rate of tax by one penny in the pound. On economic policy, the Bank of England was to be granted operational independence, and the top tax rate was to rise to 50 per cent, with the revenue being used to increase the personal tax allowance. There were radical policies on the environment and greater boldness on political reform – with a plan to move to a fully elected House of Lords and introduce PR for all elections (without specifying what system would be used). Rather oddly, the manifesto included a populist pledge to reduce the number of MPs by 200, suggesting a lack of serious thinking about the practical difficulties of moving to PR for Westminster.

On Europe, radicalism was qualified by caution. A referendum was offered if there was any substantial change in Britain's relationship with the EU. A section entitled 'Positive Leadership in Europe' included a long list of measures designed to avoid over-centralisation and appeal to the Eurosceptic voter. A section called 'Pursuing Britain's interests in Europe' offered unqualified support for the principle of joining the Single Currency, subject to a referendum.

The Liberal Democrats were using their inherently more moderate image to be a little more daring and eye-catching than Labour. The Lib Dems' clearer and bolder position on tax and spending was a potential vote winner, according to their polling. But in essence, there was not much in the two manifestos that could not be reconciled, and there were few obstacles to working together, provided the electoral reform knot could be untied: 'New Labour and the Liberal Democrats stood on platforms so similar that only close observers of politics could distinguish between them.'[25]

Ashdown fought his usual energetic campaign. Gradually, the Lib Dem poll rating began to lift into the mid-teens. And while the Lib Dems and Labour avoided any talk about pacts and deals, Chris Rennard and Paddy Ashdown had secured Mandelson's support for getting the *Daily Mirror* to encourage tactical voting. The Labour-supporting paper advised its readers to vote Lib Dem in twenty-two key seats – and the Lib Dems would go on to win twenty out of these. On polling day, the *Mirror*'s advice was reprinted on thousands of Lib Dem leaflets.

On 1 May, election day, Ashdown was campaigning in Taunton. In the late morning, Blair called, sounding confident of victory for the first time. He said he still wanted to press ahead with their common project and needed to find the right framework. He felt that a large majority gave him more scope to be bold. His view was that if the Lib Dems stayed on the opposition benches, the natural processes of politics would mean that the parties would move apart again. Ashdown said he understood this, but he was worried that the scale of Labour's win ruled out a coalition. Instead, he wondered if they might adopt an idea from the 1920s and form a Joint Cabinet Committee to look at selected issues. The precedent was perhaps not a happy one. This was all very different from the coalition that both men had considered establishing. According to Rawnsley, this might even have included Ashdown becoming Foreign Secretary.[26]

At 10 p.m., the exit polls were released. They forecast forty-five seats for the Lib Dems and a huge 159-seat majority for Labour. The Conservative vote nationally had crumbled. On an even swing, the

Lib Dems would only have finished with twenty-eight seats. Their final total was forty-six. In Con/Lab seats, the Lib Dem vote fell by 3 per cent. But in the Con/Lib Dem marginals, the Lib Dems gained around 2 per cent. Targeting and tactical voting were delivering.[27]

The Lib Dems had a successful campaign, with their vote share moving up from 10 per cent to 16.8 per cent. But this was still lower than in 1992, even though the Lib Dems might have expected to increase their vote in the context of a Conservative meltdown. Blair was hoovering up both former Conservative voters and prospective Lib Dems.

When Blair and Ashdown were able to review the final election results on the morning of Friday 2 May, they discovered that the exit polls had understated the scale of Blair's victory. Labour had achieved 43.2 per cent – way lower than its 50 per cent plus poll ratings but its best result since Harold Wilson's 48 per cent in 1966. But in 1966, the Conservatives had secured over 41 per cent. This time, they had delivered a feeble 30.7 per cent, their lowest ever vote share, and their lowest seat number (165) since their 1906 defeat (156). Not a single Conservative MP had survived outside England.

Labour had gained 146 MPs to finish with a mammoth total of 418 – greater even than the 393 in 1945. It now had a majority of 179 – also its largest ever. The result meant that the existing electoral system was now biased in favour of Labour. According to Curtice, the Conservatives would have needed to be 10 per cent ahead of Labour to secure a majority.[28] Ominously, for the Liberal Democrats, Labour had done extremely well from the existing electoral system. Their 43.2 per cent vote share had delivered 63.4 per cent of the seats. The Conservatives had bagged 25 per cent of the seats, for 30.7 per cent of the vote. The Lib Dems were still the big losers – their 16.8 per cent produced just 7 per cent of the seats.

Could Ashdown persuade a triumphant Labour Party that it was in their interests to dump the very system that had delivered such a mammoth and disproportionate seat total? After all, every general election since 1964 had resulted in Labour securing a greater share of Commons seats than their share of the national vote. And would Blair now be interested in bringing the Lib Dems into government, when he had such a huge majority?

Curtice also pointed out that since the arrival of Blair as Labour leader, the Lib Dems had seemed to many in the media and public to be 'indecisive [on strategy] and irrelevant'.[29] He noted that when the Lib Dems attacked Labour during the election campaign over their timidity on tax and spending, the Lib Dem vote share rose. This suggested policy differentiation was important for boosting Lib Dem support – as some Lib Dem critics of Ashdown had been arguing. This was the other conundrum for the Lib Dems – they needed Labour good will, and a lot of it, to deliver PR. But if PR was not going to be delivered, recent experience showed that 'attacking [Labour] looks good sense'.[30] The Lib Dems would soon discover that what matters in politics is not blue-skies thinking about political realignment but real votes in real ballot boxes, real MPs on the green leather benches of the House of Commons.

Many Lib Dems felt that the huge Labour majority had killed PR, and the best strategy was now to oppose. Labour had committed to match unrealistically low pre-election Conservative spending plans for the first two years of the parliament. This risked NHS waiting lists rising and growing public discontent about the state of other public services, such as education. The Lib Dems were now well-placed to make political hay.

But Ashdown was not about to turn away from the strategy that he had banked his whole leadership on. He still felt that the Lib

Dems and Labour were natural allies and that he could convince Blair to deliver electoral reform. In discussions between Ashdown and Roy Jenkins on 2 May, Jenkins said he thought Blair's huge mandate would make it easier for him to work with them – preferably in a full coalition. Ashdown was uncertain. Would it look odd for a coalition to deliver Labour an even bigger majority?

Ashdown didn't have to wait long for Blair's new thinking. At 6.20 p.m. on the day after the election, Blair called again. He was attracted to Ashdown's Joint Cabinet Committee idea, seeing it as a way to eventually bring Lib Dems into the government, with an end destination that could even be merger. Ashdown again baulked at the idea of merger but welcomed the notion of co-operation. After the call, he was disappointed, admitting to himself that if Blair had made him a 'big offer', he would have plunged in and taken the risk. He confided to his diary: 'My concern remains that, in the long run, we will end up reverting to opposing each other again. The moment has been lost.'

Ashdown now quickly rethought his strategy. He had to accept that, for now at least, his forty-six MPs were on the opposition benches. But he adopted a stance of 'constructive opposition', which meant supporting Labour where there was agreement while opposing in other areas – particularly over extra money for education and health. Ashdown had two aims. He wanted to ensure delivery of the constitutional reforms that had already been promised – including PR systems in Europe, Scotland and Wales. But his bigger aim was still full coalition with Blair, enabled by an agreement to introduce 'fair votes' for Westminster.

On 3 June 1997, Ashdown visited Blair in 10 Downing Street, entering through the Cabinet Office to avoid press attention. It was to be one of the most revealing discussions of their six-year liaison.

Blair was still keen on Lib Dems in government. But his staff had provided him with a briefing note highlighting that if the last election had been fought under 'PR', the Labour majority would have been only nine seats, while the Lib Dems would have finished as the big beneficiaries, with 146 seats.[31] These figures were questionable, but Blair's conclusion wasn't. He was being asked to give up a lot of his MPs in order that the Lib Dems could have more. 'Under those circumstances, why shouldn't you break away and return to equidistance? We would be tripling your seats and creating the very conditions under which we could not rely on you...'[32]

Ashdown responded with exasperation: 'I thought we had already sorted this out?' What was in it for Blair was the 'absolute certainty' of a second term. But given Blair's huge majority, was he still in need of his Lib Dem insurance policy? Blair came back to his own preferred solution: 'I believe that the only answer now is merger.' Ashdown knew he could not sell merger to his party. Blair was beginning to realise that he was similarly unable to sell PR to his, and perhaps to himself too.

Ashdown's diaries record the PM as setting out a view which had obvious implications for the next eighteen months: 'Look, I must tell you that if I give you guys PR, without getting from you a guarantee of merger, or at least some bottom-line assurance that you won't break away later, my party will think I have lost my marbles.'[33] The huge Labour majority had ensured that these two men were now not on a convergent course – why would the Lib Dems obsess over PR if they were signed up to merger? But Ashdown was invested too deeply to back out. And Blair still wanted to reunite the progressive parties and keep the Lib Dems on the hook – asking Ashdown if it would be acceptable if they took 'all the steps to PR' but delayed its implementation to the next parliament. Ashdown countered that his party needed the protective cover of PR if they were to join Labour in government – the Lib Dems would otherwise lose half their seats.

The meeting ended with Ashdown asking: 'What's behind all this? Have you now come to believe that with a majority of 179 you can win the next election by yourselves?'[34] Blair claimed that winning the next election was possible, not probable. He was still taking nothing for granted. His big tent was very much open. But the Lib Dems wanted payment for their admission and Blair was now dubious that he should meet this bill.

As Ashdown was leaving, Blair mentioned that he believed he could now deliver PR for Europe in 1999. He wanted to keep Ashdown sweet. But the omens for Ashdown's great project were not good. And in a private letter on 10 June, the PM wrote:

I explained to you why it would be difficult to move to PR at the next election. It would require me to go to my party and ask nearly 100 of our MPs to give up their seats ... There is also a serious question as to whether the country would be better off governed by perpetual coalition politics.

These were hardly minor quibbles.
The letter continued in blunt terms:

The 'project' is not PR, it is a new progressive alliance in British politics. PR may be a part of that but it is politically and intellectually absurd to say that it is the end game. The end game is for two groups of people who agree with each other to escape from the inherently unsatisfactory position of fighting one another politically ... the basic problem may be that you want coalition politics where your party can switch alliances, while I wish to build a permanent progressive alliance.

Blair understood the difficulties of Ashdown accepting merger but wanted an 'organic development of co-operation'. He concluded:

> It really would be a huge failure of history if we gave up now. I am and remain utterly committed ... But progress has to be on a basis saleable to both sides. At the moment I am being asked to sacrifice a large part of my party and accept permanent coalition politics with no guarantee that our coalition partner remains constant.[35]

That was the clearest possible indication that there would be no PR by the next election, or possibly ever under Blair.

Ashdown's reply will not have persuaded Blair: 'PR ... is the instrument of pluralism, not hegemony ... You risk losing 100 MPs. But you could (very probably will) lose them anyway under the vagaries of the present system.'[36]

Mandelson, an ally of the PM in backing a stronger relationship with the Lib Dems, judged: 'Tony was fine with introducing PR for European elections ... he was much more cautious on the domestic voting system. I know from our conversations that the most he was likely to countenance was the ... "Alternative Vote".'[37] Mandelson was also concerned that the Lib Dems were pressing for a coalition with four Lib Dem Cabinet ministers – he thought two was the maximum possible without prompting a big Labour backlash. But that was all resolvable. What was not was the stand-off on voting reform.

When Ashdown discussed the exchanges with his closest advisers, they took the view that the 'grand alliance' was no longer achievable. But, alone or not, Ashdown was determined not to give up. On 11 June, his key adviser Richard Holme reported a conversation with Roger Liddle, one of Blair's Downing Street advisers. Liddle was suggesting the parties fight the next election on a joint manifesto, with a pact where each party would give way to the other in key seats. There would be a referendum on voting reform, but no changes would be made to the voting system until the election after next. Blair put this proposal formally to Ashdown the following day.

Holme suggested that they ask Blair to appoint Roy Jenkins as chair of the Electoral Reform Commission – an idea that Ashdown instantly embraced. Ashdown and Holme now turned their minds to finding a solution to the PR conundrum. What if PR was introduced in two stages? They were convinced that the Electoral Commission would propose some form of AV with an AMS top-up. AV might be implemented before the next election, as no change in constituency boundaries would be needed. This would protect Lib Dem seats if they went into coalition. It would also avoid the need for candidates to stand down as part of an election pact, which Ashdown wasn't keen on. The parties would then fight the election on separate manifestos but on a joint programme – a Heads of Agreement. The second change (AMS top-up) would then be introduced in the next parliament, for the following election.

By the end of the day, Ashdown had secured Jenkins's agreement to chair the commission, and he put his new strategy to Blair on 12 June. Ashdown suggested that if they agreed to this, then the Lib Dems might enter a coalition with Labour that November – when Blair was planning his first reshuffle. Blair seemed interested. Mandelson and Holme were charged with thinking through the chronology that might end in 'the Big Thing', or 'the Full Monty'.

On 15 June, Holme wrote to Mandelson, setting out a plan for the establishment of the Joint Cabinet Committee and Electoral Reform Commission. The latter would start in November and be chaired by Jenkins. At the same time, Liberal Democrats would join Blair's government, with a Lib Dem–Labour policy programme. Under the Holme–Ashdown plan, the Jenkins Commission would recommend AV, with 25 per cent Additional Members, elected on a regional basis to give 'reasonable proportionality'. After a referendum, the government would legislate in two stages – AV for the 2001–02 election, and the Additional Members after the election.

The two parties would also fight the 2001–02 election on an agreed common platform. The note envisaged that the final voting system would consist of 450 AV seats and 150 'top-up' regional Additional Members. Holme's note was impressively clear and even included the wording Blair and Ashdown might use to go alongside the announcements.

In many ways, this was a good plan. It gave Labour the AV system that the party thought was in its interests. And it required no destabilising boundary review before the next election. It brought the Lib Dems into the government and gave them a good reason to stick with Labour. For the Lib Dems, AV would offer some protection in 2001–02. And they would eventually get the 'top-up' Additional Members, which would provide greater proportionality.

But, for Labour, there were still at least three major issues. Firstly, would Labour MPs back AV, and would a referendum be winnable? Secondly, would the Additional Members come largely at Labour's expense, as well as involving a messy boundary review in the next parliament? Thirdly, when the Lib Dems gained from the new AV Plus system, what would stop them going off and siding with another party? The risks were largely falling on Labour shoulders, and the rewards seemed greater for the Lib Dems.

Ashdown and Blair talked again on the way back from the handover ceremony in Hong Kong, on 1 July 1997. Blair suggested that they might go ahead with the full coalition before the end of the year. He was keen on Jenkins as commission chair but still worried that he could not get PR through his party. He suggested going with AV and then leaving the second step until later. Ashdown countered that it would be unacceptable if AV was the end position, noting again that Blair had already publicly acknowledged that AV is not a proportional system. Blair's response was that they should deliver AV with a 'presumption in favour' of the proportional top-up being introduced later. Ashdown said that both changes would need legislating for upfront. He also revealed that if there was a coalition, he would not take one of the two Lib Dem Cabinet posts – these should go to Menzies Campbell and Alan Beith. He did not want coalition to look like it was all about him getting his backside on a Cabinet seat.

On 22 July, the Joint Cabinet Committee (JCC) was unveiled, consisting of five senior members from each party and focused on constitutional reform. Ashdown envisaged that the remit would expand over time. He bounced his sceptical party into the initiative, and many MPs were furious. Alastair Campbell, Blair's pugnacious press secretary, was believed to be referring privately to the Ashdown–Blair project as 'Operation Hoover' – a process designed to suck up Lib Dem votes. At a parliamentary awayday, the senior Lib Dem MP Charles Kennedy stated that they should now be aiming to displace the Conservatives as the principal opposition party. But others in the party were more supportive of Ashdown – seeing the JCC as a limited engagement to move the constitutional reform agenda forward.

Over the summer, on holiday in France, Ashdown wrote 'Partnership for Britain's Future' – a draft coalition agreement. It was detailed and covered all main policy areas. But there was little in it that would cause problems for Blair. Like Steel in 1977, it was designed to pave the way smoothly to a deal, not be part of some tricky negotiation.

When Ashdown returned from holiday, he still hoped for coalition in November. But Blair was wobbling and suggesting delaying until the spring of 1998. His mind was on the funeral of Princess Diana, who had died in a car crash at the end of August. By 19 September, the referendums in Scotland and Wales had cleared the way for the establishment of a Scottish Parliament (with limited tax varying powers) and a Welsh Assembly, both in 1999. The Lib Dems and Labour were now trying to draft the remit of the Electoral Reform Commission, which proved a long, painful and difficult process – with Jack Straw seeking to undermine anything that hinted at a proportional system.

On 13 October, in a meeting not recorded in Ashdown's published diaries, Richard Holme met Peter Mandelson to discuss plans for coalition – the Full Monty. Mandelson asked for a Lib Dem policy wish-list 'hopefully not all involving higher taxes'. Holme repeated an earlier request that the Lib Dems should have 'three to four in the Cabinet and nine to ten others' in junior government positions. Mandelson pushed back, causing Holme to fear that Labour envisaged a 'Lib Dem bolt-on to the Cabinet', rather than a full coalition.

On 21 October, Blair met Ashdown and Roy Jenkins over dinner in his flat at 11 Downing Street. They had a wide-ranging discussion, over crab, 'some kind of chops in breadcrumbs' and 'a rather nice claret'.[38] Blair now seemed far more positive about electoral reform – in

two stages ... the first would be AV for the next election: the second, full PR after that. The Commission could recommend the ultimate destination, but ought in our view to recommend the intervening staging-post of AV as well, using the phrase 'the government may want to do this in two stages'.[39]

At last, it seemed the stars were aligning. Blair noted that he was under a lot of pressure from his party so needed the commission remit to enable AV to be considered. Jenkins said that if he chaired the commission, 'I am prepared to consider it [AV], but not as a final solution'.[40] By the end of the evening, they had agreed to Blair's suggestion that the Full Monty should be pushed back to May 1998.

By the end of the month, Blair had formally asked Jenkins to chair the commission and had given him private assurances that he would accept its recommendations if they were along the expected lines. But the battle over the proposed remit went on. At one stage, Labour was advocating a two-referendum process – one for AV and another after the next election, for the AMS top-up. Blair continued to rehearse his concerns over PR. He did not want a system that produced permanent coalition government.

On 1 December 1997, Ashdown finally had the announcement he wanted – the establishment of an Independent Commission on Voting Reform. It was a great success for him, given Blair's majority. He was delighted, confiding to his diary that 'Blair will find it almost impossible now to turn down the recommendations'.[41] He hoped the Jenkins report would be delivered in spring 1998, paving the way for coalition. But Jenkins was clear he could not finish his work until September 1998. Ashdown ended the year proclaiming himself optimistic. Over a drink with the journalist Hugo Young, he placed a bet that Blair would turn out to be a pluralist. Young put his money on the 'control freak'. 1998 would tell who was right.

Amongst Liberal Democrats, meanwhile, nervousness was growing about Ashdown's semi-secret strategy. As far back as September 1997, Charles Kennedy – seen as the most probable successor to Ashdown – had warned that the Lib Dems were in danger of 'pulling punches against Labour'. He said that the Joint Cabinet Committee should only discuss constitutional issues and there would be 'blood on the carpet' if Ashdown tried to take the party into coalition. At a parliamentary awayday in mid-January 1998, Kennedy correctly noted that the Lib Dems and Labour wanted different things – Blair sought political domination, whereas the Lib Dems wanted pluralism. And at a meeting with Earl (Conrad) Russell in February, the influential Lib Dem peer told his leader that Blair was worse than a Tory.

A meeting between Ashdown and Blair's deputy, John Prescott, on 18 February was similarly difficult. Prescott listened to Ashdown's pitch but rejected it. He considered Blair's obsession with the project as being all about 'airy-fairy ideas', and while he would accept PR for Europe, he was completely opposed to it for Westminster: 'I am a tribalist ... I think the tribe we have is the tribe we must hang on to ... I want to preserve the Labour Party ... not break it up.' Prescott was clear that he would not tolerate Ashdown joining the Cabinet in any circumstances other than a hung parliament.

Ashdown now scheduled another dinner with Blair, to discover whether Blair was serious about the Full Monty. At 4 p.m. on the day of the dinner, 4 March, the party's director of campaigns, Chris Rennard, sent Ashdown a six-page fax. Rennard was increasingly worried that Ashdown might agree to a coalition before PR was in the bag. In his note, he warned that this would be devastating for the party, drawing attention to a recent newspaper article suggesting that Blair would oppose PR in any referendum.

Rennard set out four ways in which Blair had already not delivered his promises on electoral reform: failing to endorse PR before the general election; putting Labour people on the Electoral Commission who were pro-AV but not-PR; failing to supply 'warm words' on PR for the commission launch; and failing to give pro-PR signals from the Labour 'machine', hence 'handicapping the PR campaign'. And if Blair wasn't serious about PR, Rennard was clear that the Full Monty could not safely go ahead:

> Coalition may be our end game (I agree with you that it is) – but there is a question of when. A coalition would inevitability reduce our share of support (this will be acceptable at some point) in return for a permanent share in power. But the loss of our independence and acceptance of collective government responsibility will hit us hard in the polls. We will lose significant support back to the Tories and some to Labour. This is as much a fact in my political judgement as Newton's laws of physics. You asked me to study the effects of coalition/PR elections abroad. The situation is messy … but in every case the junior coalition partner loses support … My conclusion must be that the loss of support may be acceptable in return for PR and with it permanent influence. But it is suicidal without PR … my prediction … is that with TFM 10 per cent would be our likely vote share.[42]

Rennard went on to predict that if they secured PR and fought independently at the next election, they might secure 17 per cent of the vote, 116 MPs and a large share in government. But his forecast was that a coalition without PR would lead to a big fall in the party vote and seats. The gains of 1997 would have been a 'flash in the pan'. On the other hand, if the next election was fought under AV, 'we would lose vote share but the change in system would make up for this. But Labour would probably have a 200 majority and little real need for us'. His conclusion was:

> What is really important for us ... is PR not coalition. If we achieve PR, we can afford coalition if we want to. But without it – or with AV – we simply cannot ... Of course, risks must sometimes be taken. But our reconnaissance must show that PR remains the key which unlocks the door. Without it, the prospect of TFM means that much is lost in unity, [there is] nothing to be gained electorally, and our ten years of success may end in the wilderness which befell our party in the 1920s. So, we couldn't commit to TFM without PR at the next General Election.[43]

Rennard was pressing for a PR referendum in November 1999, with Blair support, and PR delivered before the next election.

This was a timely but grim warning for Ashdown. He wanted coalition as soon as possible but knew that Blair was not about to deliver PR anytime soon, if ever. He told Rennard that he could not delay a coalition until November 1999 – he doubted he could hold the party together that long. He wanted to take a risk – coalition first, then PR.

That evening at 8 p.m., Ashdown and his wife Jane went to the No. 11 flat for a private dinner, with Blair and his wife, Cherie. Blair said he was still committed to coalition and could deal with opposition from Prescott and others. Ashdown pressed for a November 1998 date. Blair agreed that this should be their 'target'. The Jenkins report would be out in October, and they could deliver the coalition the following month. As for the PR referendum, Blair was suggesting some time in 1999 – possibly June. Ashdown thought November would be better.

Ashdown then pressed again on whether Blair would support the Jenkins proposals. Blair was clear: 'Of course I will, provided it contains what we think it will.'[44] He would also expect a single Cabinet position on the issue. The next day, the PM received a fax from Ashdown, setting out point by point what the Lib Dem leader thought he had agreed, and who Ashdown was selecting to lead the coalition policy work on the Lib Dem side.

By now, Ashdown had decided to place all his chips on his project. He had been party leader for a decade and wanted to step down soon and leave Parliament at the next election. But many in the party wanted to constrain their leader's room for manoeuvre. Even Ashdown's close ally Richard Holme told Rennard that he feared that the Lib Dems might go into coalition but fail to secure PR. Rennard himself worried that 'Paddy might be hearing what he wanted to hear. Tony Blair appeared to have some skill in achieving this with many people.'[45]

At the spring 1998 Lib Dem conference in Southport, nervous party members voted for a 'triple lock', meaning that any coalition would be subject to the support of the parliamentary party and the Federal Executive, and unless this was overwhelming would also require the approval of a special conference and potentially an all-member ballot.

Meanwhile, Roy Jenkins was well advanced in his work. He had been handed a task that could change the face of British politics but was fraught with risk. He had to find a system that would satisfy the caution of Blair, the pluralist aspirations of Ashdown, the instincts and integrity of his four fellow commissioners, the principles and self-interest of a majority in Parliament and the judgement of a perhaps sceptical public. He had also been handed carefully negotiated terms of reference that were themselves a desperate attempt to paper over competing visions of what a good alternative to First Past the Post would look like. In particular, the commission would need to 'observe the requirement for broad proportionality, the need for stable government, an extension of voter choice, and the maintenance of a link between MPs and geographical constituencies'.[46] Jenkins acknowledged very candidly on page one of his report that these were 'four not entirely compatible "requirements".' It was as if he had been handed random components from several different jigsaws and been asked to fit them together to form a new and coherent picture.

This might have seemed a difficult enough task, but Jenkins's challenge was even greater. For the Prime Minister who had commissioned the report had just been elected in a landslide that had delivered 63.4 per cent of the seats for 43.2 per cent of the vote. In the striking language that would later appear in Jenkins's report, Labour had just experienced 'a cornucopia of luscious psephological fruit emptied over its head'.

In fact, Labour had been through ten elections in a row in which their share of MPs was higher than their share of the vote. In the post-war era, only the elections of 1951, 1955 and 1959 had delivered Labour a smaller share of MPs than their vote share. It was the Lib Dems who would stand to gain most from a proportional system. And under a fully proportional system, Labour would give up over 130 of its present seats. Would Labour turkeys be keen to vote for a

Lib Dem Christmas? But Jenkins was not a man to give up easily, and in his back pocket he thought he had a commitment from Blair to support his proposed alternative.

It was easy for Jenkins to set aside some options. The Single Transferable Vote was the preferred Lib Dem policy, but not even they expected this system to be acceptable to Blair, and most commissioners were opposed to it. It would be 'too' proportional, too radical a change and would not preserve the existing constituency link. In its purist form, it also risked offering 'too much' choice, or as Jenkins was to write, it might resemble 'a caricature of an over-zealous American breakfast waiter going on posing an indefinite number of unwanted options'.[47]

Oddly, Jenkins had at one stage been attracted to the idea of STV for cities and AV for rural areas. This had been unanimously recommended by the 1917 all-party Speaker's Conference. But it didn't fly beyond 1917 and it wasn't about to eighty years later. In a confidential letter from Ashdown to Jenkins, dated 1 June 1998, the Lib Dem leader gave his thoughts on the 'AV Rural/STV Urban' system that Jenkins had raised with him at a recent lunch. He described the system as 'a potentially very attractive option', but the remaining two pages of his letter only served to highlight some of the complexities of defining which seats would fall into each category. It would also not be possible to introduce the system for the next election, though Ashdown didn't mention this in his letter. In any case, Blair didn't remotely like either the notion of different voting systems in different constituencies, or the idea of enabling the Conservatives to win back seats in the urban areas that they had now mostly been expelled from. At a meeting with Ashdown on 7 July, he noted: 'I am a bit worried about some of the things that are coming out from the Jenkins Commission. There is some proposal about two different kinds of voting. I think that is a load of rubbish.' Ashdown did his best to defend the Jenkins plan, arguing that it would avoid having two classes of MPs – one constituency-based, the other a list-based group. Blair promised to 'get someone to look at it'. But he must have instantly considered it unsellable. Ashdown omitted details of this initial Jenkins plan from his published diaries, referring to some of the conversation with Blair on 7 July but without details of what it was that Jenkins was considering.

What about AV? This was the system favoured by many in the Labour Party, and it was already used by the Conservative Party to elect its leaders. It would require no redrawing of constituency boundaries and would keep the existing constituency link. It would allow voters to rank their preferences and help ensure that the elected MPs had broader support than under FPTP. But AV was most definitely not a proportionate system, and Jenkins knew that by itself it was not going to be acceptable to the Lib Dems. Indeed, in landslide election outcomes, it could even have an 'unfair' impact on the losing party. And one of the commissioners, Lord Alexander, was opposed to AV.

Jenkins looked at what would have happened to the 1997 election result, under AV. No wonder Labour was attracted to this option – in the context of tactical voting to throw out the Conservatives, he found that AV would have delivered 452 Labour MPs, even more than their current 418. The Lib Dems would have got a fairer share of eighty-two, rather than their actual total of forty-six. The problem was that the Conservatives would have plunged to ninety-six MPs, almost half the 165 they had secured. A Tory vote share of 30.7 per cent would have delivered just 14.6 per cent of the seats. No doubt the control-freak PM would love this outcome, but it would be tough to sell to the public and to Ashdown.

After eliminating various other obscure and obviously unlikely options, Jenkins closed in on the system that he, Blair and Ashdown had been discussing over the last eighteen months – AV, with a 'top-up', elected to ensure greater proportionality. This was the option that Jenkins settled on. He spoke privately to Ashdown on 22 July, having also just updated Blair. He had now dropped his AV/STV plan, saying that he could not get it through his committee, given Labour opposition (this was also omitted from Ashdown's published diaries). It is, frankly, extraordinary that he tried. Instead, he told Ashdown that he was now proposing a 'very decentralised' Alternative Member System to deliver greater proportionality. This would consist of around one AMS member per 'county'. Ashdown was worried that 'there had been such a turnaround without me knowing'. He sought advice from Chris Rennard, who was concerned as to whether it would be proportional enough. Jenkins thought it would have delivered Blair a majority of around fifty in the context of 1997. He knew that there was no way that he could persuade Blair to sign up to a system that would have failed to give him a comfortable majority even in this 'landslide' year.

There was some debate in the Commission on the phasing of this plan and whether the 'base' system should be FPTP or AV. Ashdown really needed AV to be the 'base' system, if this was the only change that could be delivered by the next general election. He made that point to Blair in a meeting on 23 July. Blair could see the argument – but also that this might look to the public too self-interested, given that AV in 1997 would have cost the Conservatives more seats.

On the commission, David Lipsey wanted AV to be introduced first, with the top-up component being considered later as a second phase reform.[48] He would later reveal that there had been 'a tremendous tussle within the Commission' on this issue, with some members (such as Alexander) much keener on proportionality. Whatever was proposed would be hugely controversial within the Labour Party, including with MPs who might fear their own seats would at some stage be at risk. By now, there was a 'Keep the Link' group, which had the support of around eighty Labour MPs. This was centred on preserving the 'constituency link', but most support-ers were opposed to any move away from FPTP.

Rennard – a shrewd tactician and strategist – considered that the final Jenkins proposal – AV Plus AMS – was 'the best that we were likely to achieve in the foreseeable future'.[49] It was also not wholly dissimilar to the system that had been selected for use for the Scot-tish Parliament and Welsh Assembly. Under the final commission recommendation, 80–85 per cent of MPs would continue to be elected at a constituency level, by AV. The other 15–20 per cent of MPs would be elected as a 'top-up' to achieve greater proportion-ality, and as this would happen at a relatively local level, this would help to avoid small fringe parties entering Parliament. The limited size of the top-up would reduce the degree of proportionality but help to deliver on a key Blair requirement – that a majority govern-ment could still be elected on a high proportion of the total vote, without needing to exceed the 'impossible' bar of 50 per cent.

It was an ingenious solution – perhaps close to the best available, given the circumstances.

But was it good enough? The answer was no.

The failure was not in Jenkins's ability to unite the commission. Only one member, the Conservative peer Lord Alexander, took a slightly different view. In a 'Note of Reservation', he set out why he thought FPTP was a better system than AV, at the constituency level. He pointed out that FPTP would be used for this purpose in the new systems for both the Scottish Parliament and Welsh

Assembly. He also thought AV was unfair – only considering the second preference votes of those who had voted for the least popular candidates. He quoted Churchill, who in 1931 had described AV as a system based on 'the most worthless votes of the most worthless candidates', and he pointed out that it would be simpler to keep FPTP as the base system. Alexander's case was a powerful one, but it did not appeal to Labour, and it was directly contrary to what Ashdown and Blair had discussed.

But there were other, bigger problems with the system that Jenkins had so elegantly designed. He and the other commissioners had decided that bringing reform in in two stages would seem unfair. That instantly scuppered the two-stage Lib–Lab plan. In addition, Jenkins argued that the total number of MPs should stay at the present number. As this number would include the extra top-up MPs, this would require a review of parliamentary boundaries and bigger constituencies. Instantly, this would take more time and upset existing MPs, who would find their seats abolished. Consequently, Jenkins advised that it would take eight whole years before for the new system could be used in a general election. From Ashdown's perspective, that was hopeless. If the Lib Dems entered coalition in 1998 or 1999, they would have no protection from the expected decline in their poll ratings.

If all that was not enough to deter Blair from proceeding, Table 3 on page forty-six of Jenkins's final report contained some killer statistics. It recalculated the 1997 general election result, using the proposed new voting system. The Conservative seat number would stay pretty much the same. But Labour would lose fifty-one seats and pass forty-three of these to the Lib Dems and five extra to the SNP. Blair was a control freak. He had sweated blood to modernise his party and get them into government. Now he was being asked to transfer almost one in eight of his seats to other parties, whose long-term loyalty could not be guaranteed.

As Jenkins wrote his report over the period from December 1997 to October 1998, all of this would have gradually dawned on Blair and his advisers. Jenkins was doing his best. But he had not been able to assemble an attractive new picture from the disparate jigsaw pieces.

Despite this, Ashdown continued to plan for an autumn 1998 coalition. On 7 July, he took his closest advisers with him to Downing Street to make final arrangements. Now, Blair sounded a more uncertain note. He wasn't sure the November target date was deliverable. Mandelson wasn't convinced that the Cabinet could be persuaded on PR. When Ashdown met Blair again on 23 July, there was more backsliding. Blair couldn't deliver coalition in the autumn and was asking if the PR referendum was urgent, as the Jenkins system would not be in place for the next election. He was not keen on Ashdown's suggestion that the new voting system would require a party to secure as much as 45 per cent before getting a working majority.

When Ashdown later reflected on his dealings with Blair, he noted three problems – a tendency to say what people want to hear, a failure to have officials present to follow through on agreements and too much attention to the big picture rather than the means of achieving it. Ashdown liked decisions. Blair liked to chew over issues, give an impression of support, then wriggle away later. And Ashdown had faults too. He struggled to see just how large the concessions were that he was asking Blair to make. And his forceful, alpha-male style, married to Blair's desire to please, often meant that he left meetings feeling he had secured guarantees from Blair, which were in fact much less bankable than he liked to think.

Over the summer, Blair finally applied his mind to the PR issue.

In the middle of the summer recess, on 18 August 1998, Blair's office called Ashdown. The PM, also in France, wanted to send him an important fax. Could he switch his machine on? Ashdown was at his daughter's house, and she was unprepared for an urgent missive from the PM. Her machine almost immediately ran out of fax paper. The agitated but tech-friendly Lib Dem leader arranged to receive the message on his laptop instead.

It was not good news. Blair recapped on progress to date. Initially, they were thinking of AV first, plus an 'AMS' top-up. The problem here was that the system might look unfair – AV delivering an even bigger Labour majority. Then they had looked at AV for rural areas and STV for urban areas, 'but the logistical difficulties of that seemed too great'. So, the Commission was now considering FPTP for 80–85 per cent of seats, with an AMS top-up for the rest. (Ashdown's published diary diplomatically avoids recounting the evolution of commission thinking on reform.) Blair felt that their two-stage plan – AV first, then a top-up later – would be difficult to sell to the country and would appear unfair to the Conservatives. Instead, they needed to move in one leap to either FPTP with a top-up or AV with a top-up. But this would have problems: two tiers of MPs, near-permanent coalitions, the loss of many Labour MPs and difficulty getting it all through Parliament. Would it not be better, he suggested, to delay the referendum to the date of the next general election?

Ashdown replied within twenty-four hours. He was still keen on the two-stage reform process, with AV first. He thought AV rather than FPTP would be the better system for direct elections, as it increased voter choice and was already popular with many Labour people. He did not favour delay, as this risked the 'rats' getting at the

Jenkins proposals and would make moving to a coalition impossible. The next day, Roy Jenkins called Ashdown: it was now likely the commission would plump for AV Plus. But the timing of any change was unclear.

It was all coming to a head. Either Blair would support the Jenkins conclusions in October and a coalition would begin soon afterwards, or Blair would pull back, in which case, Ashdown would swiftly resign. The stakes were high.

By the time Ashdown was back in London, in early September, Blair was still inching away. And Jenkins had confirmed that he could not now support a two-stage process – feeling it would look like a conspiracy against the Tories.

In early September, the ingenious Rennard sent Ashdown a private paper that sought to break the logjam. He noted that Jenkins was considering a 115 AMS top-up to 543 MPs elected by FPTP or AV. Rennard suggested the immediate introduction of the 115 top-up, to avoid the need for a swift, and probably undeliverable, boundary review. The problem was that this would increase the size of the Commons from 658 to 773 MPs – even if for one parliament only. Rennard suggested countering this by removing the hereditary peers from the House of Lords. There would need to be an early referendum both on the Jenkins recommendations and on the Lords changes. He estimated that the interim reform would deliver Labour a Commons majority on 40 per cent of the vote. The boundary review would then take place after the election, reducing the Commons to its existing 659 seats. Either FPTP or AV could be used for the single-member seats. This memorandum was excluded from Ashdown's published diaries. It is not clear if the idea was put to Blair or not. It was clever, but from Blair's perspective, it still had two huge disadvantages: he wasn't ready to move quickly to a PR system, and increasing the number of MPs (even for one election) would be savaged by the Conservative-leaning media.

By 6 September, Ashdown was 'in the blackest, deepest mood of depression'.[50] He needed to write his conference speech, but what would it say? That he had achieved everything he had worked for, or that he was resigning? On Wednesday 9 September, Ashdown would meet Blair again, for what he expected to be the 'crunch meeting'. He had an ambitious shopping list, including 115 (150 in his published diary but 115 according to Ashdown's unpublished diary, and a note of the meeting made by Jonathan Powell) top-up MPs, with open lists, an early referendum, at least some change in the voting system before the next election and AV as the base system. All other than the last would be tough sells.

For three and a half hours, Blair, Ashdown, Mandelson and Holme talked through the issues. But it was soon clear that Blair had not reached a conclusion and that 'we were here … to join him in yet another long perambulation around the issues'. Blair was not willing to deliver AV Plus immediately and repeated that he felt AV first, by itself, could not be sold to the public. He suggested that he might only have the support of two members of his Cabinet for the proposals. Ashdown countered that he could not go into coalition without the protection of at least AV. Blair now suggested instead, according to Ashdown's unpublished diary, that there should be 'say, twenty seats where we won't stand against each other. I can carry that in my party'. Ashdown rejected the offer, citing all the difficulties that the Alliance had experienced in 'dividing up' seats. Richard Holme later complained that it was 'like being condemned to attend endless repeats of *Hamlet*'. Ashdown confided to his diary that night 'Waiting for Blair is like waiting for Godot!'

On Friday 11 September, Blair finally gave his decision. This time it came not at an intimate dinner or on the Downing Street sofa, but in a fax of a few pages in length, with eight numbered bullets. It was sent through just before 9 p.m. And it was the great Blair let-down.

It started well enough, with a commitment to 'a great progressive alliance', but by point two the back-peddling was evident. The Jenkins solution could not be introduced for the next election. They needed other constitutional changes to bed in – a particularly feeble point. Their parties would be tough to win over. This all pointed to delaying the referendum.

Blair's alternative was some warm words on Jenkins ('if there is to be change … this is the best system'), and a referendum delay until 'shortly after the next election'. There wouldn't be a coalition, but there would be 'strengthening of joint co-operation', and Blair would say it was 'possible to contemplate Lib Dems in the Cabinet'. Then they could work to encourage tactical voting in seats where Lib Dem MPs were vulnerable. He had considered a Lib Dem suggestion to move immediately to AV at the next election with no referendum but had decided this would not be sellable.

For Blair, this was 'the only realistic path forward'. For Ashdown, it was 'dreadful … this will crucify me … This is the end.'[51] For the past four years, he had been trying to convert Blair the control freak into Blair the pluralist. He had failed. The 1997 landslide had made the Lib Dems less important and had confronted Blair with the prospect of having to cull up to 100 of his own MPs to deliver an outcome where his majority would be similar but he would be dependent on another political party. The election result had left Ashdown with an incredibly weak hand. After this, the failure of his project was always likely. But he was determined to take risks to pursue the opportunity to the very end. He had now reached that point. In his diary that night he recorded: 'It ends here ... The project is dead in the water, probably for another generation – or at least until the next time Labour needs us ... it will now only happen when the electoral arithmetic makes it necessary. Then, and only then, will we get PR'.[52] Shortly after, in his party conference speech, he said he had 'one great question' for Blair: 'Are you a pluralist, or are you a control freak?' But by then, he had already had his answer.

Ashdown decided to delay his resignation to January and leave after the June 1999 elections to the Scottish Parliament and Welsh Assembly. The Jenkins report was due to be released on 29 October. On 19 October, senior Labour sources were saying that the PR referendum would be kicked into the next parliament. On 22 October, Blair met Ashdown and told him that on Jenkins he could move from 'No, but...' to 'Yes, but...' but no further. On 27 October, Blair shared with Ashdown the words he planned to use in responding to Jenkins. They were completely neutral, 'entirely contrary to what you and I said at Chequers [just a month before]', noted Ashdown.[53] Blair claimed his words were 'a massive move forward ... from "No, unless" to "Yes, unless"'. But he admitted he was facing major Cabinet opposition. He claimed that Mandelson and Brown believed a referendum would be lost while Straw and Prescott were opposed to the Jenkins solution. When Alastair Campbell was called in, he said that his press briefing would be neutral on both Blair's position on PR and on the referendum timing.

When the final Blair wording on Jenkins was released with the report on 29 October, it was a long page of prose that committed to nothing. Jenkins, Ashdown and others met for a 'celebratory' glass of champagne in the Lib Dem leader's office, but there was no disguising their disappointment. It was a learned, thoughtful and convincing report, but it was only hours old and already gathering dust. And in the Chamber of the Commons and on the media, Jack Straw was damning the proposals with very faint praise.

Robin Cook phoned Ashdown that afternoon to express regret. He revealed that the Cabinet had that morning discussed the report, which he and Mo Mowlam had supported. But, in the absence of any lead from Blair, 'the debate swung the other way, and the best Mo and I could get was that the Cabinet's position should be neutral'.[54]

In the weeks ahead, Mandelson suggested that reformers should switch to supporting only an AV system, without the 'Plus'. In his memoirs, Chris Rennard records:

> Several times in Paddy's office I argued strongly with him that we should now accept the offer of AV, at least on the basis that 'a bird in the hand is worth two in the bush'. In response, he would only keep repeating that 'Roy Jenkins is not in favour'. In turn, I kept saying that this in itself 'is not a reason at all'. Roy himself later considered that not accepting AV when it was offered at this point was one of the greatest mistakes of his political life.[55]

Rennard's view is:

> A referendum at this time, if it had been strongly backed by a popular Labour government … with the Lib Dems also remaining in a very popular position, and with the Conservatives marginalised, would have been won. But we failed to seize the opportunity that we had then … Not trying to achieve the introduction of the Alternative Vote system for Westminster in 1998 was later to prove a costly mistake.[56]

Had the Lib Dems decided to settle for AV in 1997, after the size of Blair's majority became clear, it seems likely that they would have been able to persuade Blair to deliver the referendum. And a referendum in the circumstances of 1998–99 would have had a much greater chance of success than the AV referendum that was to come twelve years later. Lord (David) Lipsey considers that an AV referendum in 1998–99, backed by Labour and the Lib Dems, would have been 'a shade better than odds on' to win public backing.[57]

But once Jenkins had dismissed AV in his 1998 report, it was much more difficult for Ashdown and Blair to argue for this as a standalone solution, and the risk of a referendum defeat was greater. By late 1998, it also appears that Blair had rejected AV by itself. An opportunity for a modest first step to a fairer voting system that probably existed in the first year of the parliament was gone by the autumn of 1998. Ashdown had often been criticised by his party for being too keen to 'get into bed with Blair'. But it was his insistence and that of his colleagues that any new voting system must be proportional that almost certainly sank reform and made coalition impossible. Ashdown's mistake was not to have accepted too little, but to have insisted on so much – more than Blair could or would deliver.

In any case, Ashdown's project was now dead. But on 11 November, he and Blair announced the extension of the Joint Cabinet Committee into new policy areas, causing a huge row in the Lib Dems. The Bill for PR in Europe was also pushed through.

For Ashdown, there was to be one hugely positive note to end on. For forty years, the Lib Dems had been seeking to secure a Scottish Parliament, elected by PR. Blair's government, with Lib Dem support, now delivered this and on 6 May 1999, the elections to the new Scottish Parliament took place. What Ashdown and Blair could not achieve for the UK – a coalition – was now delivered by their Scottish leaders – Jim Wallace and Donald Dewar.

Using the new 'Mixed Member Proportional Representation system' – seventy-three First Past the Post constituency MSPs, combined with fifty-six top-up 'Additional Members' – the election on 6 May delivered a result close to expectations. Labour emerged with fifty-six seats, well ahead of the SNP on thirty-five. The Conservatives had eighteen, the Lib Dems seventeen. The Lib Dems had polled 14.2 per cent in the constituency election, and 12.4 per cent in the regional top-up vote. This was enough to give them the balance of power.

Dewar and Wallace immediately entered talks to establish a coalition with a detailed programme – the first of its kind in the UK. But the talks weren't easy. Dewar tabled his own proposed 'Statement of Co-operation', which ran to just four sides of A4. Although this proposed a 'full and genuine coalition', the second paragraph underlined Labour's tendency to control freakery, suggesting the election result implied 'the Scottish people wish to see a new Labour-led administration in Holyrood implementing Labour's manifesto.' This was not the way for a party with just one third of the regional vote to pitch its partnership to the Lib Dems.

Jim Wallace and his party were determined not just to be lobby-fodder for a Labour government – they wanted the policy programme of the new government to bear their stamp. Meanwhile, Blair and Brown were still demonstrating their control freakery – insisting that Scottish policy on issues such as university tuition fees should not diverge from that south of the border. On Friday 7 May, just hours after the election results, Blair was on the phone to Ashdown, telling him: 'You can't have Scotland doing something different from the rest of Britain.' Blair did not seem to understand the implications of devolution. Ashdown insisted these were matters for his Scottish party and that he would not try to impose solutions. Later that day, Gordon Brown was also on the phone to Ashdown, claiming that free tuition would be too expensive and was wrong in principle. Ashdown wanted to know if the issue was the principle or the money. 'Well, the principle is the money.'

Ashdown was determined that Scotland should deliver the coalition and progressive realignment that he had not been able to achieve at Westminster. He remained constantly in touch with party advisers in Scotland and with Jim Wallace and did his best to urge patience and co-operation, in what became increasingly fraught, prolonged and painful negotiations.

By Tuesday 11 May, there was still no deal, and both sides were exhausted and losing patience. For a while, it looked as if the talks might break down. At that stage, Donald Dewar and Jim Wallace met privately over a bottle of whisky. Suddenly, the tectonic plates moved. Labour sent through a short paper, conceding extra money for schools, a freeze on tolls on the Skye Bridge and – crucially – a review into the system of student support, during which both parties would argue for their existing positions. The Lib Dems also wanted a clear commitment to PR for local elections. Dewar told Wallace that this would cause him significant problems with his party but said he would privately undertake to Wallace to support the policy.

At last, at 1 a.m. on Wednesday 12 May, they had a deal. Ashdown was delighted. He phoned Blair at 1.30 a.m. to share the good news. Cherie answered the phone: 'Good morning, Paddy.' 'Good god, are you two in bed?' 'Yes, of course we are.' The phone was passed to Blair. At last, the two leaders had something to celebrate. They were, metaphorically speaking, finally in bed together.

The next day, the full coalition agreement – 'Partnership for Scotland,' running to over twenty sides of A4 – was agreed by both parties. Three of the seventeen Lib Dem MSPs voted against, with another three abstaining. But Wallace had the backing he needed. On Thursday 13 May, the agreement was published, and Donald Dewar became Scotland's First Minister, with Jim Wallace as his deputy. It was, in Scotland, everything that Ashdown had wanted for the UK.

Those who worried that coalition would undermine Liberal Democrat identity and support now feared that their party would pay a high price at the next Scottish Parliament elections in 2003. And in the Hamilton South UK by-election in September 1999, the Scottish Lib Dems fell into sixth position – polling a miserable 3.3 per cent and beaten even by a candidate protesting against the ownership of the local Hamilton Academical football club.

But the May 2003 Scottish Parliament elections saw the Liberal Democrats do surprisingly well. They held on to their seventeen seats, and their constituency vote rose to 15.4 per cent, up 1.2 per cent. It was Labour whose support fell – losing six seats to finish with fifty. The Greens and Scottish Socialists gained from Labour's losses. A second Lib Dem–Labour coalition was agreed, with Jack McConnell as First Minister. As part of the agreement, Labour would now concede to the Lib Dems PR for local elections.

How did the Lib Dems manage to hold their vote up in Scotland? Even in 2007, eight years after the first Scottish coalition, the Lib Dem constituency vote rose to 16.2 per cent, from 15.4 per cent in 2003 and 14.2 per cent in 1999. Their number of MSPs in 2007 was sixteen, down just one from 1999. Was there something particular about the Scottish coalitions that allowed the Liberal Democrats to defy the usual third-party 'hit'? Several factors seem to explain this.

Firstly, the Lib Dems were still in opposition in Westminster, so they did not suffer the same loss of identity that can arise in Westminster coalitions. Indeed, between 1999 and 2007, the national Lib Dem vote share was rising – helping to protect the party in Scotland. In 1997, the party polled 16.8 per cent in the UK-wide general election, and this rose to 18.3 per cent (2001), 22 per cent (2005) and 23 per cent in 2010. So, the rise in the national Lib Dem support was cushioning the impact of the coalition in Scotland. The big decline in Scottish Lib Dem vote share in came in 2011, when the Lib Dems were no longer in coalition in Scotland but were in Westminster. At that point, their poll share halved at a constituency level, from 16.2 per cent to 7.9 per cent, and their seat numbers fell from sixteen to just five.

Secondly, the Lib Dems were widely expected to go into coalition with Labour in 1999, so they may not have suffered defection from supporters who voted Lib Dem and ended up with a Lib–Lab partnership. Crucially, with a PR system, voters were already able to express their preferences between parties without the same extent of tactical voting. This meant that there were fewer 'swing' voters to lose.

In the run-up to the 2010 Westminster coalition, the Lib Dems would emerge as the main opposition to Labour for centre-left voters who opposed government policy on issues such as Iraq. These voters may have been unhappy to find that the party they had supported was now in coalition with the 'hated Conservatives'. But in Scotland, the Labour–Lib Dem pact was less surprising and probably less uncomfortable for Lib Dem voters.

The Lib Dems had long had a problem that many of their voters could not be relied upon as solid, long-term supporters. Dutton estimates that between 1959 and 1979, less than 50 per cent of Liberal voters in one general election remained loyal in the subsequent election – compared with around 75 per cent of Labour/Conservative voters.[58] And in the 1970s, only 2 per cent of the electorate backed the Liberals in all four of the decade's general elections. Easy come, easy go. But less so in PR elections.

A third factor in explaining Lib Dem resilience in Scotland is that the economy was doing reasonably well between 1999 and 2007, and the Westminster government was handing out increasingly large sums to fund public services. The Lib Dems in Scotland were not having to deliver austerity. Torrance sums up the overall position well: 'Not only had the Labour–Liberal Democrat coalition involved two parties with a similar ideological outlook, but the economic climate was such that money was easily found for Scottish Liberal Democrat commitments. Importantly, neither had been true of the 2010–15 UK Conservative–Liberal Democrat coalition.'[59]

Finally, the Lib Dems may have done a better job in maintaining their distinctiveness in Scotland, with rows with Labour over issues such as university tuition fees. There was no equivalent of the 2010 'Rose Garden' Clegg–Cameron moment.

And then there was further cheer for Ashdown in June 1999, in the elections for the European Parliament. Though the Lib Dem vote share was a disappointing 12.1 per cent, the fairer voting system saw the party increase its number of MEPs from two to ten. By October 2000, Ashdown was no longer leader, but the Lib Dems also went into coalition with Labour in Wales. Thanks to Blair and Ashdown, the UK was experiencing a new politics, one built on devolution and PR. But it was not the national coalition that Ashdown had hoped for.

In Blair's memoirs, it is clear that the Lib–Lab project was always secondary to his main mission: 'I wanted to modernise the Labour

Party so that it was capable, not intermittently but continuously, of offering a progressive alternative to Conservative rule.'[60]

All the liaisons with Ashdown, which seemed so important at the time, are covered briefly in just four and a half sides. Blair explains candidly that he 'wanted to have [the Lib Dems] in the big tent ... Reuniting these two wings of progressive social democracy appealed to my sense of history ... In terms of values and ends, it was hard ... to see where the great point of fundamental difference lay. Hence the decision to try to co-opt them.'[61] There is no mention of AV or the tensions between pluralism and control freakery, but the gulf between Ashdown's vision and Blair's is highlighted by that casual reference to 'co-opting' the Lib Dems – that is what Blair wanted but Ashdown fought against.

Blair's explanation for the project's failure is much less plausible and honest. In his account, this is not attributed to his inability or unwillingness to deliver on voting reform but to his conclusion that the Lib Dems lacked 'the necessary fibre to govern ... In the ultimate analysis, the Lib Dems seemed happier as the "honest" critics, prodding and probing and pushing, but unwilling to take on the mantle of responsibility for the hard choices.'[62] This is nonsense. One thing that Ashdown did not lack was 'fibre to govern'.

Ultimately, Blair followed a perfectly sensible short-term strategy for himself and the Labour Party. Pre-1997, he needed to get close to the Lib Dems to encourage tactical voting, to hoover up Lib Dem votes and to hold the Lib Dems in reserve in case there was a hung parliament or small Labour majority. In the medium and longer term, Blair wanted to realign British politics by folding the Lib Dems into the Labour Party – creating a more powerful, and more moderate alternative to the Conservatives. His huge 1997 majority meant that he didn't need the Lib Dems, but he wanted them again in reserve for 2001 and sought a close enough relationship to tempt the Lib Dems into his tent. But with a massive majority, Blair was not about to switch to PR. All he was willing to concede was AV, which would consolidate his position and help encourage close Lib–Lab co-operation.

Blair wanted a fusing together of the Lib Dems and Labour, and as Rentoul has noted:

> Only merger between Labour and the Liberal Democrats would achieve that. Merger, however, was never possible. This was not simply because the parties competed so fiercely on the ground and in local government, but because it would fall victim to the electoral reformer's catch-22. In order to merge, the parties would have to first join in a coalition. And the price of coalition was a proportional voting system, which would render merger unnecessary.[63]

Peter Mandelson was to conclude:

> Looking back at the many discussions we had with Paddy Ashdown, Roy Jenkins and others, I did not see them so much as a missed opportunity as an opportunity that was never really there to be grasped. The forces against it at the time, in both our parties, were too strong, and the circumstances were never propitious enough to overcome them.[64]

Mandelson's view is that Ashdown pushed for an agreement that was beyond Blair's willingness or ability to concede. He thought Blair was up for 'a gradual move towards a simple AV voting system', with two Lib Dems joining the Cabinet. But he claimed that 'Paddy insisted on a larger number of Cabinet seats, a governing "coalition", and a proportional voting system, not just AV'.[65]

In his memoirs, Ashdown regretted the decision not to go into coalition with Labour in May 1997, seeing it as a lost opportunity to realign British politics. He understood that

> Blair's heart was never really in the constitutional reform agenda … he went along with Cook/Maclennan … not because he really believed in it, but because it was a legacy from John Smith that he felt duty-bound to honour and a framework within which to build a closer relationship with us.

But did Ashdown miss a major opportunity? Should he have settled for AV? Ashdown rightly felt he had to push for a more proportionate system and came close to persuading Blair to back this – phased sensibly over two elections. But he was defeated by Jenkins's unwillingness to back a staged process, combined with Blair's caution that any kind of electoral reform would be deliverable or worthwhile.

A small minority of Lib Dems, including the then environment spokesperson, Matthew Taylor MP, thought that the Lib Dems should settle for AV. And Rentoul argues that Ashdown and Jenkins made a 'serious strategic error in rejecting the Alternative Vote option. As a result of their purism, they lost the chance of a partial reform which would have almost certainly given the Liberal Democrats a fairer share of seats.'[66]

With the benefit of hindsight, this seems an accurate assessment. But once Jenkins had reported and rejected AV as a standalone system, it was very difficult to disinter this potential solution. Blair had lost interest in any measure of electoral reform, and Ashdown was standing down as leader.

To secure PR, Ashdown had needed the 1997 election to deliver him an effective negotiating position, with a hung parliament or more probably a modest Labour majority. Instead, he faced a landslide Labour win. After that, he was like a card player who needed to hold a string of aces, but whose best card was the three of clubs.

Twelve years later, after no progress on electoral reform, a more pragmatic Lib Dem leadership was to reconsider the AV compromise. But in 1999, all that was in the future. The progressive renaissance was over.

CHAPTER 8

'DIVERGENCE, DISILLUSION AND THE ZUGZWANG' 1999–2019

With the election of Charles Kennedy as Lib Dem leader on 9 August 1999, the era of intense Lib–Labbery came to an end. The Joint Cabinet Committee was not immediately put out of its misery, and both Kennedy and Blair attended a meeting on 13 December to discuss constitutional issues and Europe. But both men were content to let the initiative wither away.

When Blair telephoned the Lib Dem leader on 3 February 2000, to see if Kennedy would be willing to lean on his Welsh Assembly members to prop up Labour's Welsh First Minister, he received a polite brush-off. Without Lib Dem support, Alun Michael – Blair's man in Wales – was forced out. Later that year, the Welsh Lib Dems would negotiate a coalition agreement with the new Labour First Minister, Rhodri Morgan, no ally of Blair. The agreement provided stable government in Wales until the Assembly elections of spring 2003. Kennedy had shown that he was no pushover. Labour had decided not to deliver on the Ashdown agenda. There was a price to pay.

It was not that Kennedy was anti-Labour – if anything, he was more on the left than Ashdown, and at the age of fifteen he had even joined Labour and remained a member for six years. But he switched to the SDP in November 1981 and was attracted to the politics that Roy Jenkins espoused. Kennedy liked Blair personally but was sceptical of him in two respects. Firstly, he considered the PM had been stringing Ashdown along. Secondly, he felt that Blair was moving his party too far to the right.

Kennedy had described Ashdown's 'constructive opposition' as 'a contradiction in terms if ever I heard one'. He now sought to position the Lib Dems as the 'effective opposition', to take votes both from Labour and the Conservatives. Blair was not ready to completely give up his project, and in April 2000 he was telling one interviewer that Labour and the Lib Dems were 'basically driven by the same value systems'. But his instinct was still 'hegemony, not pluralism', and the two parties were on separate and diverging paths.[1]

The first Blair government dominated UK politics and benefited from a recovering economy. The Prime Minister was desperate for a multi-term administration and decided he was in a strong enough position to follow the Thatcher formula of holding general elections after four years in office – on 7 June 2001. The Conservatives were still in a fragile state, and their leader – William Hague – was not regarded as a credible Prime Minister. Hague fought a 'Save the Pound' campaign, but as Labour were not planning to join the euro any time soon, this had little traction.

Kennedy was regarded favourably by the public – he seemed warm, humorous and straightforward. His manifesto was centrist but still modestly to the left of what was now a distinctly 'Blairite' Labour Party. The Lib Dems continued to argue for modest increases in taxes, earmarked for investments in education and the NHS.

Kennedy did not want to completely discount the possibility of electoral reform, and in March 2001 he had a private meeting with Blair, along with his key advisers, Lord Newby and Lord Razzall, to agree a form of words for Labour's manifesto. Blair still wanted his insurance policy. He was unwilling to commit to a referendum but agreed to include a pledge that 'we will review the experience of the new voting systems [in Scotland and Wales] and the Jenkins report to assess whether changes might be made to the electoral system for the House of Commons. A referendum remains the right way to agree any change for Westminster.' It was vintage Blair – hinting at much, keeping the Lib Dems hopeful but promising absolutely nothing.

The words were proved to be hollow after Labour's second landslide win. The 'review' was never delivered by Blair, but a similar product emerged in January 2008, by when Gordon Brown had become Prime Minister. It ran to 197 pages, including an introduction by the then Lord Chancellor – one Jack Straw, still no fan of voting reform. The review, as Straw noted, 'does not make any recommendations for reform'. It was just a boring analysis, calibrated to paper over Labour divisions while reverting to the strategy of keeping the Lib Dems as insurance.

The 2001 election was widely regarded as a foregone conclusion, and there was a high level of public apathy. Turnout plunged from 71.6 per cent in 1997 to just 59.4 per cent – the lowest since the 'coupon election' of 1918. The result was dubbed by some the 'quiet landslide'. Labour secured a mammoth 412 seats, down just six. The elections of 1997 and 2001 were, until 2024, the only post Second World War elections in which any party had secured more than 400 seats. The swing to the Conservatives was a measly 1 per cent, delivering them one extra seat.

Kennedy increased the Lib Dem vote share by 1.5 per cent, and their seats by six, to fifty-two. It was the first election since 1983 in which the Lib Dem vote share had risen. The Lib Dems were for once picking up some of Labour's working-class vote and starting to compete with Labour in its heartlands. According to Curtice, Lib Dem voters in this election were slightly to the left on average compared to Labour supporters – on issues such as rail nationalisation, 'tax and spend' and the role of the private sector in health and education.[2] Blair's shift to the right had placed the Lib Dems to his left on many issues.

Before and during the election campaign, there had been some discreet co-operation between the Lib Dems and Labour. Kennedy met Blair privately and the two men discussed how they could loosely work together to focus attacks on the Conservatives. Trusted confidants of both leaders would liaise to discuss campaign themes and the timings of their policy launches. They were still largely committed to the 'two against one politics' that had served both parties well since the 1997 landslide.

But the degree of co-operation was limited, and in September 2001, the Joint Cabinet Committee on constitutional reform was quietly shelved, though Blair and Kennedy described it as being 'suspended' to save blushes on both sides. Kennedy had astutely kept Lib–Lab co-operation on life support while Blair was still popular and while tactical voting might help the Lib Dems. But the longer Labour were in office, the more likely they would become unpopular, and the Lib Dems needed to be ready to exploit that opportunity.

But as the parliament of 2001–05 began, Labour was still in a dominant position. This was a period of solid global growth and low interest rates. Blair and his Chancellor, Gordon Brown, claimed to have ended the 'boom–bust' cycles of the past. With a healthy economy, they could pour increasingly large amounts of money into the public services, which meant that the Liberal Democrat critique of Labour from 1997 to 2001, that they were not doing enough to improve education and health, was becoming less convincing.

And then, everything changed. The Lib Dem peer Conrad Russell, writing at a time when the Lib Dems and Labour seemed increasingly aligned, recalled an earlier period when his party seemed to have few differences with the government of the day.[3] This was 1955, with the Conservatives in power. But he noted that proximity 'is not eternal' and that in 1956, the Conservative government became embroiled in the Suez crisis and suddenly 'closeness vanished in a puff of smoke'. He asked himself, in 1999, what the next such event might be.

In 2001, he would find out. This time, the game-changing event also originated from abroad. On 11 September, terrorists flew passenger planes into the World Trade Center in New York and the Pentagon. Afghanistan was invaded by the US and its allies, and President George W. Bush committed to deal with other 'rogue nations'. In 2003, his attention moved to Iraq, where he claimed Saddam Hussein was hiding weapons of mass destruction.

A key element of 'Blairism' was for Labour to cease to be the anti-US, unilateral, 'soft on defence' party of 1983. Blair was determined to support Bush come what may. While demanding that Saddam Hussein give up his alleged weapons of mass destruction, the real US (and therefore UK) strategy was to achieve 'regime change'. This meant sending a large army into Iraq.

In the UK, opinion was deeply divided. Many were not convinced that this was a war worth fighting. They thought Blair was becoming a poodle of Bush and that the evidence for weapons of mass destruction was weak. Nevertheless, under Iain Duncan Smith, most of the Conservative Party rowed in behind Blair. In Parliament, only the Liberal Democrats were united against the Blair strategy – 'united in opportunism', as Blair was poisonously to declare in the House of Commons debate over whether to commit British troops. It was a low blow, and the days of the Blair–Lib Dem 'love-in' were well and truly over. On 18 March 2003, fifty-two Lib Dem MPs voted against the government's decision to go to war, with just one abstention. Labour was badly split. Only 254 of its MPs voted with Blair. Eighty-four voted against and sixty-nine abstained.

One day later, US, UK and 'coalition' troops invaded Iraq. Hundreds of thousands of deaths and injuries would result. Saddam Hussein was tracked down, tried, and hanged on 30 December 2006. But no weapons of mass destruction were ever found.

Blair would never be forgiven for Iraq, by his party, and by many voters. As the only party that had opposed the war, the Liberal Democrats now attracted new support. Political popularity cannot defy gravity forever, and as Labour had now been in office for six years, they started to do what all governments do: create enemies and disillusion. University tuition fees were tripled. Council tax was rising.

In 2005, Blair still seemed, though, to be on track for another Labour victory. In the election that year, the Conservatives were led by Michael Howard, an unpopular remnant of the Thatcher era. He fought another right-leaning campaign, under the slogan: 'Are you thinking what we're thinking?' – an attempt to whip up concerns about immigration and crime. It turned out that most voters were not thinking what Howard was thinking, and the Conservatives suffered a third mighty defeat. Their vote share was just 32.4 per cent, up a piffling 0.7 per cent.

There was still some liaison during the election campaign between the leaders' senior advisers – Sally Morgan for Blair, and Tim Razzall for Kennedy. But in practice, the degree of co-operation was again limited. The parties were now competitors in many parts of the country. At one stage in the campaign, Blair suggested to Kennedy that both parties should focus on the benefits of immigration on the same day, to combat Conservative attempts to stir up the issue. But despite Kennedy's apparent agreement, the Lib Dem team did not proceed with the plan – judging that this was not an issue that would help their campaign.

When the results were declared, Labour had won again. For the first time in its history, it had recorded a third successive victory. It had secured 355 seats and a majority of sixty-six, but vote share was down from 40.7 per cent in 2001 to just 35.2 per cent.

The big winners were the Lib Dems, whose vote rose by 3.7 per cent to 22 per cent. But under First Past the Post they gained only eleven seats and finished with sixty-two. They had won eleven seats from Labour – breaking through in constituencies not held for almost 100 years. Blair had again triumphed under FPTP. Labour polled 9,552,000 votes and 55 per cent of the MPs. Blair had therefore secured a majority on the lowest vote share of any party in UK history.

The parliament of 2005–10 saw all parties elect new leaders. David Cameron replaced Howard on 6 December 2005 and immediately started to move his party back towards the centre ground. Charles Kennedy seemed to have had a relatively successful election, but at the launch of his party manifesto, he appeared confused and unfocused about party policy on replacing council tax with a local income tax. Only his closest advisers and a few other senior Lib Dems knew that their leader was an alcoholic who had consumed too much the night before.

Kennedy's parliamentary party was now stuffed full of talented MPs who were ambitious for their party. His laid-back style, which contrasted so strongly with Ashdown's hyper-activity, and his lack of interest in policy detail were already a concern to these MPs. But it was the increasing knowledge of Kennedy's battle with alcohol and its consequences (missing important Commons Statements on the Euro and the Budget, with little notice) that finally led to a coup against him by most of his shadow Cabinet. He resigned on 7 January 2006 and tragically died nine years later, aged fifty-five.

Blair was next to go – forced out by his party. He departed on 27 June 2007, after over ten years as Prime Minister and thirteen as Labour leader. Gordon Brown was elected unopposed. Brown had always kept his distance from Lib–Labbery. He was tribally Labour, suspicious of 'the Liberals' and not keen to concede any power. He had been frequently criticised in opposition and early in government by Malcolm Bruce, the Liberal Democrat Treasury spokesman, which had not served to increase his enthusiasm. Now, however, Brown was taking over as Prime Minister after Labour had been in office for a decade. It would not be easy to retain power. He realised he had to build bridges.

The new Lib Dem leader, from March 2006, was Menzies Campbell. Campbell was much more sympathetic to Labour than the Conservatives and was one of those Lib Dems whom Ashdown and Blair would have appointed to the Cabinet had there been a coalition after 1997. Just before Brown became PM in late June 2007, he decided to reach out to Campbell and his party.

On 18 June 2007, Paddy Ashdown arrived in the House of Lords to find a small pink telephone message slip in his mailbox.[4] It asked him to call Brown's private office, still in the Treasury. A meeting was fixed for him to see the Chancellor two days later. Ashdown immediately went to see Menzies Campbell to inform him of the approach. Campbell told him that he was aware it was coming, as the day before Brown had called and asked if various Lib Dems – including Lords Lester and Carlisle, as well as Baronesses Shirley Williams and Julia Neuberger – might be willing to chair various government commissions. This sounded acceptable to Ashdown, but Campbell then revealed that Brown was also proposing to bring several senior Lib Dems into his government. Brown had even raised the possibility of Ashdown joining the Cabinet as Secretary of State for Northern Ireland.

Campbell confirmed that there was no talk of a formal coalition, or of Labour offering PR or AV. Ashdown was concerned – rightly concluding that what Brown was offering was 'a deadly suicide pill that would diminish our ability to oppose the Government … and could seriously damage us in the polls'.[5] He told Campbell that they should decline the offer.

The news of the secret Campbell–Brown talks leaked almost immediately. Campbell was forced to deny publicly that Lib Dems would be entering the Cabinet. But amongst Lib Dems, there was deep concern and suspicion. Ashdown's meeting with Brown still went ahead at 2 p.m. on 20 June. Brown offered the Northern Ireland job, as Campbell had suggested he might. Ashdown categorically rejected this, asking Brown if his aim was the emasculation of the Lib Dems. Brown said that Ashdown's involvement in his government would open the way for future Lib–Lab co-operation. He must have calculated that Ashdown was ambitious for a senior job before his political career ended. He was wrong: 'I am not willing to be locked in a Lib Dem garden shed in the grounds of your Labour mansion. I believe in partnership politics, but it has to be based on policy agreements.' Ashdown quizzed Brown on why if he now wanted partnership with the Lib Dems, he had opposed this a decade before. Brown responded that in those days, he could not trust the Lib Dems – hardly convincing. It was not partnership politics but an attempt to reopen and expand the Labour 'big tent' and buy off opponents – Blairism, without the subtlety.

The meeting lasted half an hour. Ashdown concluded that Brown was amazed by his rejection and unlikely to forgive the snub. Brown's ill-considered and ham-fisted offer also served to damage the leadership of his potential Lib Dem ally Menzies Campbell, who had already had a tough first year as leader. When Brown ducked the opportunity to call a general election in late 2007, Campbell decided to step down.

On 18 December 2007, the Liberal Democrats elected Nick Clegg as leader. Clegg was only forty and had served in the Commons for just two and a half years. He was – like Campbell, Kennedy and Ashdown – a passionate internationalist and pro-European. But he was from a different political generation and did not share the instinctive pro-Labour bias of each Lib Dem leader from Steel onwards.

Clegg's career to date had been defined against Labour rather than the Conservatives, as they were the party in power. He saw Labour, under Blair and Brown, as unsound on civil liberties, wrong on Iraq, timid on Europe, wedded (particularly under Brown) to 'big government' solutions and fundamentally illiberal. Clegg had been one of the contributors to *The Orange Book*, a 2004 collection of essays by MPs and two MEPs (Clegg and Chris Huhne). *The Orange Book* was an attempt to 'reclaim liberalism' in all its forms – political, personal, social and economic. And to the extent that at times the Liberal Democrats and Liberals of earlier years had become committed to rather soggy, statist approaches to economic and social policy, *The Orange Book* served to push the Liberal Democrats back towards economic liberalism and nudge them further away from traditional Labour thinking.

The significance of Clegg becoming leader in 2007 and Cameron taking over the leadership of the Conservative Party in 2005 was not that it made relations between these two parties positive or close. On Europe, public services, taxation, the constitution, the environment and personal liberalism, the two parties were still very far apart. The Liberal Democrats fought Conservative challengers in most of their seats. And Liberal Democrat MPs and supporters saw the Conservatives as their principal political opponents – as the party of privilege, the status quo, nationalism and inequality of wealth and opportunity.

But the new Clegg and Cameron leaderships had changed one thing. Before these two leaders, for at least thirty-five years it had been impossible to imagine any Liberal Democrat–Conservative governing arrangement. Steel was never going to unite with Heath or Thatcher. Ashdown, Kennedy and Campbell were never going to work harmoniously with Major, Hague, Duncan Smith or Michael Howard. And nor was Campbell ever going to make common cause with Cameron.

Now, things were different. Labour had been in power (by 2010) for thirteen years. There had been no PR, no serious Lords reform, no euro, no Lib–Lab partnership. What there had been was Iraq, top-up tuition fees and assaults on civil liberties that offended Lib Dem principles. And in 2007–08, there was the world financial crisis – the 'Great Recession' – which saw growth plunging, living standards squeezed, borrowing soaring and governments everywhere becoming unpopular.

Against this troubled background, Gordon Brown played for

time. The parliament would go its full term – until 6 May 2010. When it came, the election campaign was inevitably dominated by the parties' differing economic strategies. The Conservatives were promising to cut government borrowing by immediately slashing spending. The Lib Dems wanted to delay the major deficit reduction until the economy was recovering, as well as ensuring that higher taxes on the rich played some part in reducing borrowing. Labour was also proposing to cut some spending and halve the budget deficit in four years, but their plans were the least ambitious. Brown found it difficult to move away from his usual 'Tory cuts versus Labour investment' narrative.

On 6 May, at 10 p.m., the exit polls were released. It was a hung parliament, for the first time since February 1974. After decades of Lib–Labbery, would a full coalition finally be formed?

During 2009, Brown was considering whether he could strike a post-election deal with the Lib Dems. At the September 2009 Labour conference, the party dusted off its commitment to a referendum in the next parliament – on AV, not PR. Brown followed up with a speech in February 2010 arguing the case for AV. He was now pledging an AV referendum no later than October 2011, should Labour still be in power.

Even Mandelson would later admit though that 'the conversion looked a little belated, a little shallow'. Chris Mullin MP, speaking at a meeting of Labour's parliamentary party, noted that it all 'stinks of desperation and self-interest'.[6] And there were many Labour MPs still bitterly opposed to change. The division extended to Labour's Cabinet, where Brown, Mandelson, Ed and David Miliband, Alan Johnson, Peter Hain, Ben Bradshaw and Lord Adonis were all backing AV, but Ed Balls, Jim Murphy and Andy Burnham were thought to be against.[7]

On 9 February 2010, Brown tabled a Commons vote on a referendum on AV, to be held after the general election, by 31 October 2011. He hoped this might facilitate a post-election deal with the Lib Dems and encourage Lib–Lab tactical voting. A Lib Dem amendment backing STV was rejected, but the AV motion passed by 365–187. However – predictably – there wasn't time for the legislation to be approved by the Lords before the election was called. It was all too little, and much, much, much too late.

Research after the 2010 election would show that if it had been fought on an AV system, it might have enabled a Lib–Lab administration, with the Lib Dems gaining up to thirty-two extra seats and the combined Lib Dem–Labour total being 337 versus 283 Conservative. Curtice provides a similar estimate of the likely share of MPs under AV as: Conservative 281; Labour 262; Lib Dem seventy-nine.[8] This would have enabled the Lib Dems to go into coalition with either other party. In practice, it would almost certainly have led to a Lib Dem–Labour coalition, but with Gordon Brown replaced as PM.

In any case, the 2010 Labour manifesto was now promising two referendums, held on the same day, and by October 2011, to introduce the Alternative Vote and move in phases to a fully elected House of Lords, using PR. Both policies were designed to appeal to the Lib Dems, though senior Labour ministers also admitted privately that AV was opposed by as many as seventy of their MPs.[9]

In late 2009, Nick Clegg had appointed a small team to plan for hung parliament scenarios. This outcome already looked quite likely, but it seemed probable that Labour would not have enough MPs to form a government, even in coalition. This might leave the Lib Dems only talking to the Conservatives. But the Lib Dems feared that any post-election pact with the Conservatives (as with

Labour) would lead to a dramatic decline in Lib Dem support. As ever, partnership or coalition would only make sense if electoral reform could be secured. It seemed to Clegg's team unlikely that the Conservatives would concede any form of electoral reform, which pointed to either a minority Conservative government or a short-lived 'Confidence and Supply' arrangement, followed by a second general election. In this scenario, the Lib Dems considered it vital that they should not be seen to be at fault for the failure to create a stable government.

The election results were broadly in line with Lib Dem expectations. Labour's vote fell from 35.2 per cent to 29 per cent – their second lowest share since 1918. They had lost ninety-one seats and now had 258 MPs. In the south, beyond London, Labour had been almost wiped out – holding only ten of the 197 seats. The Conservative vote was back up to 36.1 per cent – better than any election since 1997 but well down on the 42 per cent of 1992. They had gained ninety-six seats, but at 306 MPs they were still short of a majority.

The Lib Dems had an excellent campaign, with Nick Clegg emerging victorious in the first televised leaders' debate. But their vote was up only 1 per cent and the number of Lib Dem MPs had fallen from sixty-two to fifty-seven – a huge disappointment. Nevertheless, the outcome was a hung parliament, and Clegg now had to honour his pledge, to talk first to the party with 'most votes and most seats' – the Conservatives.

While many Labour MPs felt that they should now accept defeat, Brown wasn't giving up. In a 23-minute telephone call the day after the election, he told Clegg that he wanted a coalition and would deliver the referendums on electoral reform and reform of the Lords. Brown suggested there were no big policy differences between the two parties. Clegg was worried about the optics of two parties that had come second and third forming a government – but Brown noted that together they had over 50 per cent of the vote, versus 36 per cent for the Conservatives.

Brown claimed that even though the Lib Dems and Labour combined had too few seats to form a majority, they could rely on the Northern Ireland parties. He was desperate to retain power and wanted Lib–Lab talks to run in parallel with any with the Conservatives:

> Nick, I have studied history ... I approached Ming in 2007 on this. I know that the future of our country is a progressive alliance between two progressive political parties. The election has provided an opportunity which will not return. We could miss this opportunity forever ... The possibility has eluded us before Nick, for various historic reasons [he did not mention that his own determined opposition had been one of these] ... you would get electoral reform, it would be a pro-Europe government and we would have a progressive economic policy.

But Clegg was now getting frustrated and was determined to stick to the order of talks that he had previously announced: 'Yes, I see the pot of gold at the end of the rainbow but...' It had been a long lecture by the great Labour tribalist, and it offered a vision of a progressive alliance that Liberals had dreamt of since the days of Grimond. But it was a deathbed conversion that had come too late.

The Lib Dems held the balance of power, but they were not in an easy position. If they formed a coalition with Labour, they would have no working majority and would be accused of propping up a defeated Prime Minister in a 'Coalition of Losers'. If they went into coalition with the Conservatives, they would be in alliance with their oldest political enemies, a party that had never even pretended to believe in electoral reform. But if they declined coalition with either party, then inevitably there would soon be another election in which the Lib Dems would likely be badly squeezed as voters sought to break the deadlock. Professor Philip Cowley later described the Lib Dem predicament as 'Zugzwang' – a term used in chess to describe a situation in which a player must make a move, but where every available option leads to a bad outcome.

Ashdown, advising Clegg, accurately observed that voters had 'invented a deliciously painful torture mechanism for the Liberal Democrats because our instincts go one way [Labour] but the mathematics go the other [Conservatives]'.[10]

Over the next few days, the two sets of talks would reveal a Conservative Party desperate for power and willing to concede even an AV referendum to secure it. The talks with Labour, by contrast, highlighted a party that was split on the merits of staying in power and uncomfortable about making concessions.

In talks with Labour, the Lib Dems pressed for a two-question referendum – the first on the principle of changing the voting system, and the second on a choice between PR and AV. The Labour negotiating team (Peter Mandelson, Harriet Harman, Ed Miliband, Ed Balls and Andrew Adonis) made clear that they could go no further than AV. Ed Balls highlighted that even that might be a bridge too far for many Labour MPs, and he pointed out that the Labour Chief Whip could not guarantee their MPs would back a referendum as Adonis had warned Lib Dems some months beforehand.[11]

It was a deadly intervention by Balls. If the Lib Dem minimum price for coalition was an AV referendum, why would they join a coalition with a party that was not able to deliver one? The Lib Dem negotiators reached the conclusion that Labour was divided over whether a coalition was desirable and could not ensure that even an AV referendum would be delivered. 'We would be chaining ourselves to a decaying corpse,' was the conclusion of one.[12]

But ultimately, it was not the talks on policy that blighted any Lib–Lab deal, nor was it Gordon Brown, who swiftly agreed to Lib Dem demands that he should hand over to another Labour leader if a deal was to be possible. What killed a Lib–Lab deal was the election result. Labour had lost. It had polled only 29 per cent. Most people now expected it to leave office. The right-wing press were characterising Brown as a 'squatter' refusing to leave Downing Street. Could the Lib Dems really afford to put such a party back into power? They were dubious, but what made them definite was the arithmetic. Even adding together all the Labour and Lib Dem MPs totalled only 315 in a Commons of 650. There were also three SDLP MPs, one Alliance and one independent – Lady Sylvia Hermon. That might deliver 320 MPs. The Democratic Unionist Party had eight, but could they really be relied upon? Around 316 MPs seemed likely to oppose such a coalition on key issues– 306 Conservatives, nine Scottish and Welsh Nationalists and one Green. So, the DUP would potentially have the casting votes in every division.

And this would be no parliamentary walk in the park. With a public sector deficit of 10 per cent of national output, hard decisions would be needed. Who was to say that all Labour and Lib Dem MPs would follow the party line? Almost certainly they would not. And given that the only protection for Lib Dem MPs would be delivered by securing a yes vote in an AV referendum, how could the Lib Dems rely on the votes of up to seventy Labour MPs who even Labour's leaders admitted were bitterly opposed to this change? Under these circumstances, there seemed little or no chance that an AV vote would get through Parliament. The Lib Dems had been strung along before on voting reform – first by Ramsay MacDonald, to some extent by Harold Wilson and Jim Callaghan and most recently by Tony Blair. They were not about to make the same mistake again.

If a Lib–Lab coalition had been formed, it would likely not have lasted. It would have stumbled on for a few months and probably been defeated on its economic programme. And then there would be another general election, in which the Conservatives would be swept in and in which Lib Dems would go out on the anti-Labour, anti-coalition, tide.

As Baston and Ritchie wisely concluded:

Night after night, such a government would have to corral Jeremy Corbyn, David Laws, Sylvia Hermon and David Blunkett into the same division lobby. It would never have worked, even in relatively placid times – let alone a period of some financial instability … It would have been impossible for Labour's leaders to deliver electoral reform given the tight numbers and the near certainty that there would be enough anti-reform backbenchers willing to rebel and scupper the plan.[13]

Andrew Adonis could not accept this analysis and claimed: 'It was … not preordained that Britain should have taken the Tory road in 2010 … the critical determinant was Nick Clegg's instinct to go right rather than left.' But it was not basic instinct but basic maths that determined the views of both Nick Clegg and his parliamentary colleagues.

While Gordon Brown could never understand or accept the Lib Dem decision to reject a coalition with his party, many other senior Labour leaders recognised that a deal was never on. That included both Peter Mandelson and Ed Balls – two key members of Brown's negotiating committee. Mandelson has written in his memoirs: 'I thought a deal between us and the Lib Dems was highly unlikely.' He had already received a phone call from Tony Blair who was 'firmly opposed to even thinking of a deal'.[14] Blair noted in his own memoirs: 'There's been lots of speculation about the possibility that there could have been a Labour–Lib Dem coalition. In my view, it was never on. The people would have revolted; the votes weren't there. The truth is … we were hammered.'[15]

Even Ed Balls – no fan of the Liberal Democrats – concluded:

> Many of my Labour colleagues, not least Gordon, were angry with the Liberal Democrats for making that choice … But the Liberal Democrats had a chance to be in government and they took it … Nor do I have any problem that he [Clegg] shared power with the Conservatives. There was realistically no prospect of a workable Labour/Lib Dem majority.[16]

Labour was heading into opposition. And this was not because of stitch-up by right-wing Lib Dem MPs, but because it no longer had the votes to stay in office, the will to stay in office, the unity to stay in office, and the willingness to compromise to deliver an agreement. But mainly it was just because of votes. Whichever way you looked at it, the numbers didn't add up. When Labour had the votes, between 1997 and 2010, they did not have the will to do a deal. Now, some of them had the will, but they lacked the votes.

And so it was that after all those years of waiting and hoping for the great reuniting of the centre-left, it all came to nothing. And the irony is that the first real, properly structured and negotiated, peacetime UK coalition government was a Lib Dem–Conservative administration, just as Churchill had hoped ninety years before. For almost 100 years, those on the left and centre of politics had been anticipating a 'progressive alliance' in the shape of a full-scale, formal, coalition government. But when the coalition finally arrived, in 2010, it was what David Steel was to describe as an 'unfortunate but necessary coalition with the wrong party'.[17]

And so it was too that the first referendum on voting reform for Westminster was delivered not by a Lib–Lab arrangement but by a Conservative PM. The irony was also that the Lib Dems had negotiated hard to deliver a referendum not on PR, which they believed in, but on the AV system, which they had so strongly rejected when Labour might have offered it in 1997. Indeed, Nick Clegg had even, unwisely, used an interview in *The Independent* on 22 April 2010 to describe AV as a 'miserable little compromise thrashed out by the Labour Party.' Many in Labour would now fail to support their own pro-AV policy, while the Conservatives campaigned consistently against all change.

With a Conservative Party bitterly opposed to change, a Labour Party split down the middle and the Lib Dems left advocating a non-proportional system (the only possible change they could secure a referendum on), the prospects for the referendum were poor. And when the vote was held in 2011, AV was decisively rejected by the public – by 13 million votes (68 per cent) to just 6.2 million (32 per cent). The Lib Dems had waited for this moment for almost 100 years, and when it came, it was a crushing defeat – with a majority for change in just ten of the 440 UK voting areas.

The Lib Dems and some in Labour might have understood the benefits of the Alternative Vote, but it seemed that most of the public did not. And a majority of Labour MPs also opposed change – confirmation that a Lib–Lab coalition would not have survived long.

Political analysts played down the impact of the lost AV vote – Vernon Bogdanor calculating that AV would 'not have transformed the result in any of the twelve post-war elections that yielded large working majorities. But the Parliaments of 1951 and 1992 might have been hung, and AV might have given Labour a working majority in the indecisive elections of 1950, 1964 and February and October 1974.' Significantly, though, AV would almost certainly have led to a Lib–Lab coalition in 2010, with a newly elected Labour Prime Minister replacing Gordon Brown. Britain's recent political history would then have been very different. But Labour's (partial) conversion to voting reform came too late to achieve this.

For the Lib Dems, the referendum defeat of 2011 was a huge blow. AV was supposed to provide at least some protection from the negative electoral consequences of coalition. With AV dead, many Lib Dem seats were almost certainly going to follow. The only small, long-term consolation for the Lib Dems was that it was AV that was rejected and not PR.

Despite this blow, the Lib Dem–Conservative coalition proved to be far more stable and enduring than many expected, surviving its full five-year term. But in the 2015 election, the Lib Dems suffered badly for joining the coalition and being in government at a time of austerity. Many former disillusioned Labour voters who had moved to support the Lib Dems in 2010 now withdrew that support. And the Lib Dems also lost the weakly aligned voters who had backed them as an 'anti-establishment' party only to find them in government.[18] By 2015, many of these gave their support to the Greens, the nationalists or even UKIP.

In the general election of 7 May 2015, Lib Dem support plummeted from 6,836,000 votes in 2010 to just 2,415,000. Forty-nine of the fifty-seven Lib Dem MPs lost their seats. Their vote share dropped by a monstrous 15.1 per cent to just 7.9 per cent – the lowest since 1955. The Conservative vote rose only marginally from 36.1 per cent to 36.9 per cent, but this yielded twenty-four more MPs and delivered a small Conservative majority. Labour was up from 29 per cent to 30.4 per cent – but its seat number fell from 258 to 232.

The winners in 2015 were the smaller parties. The SNP gained fifty seats and surged to 4.7 per cent of the national vote and fifty-six MPs. UKIP took a mighty 12.6 per cent but finished with one MP. The Greens rose to 3.8 per cent but also had only one MP. The smaller parties (now including the Lib Dems) had secured one third of the votes.

After the 2015 election, David Cameron was back in power, this time leading a Conservative majority government. But in his manifesto he had pledged a referendum on UK membership of the EU – concluding that he had to concede this to stop Conservative support draining away to UKIP. Having won referendums on AV (2011) and Scottish independence (2014), he was confident that he could deliver on Europe too. He was catastrophically wrong. On 23 June 2016, the UK voted 51.9 per cent to 48.1 per cent on a 72.2 per cent turnout to leave the European Union. David Cameron immediately resigned and was replaced by Theresa May.

Labour had by now also changed leader, electing Jeremy Corbyn on 12 September 2015. Corbyn was the most left-wing Labour leader in the party's history. Indeed, he was the most rebellious Labour MP during the period 1997 to 2010, voting 428 times against his party.

He was a supporter of unilateral nuclear disarmament, withdrawal from NATO and nationalisation. He was half-hearted in his support for the European Union and kept a low profile in the debate about 'Brexit'. Earlier in his career, he had opposed the expulsion of Militant from the party and backed the 1984–85 miners' strike.

In the space of just eight years, Labour had lurched from its most right-wing leader to its most left-wing. The Lib Dems were suddenly again as distant from Labour as they had been when Michael Foot was leader.

In 2017, Theresa May called an election to secure a larger majority with which she could push her Brexit policies through Parliament. May increased her party's vote by 5.5 per cent to 42.3 per cent but lost thirteen seats and ended on 317 – just short of a majority. The Lib Dems fell 0.5 per cent to 7.4 per cent and increased their seats from eight to twelve. In July 2019, May stood down as PM, after failing to get her Brexit deal through the Commons. Boris Johnson replaced her and called a general election for 12 December, to secure a majority to 'get Brexit done'.

This time the Conservatives gained forty-eight seats, finishing with 365. Labour lost sixty MPs, ending with only 202. The Lib Dem vote share rose into double digits – to 11.6 per cent, up 4.2 per cent. But the party experienced a net loss of one MP, finishing with only eleven, and its leader, Jo Swinson, lost her own seat.

Jeremy Corbyn resigned as Labour leader on 4 April 2020 and was replaced by the moderate Sir Keir Starmer. The Lib Dems elected the equally moderate Sir Ed Davey on 27 August 2020. Within just a few months, Labour and the Lib Dems found themselves moving from irreconcilable policy differences to being led by two Oxford-educated, centrist, pro-European, male, London MPs, both of whom were knights, of a similar age and political outlook.

What this will mean for future relations between Labour and the Liberal Democrats, only time will tell.

CHAPTER 9

REFLECTIONS AND LESSONS

What can we make of the history of the past 120 years of Lib–Lab relations? Are these two separate parties essentially part of the same progressive cause, pulled apart by historical accident? Or do they represent distinct political ideologies that are as far apart as, say, liberalism and conservatism? What do the experiences of the past 120 years tell us about the potential of both parties to work together and how this might be achieved – through voting pacts or by co-operation or coalition within Parliament? And what does this story tell us about the prospects for electoral reform? Are reformers condemned for ever to wait, hope and suffer disappointment?

Let us first consider what political history tells us about whether and when these two parties can work together. We can then turn to consider the means – constituency voting pacts, deals at Westminster or perhaps, ultimately, electoral reform.

Looking back over the period since 1903, we can see that there have been many distinct phases of Liberal–Labour relations. The two parties have been in very different proximity to each other at different times. No simplistic schema is ever going to perfectly describe and delineate how this relationship has evolved over time, but I have suggested that it makes sense to break up the past 120 years into eight separate periods: 1903–14, 1914–31, 1931–56, 1956–74, 1974–79, 1979–92, 1992–99 and 1999–2019.

During some of these periods, the two parties have been closely aligned and the scope for co-operation has been great. The outstanding examples of this proximity would be 1903–14 and 1992–99. At other times, the two parties have been far apart in their policies and strategies, and the scope for and degree of actual co-operation has been very limited. The periods of 1931–56 and 1979–92 are the best examples of this.

In Appendix 2, I have attempted to provide a simple measure of the enablers of Lib–Lab cross-party co-operation for each of these eight periods, using five measures that seem to have been particularly important since 1903. These are: the degree of policy and ideological alignment between the two parties; the political strategies of the parties and their willingness to co-operate rather than compete; the size of governing majority of the larger party when in power; the size and therefore 'clout' of the smaller party; and the willingness of the larger party to embrace or at least consider electoral reform.

The reason for the selection of the first two of these is rather obvious. It is easier for parties to work together when their policies and ideologies are more aligned and when their political strategies include co-operating with each other rather than intense competition.

The third 'enabler' relates to the size of the governing party's majority. I have determined this to mean that when the larger party has a small majority or is in a minority position, it is more likely to be inclined to co-operate with the smaller party. The evidence of the past 120 years seems to support this conclusion. But it is worth noting that to the extent that co-operation over time may be linked to ability to deliver electoral reform, a small majority or no majority might tend to make this more difficult to deliver in Parliament.

The fourth enabler is the size and clout of the smaller party. Of course, it is possible that a very small party could still exercise a lot of power in a hung parliament, but on balance a larger party is more likely to have influence and is more likely to be able to deliver meaningful concessions, which are themselves a likely driver of co-operation.

The final enabler is the willingness of the larger party to embrace electoral reform, and we can see from the post-1922 period that this has usually been a key demand of the smaller party.

Some of those consulted during the writing of this book have suggested a sixth enabler – the relations between the party leaders. It is tempting to include this additional factor, and there is a strong case for believing this was important in the 1992–99 period, when Tony Blair and Paddy Ashdown were working closely together and seemed to like and respect each other.

But when we look at other key periods, including 1929–31 and 1977–78, it seems less convincing that this should be considered a key enabler. Ramsay MacDonald intensely disliked Lloyd George but still came very close to delivering him AV. And although David Steel and Jim Callaghan grew to like and trust each other over the course of the Lib–Lab Pact, this was not so much the case when the pact was formed, when Callaghan initially felt that he would get along better with the Ulster Unionists. Ultimately, party policy, strategy, self-interest and electoral strength are likely to prove more powerful than personal relations, though that is not to suggest these are unimportant.

What this simple schema serves to highlight is that there have only been two periods of time, of these eight, that were highly conducive to Liberal–Labour co-operation. These were 1903–14 and 1992–99. There was also a small sub-period, 1929–31, when the stars were broadly aligned. So, in the 116 years covered by this book, only twenty years presented highly favourable circumstances for

Lib–Lab co-operation – and eleven of these were when the Liberals were the larger party.

In 1903–14, Labour had not yet fully developed its socialistic policy agenda, nor had it adopted its Clause IV commitment to nationalisation, which created such a significant dividing line with a liberal party. Instead, the Labour Party was a mixture of pragmatic trade unionists and more radical socialists. Meanwhile, the 'New Liberalism' of Lloyd George and others, combined with the major policy issues of 1903–14 – free trade, progressive taxation, pensions, Home Rule, Lords reform, social reform – meant that there was a significant overlap between the Labour and Liberal programmes.

The two parties had also decided in 1903 and until the First World War, rightly or wrongly for their long-term interests (we shall return to this issue), that they had an interest in working together to defeat the Unionists at a constituency level. The Liberals had done badly in four general elections in a row and felt they needed allies. The two parties co-operated closely in Parliament, with Labour MPs even sitting on the government benches after 1910.

Co-operation was facilitated by two other factors in our schema – that in 1910 the Liberals had lost their majority and needed Labour support, and that the size of the smaller party (thirty to fifty MPs) was material and of real value to the Liberal government.

Only the lack of commitment to electoral reform from the larger party (then the Liberals) fails our five tests of the enablers of Lib–Lab co-operation, but this was less of an issue at a time when Labour was in any case split on the merits of changing the electoral system and generally saw MacDonald/Gladstone-type arrangements as the means of achieving a parliamentary breakthrough.

Had the First World War not intervened, it seems likely that the two parties would have fought the next election with some continuing form of constituency pact, and there were even approaches from senior Liberals over 1911–14 suggesting to Labour a post-election coalition or partnership.

In 1992–99, there was also huge potential for the two parties to work together. Labour had, by 1992, lost four general elections in a row and was moving back to the centre ground to maximise its electoral appeal. It was also actively considering whether it would need to forge an alliance with the Liberal Democrats to get back into power. By 1995, Tony Blair had dropped Labour's Clause IV commitment to public ownership and had moved the party away from its past socialist agenda. In the 1997 general election, the Liberal Democrats and Labour presented highly aligned policy platforms. Both Blair and Ashdown were keen on co-operation, and Blair set out explicitly to bring the two parties together, even contemplating merger. The size of the smaller party (now, of course, the Lib Dems) was sufficient to be of potential importance in any hung parliament scenarios, and Labour had been willing from 1990 onwards to consider voting reform, though this was always more likely to be limited to AV or SV, rather than STV/PR.

This means that all the key enablers of Lib–Lab co-operation were flashing green during 1992–99, except for one – the size of the majority in Parliament achieved by the larger party. The 1997 election handed Blair a huge majority of 179, and this was still 167 after the next election in 2001. The two parties did co-operate closely on the constitutional reform agenda, including introducing PR systems for Europe, Scotland and Wales, and London. But there was no Westminster coalition and no voting reform, and the culprit was predominantly the size of Blair's majority.

By contrast, in Scotland in 1999, all the enablers of co-operation were flashing 'green' and it is unsurprising in this context that there was a long-lasting and successful Lib–Lab coalition government.

If we look at the other six periods of Liberal–Labour relations since 1903, we can see that all of them were in multiple respects not conducive to co-operation.

The period 1979–92 emerges clearly as the least favourable and aligned period for Lib–Labbery. Labour had moved sharply to the left on economic policies, including nationalisation, and was anti-European. The two parties were therefore not aligned on policy, and far from having any willingness to work together, they were fighting each other for the right to be the main challenger to the Conservatives. Labour was wholly opposed to PR and was out of power, while with just twenty-two to twenty-three MPs, the Liberals/Alliance lacked the size to have real clout at Westminster. Not a single enabler of co-operation was showing 'green'.

1931–56 emerges as the second least likely period for co-operation. Labour had moved left after the collapse of its second minority administration and following MacDonald's departure to lead a National Government. It was now advocating a major programme of nationalisation and state involvement in the economy, which was anathema to most Liberals. Neither Labour nor the Liberals were keen to co-operate with the other, and Labour had no interest in electoral reform. While the Liberals were large enough to have some limited influence and value in 1931, by 1935, the official Liberals had only twenty-one MPs. This had fallen to twelve by 1945 and to six by 1951. It is indeed notable that during this period what cross-party co-operation existed was more between the Conservatives and Liberals than between Labour and the Liberals. Many Liberals MPs were reliant for their survival on the Conservatives not standing candidates in their seats. And from 1946 to 1951, Churchill was seeking to persuade the Liberals to enter first an electoral pact and then a coalition. This was, then, another period when all the 'enablers' were on red.

The periods 1956–74 and 1974–79 were arguably quite similar in relation to the enablers of co-operation. In both periods, the Liberals were relatively keen to work with Labour, but Labour wanted to follow a separate course as far as it could. While both parties had some overlapping agendas, not least in relation to social policy, there were major divergences on issues such as nationalisation and Europe. And in both periods, Labour was an unsettled coalition of socialists and social democrats, with Liberal proximity only to the latter grouping. In neither period was Labour enthusiastic about voting reform, and throughout this time the Liberal grouping was very small – with between six and fourteen MPs. The only positive enabler of co-operation in both periods was the size of Labour's majority. This was very small in 1964 and October 1974; and in both February 1974 and from early 1977 Labour was in a minority situation. It was the minority position of 1977–79, combined with Steel's determination to have influence in government, that delivered the Lib–Lab Pact. But it is notable that this pact took place when most enablers of co-operation were on red or amber at best, and this gives us a strong indication of why the pact was not a success for the Liberals, and indeed why it was likely a mistake.

This leaves us with just two periods to consider, and these periods of years are less homogenous in relation to the 'enablers' than the other six periods we have so far considered. The enablers varied at times over each period.

The period 1999–2019 was not hugely conducive to co-operation, but for varying reasons. From 1999 to 2010, the parties had both lost interest in co-operation after the failure of the Blair–Ashdown project and the lack of movement on electoral reform. The war in Iraq also divided the Lib Dems from Labour. The Lib Dem Parliamentary Party was of adequate size to be influential, but Labour continued to conclude that their majority was large enough not to need the Liberals, until it was too late. By 2010, however, four of the enablers had moved to green (not least because of Gordon Brown's sudden conversion to the cause of AV), but the fifth one (size of the Labour majority) was red – Labour had not only lost its majority but could not assemble one even with the addition of the Lib Dems. From 2015 to 2019, Labour was led by Jeremy Corbyn, its most left-wing leader ever, and during this period all the enablers were very firmly on red.

This leaves us only with the period of 1914–31 – the period of political flux in which the Liberals were imploding and Labour was emerging as the main challenger to the Conservatives. In this period, neither Labour nor the Liberals saw each other as ideological allies. They were both competing to try to knock out the other. Following the new 1918 Labour Party constitution, Labour was moving to the left and evolving as a socialist party, committed to some measure of public ownership. But MacDonald and his Chancellor, Snowden, were still seeking to pursue a relatively moderate policy course, in part to persuade the electorate to trust them. The parties were therefore not aligned on policy and ideology, but it was not as difficult to work together on common programmes as it was later to become. The Liberals were now (for most of the period) the smaller party, but they had more than enough MPs to be influential. Where the enablers were clearly flashing green was on the size of Labour's majority – in both 1923–24 and 1929–31 it was in a minority position and desperately needed Liberal support. And though Labour was not enthusiastic about electoral reform, it was willing to be pragmatic and by 1931 had pushed an AV Bill through the House of Commons. Had the government not collapsed over the economic crisis, it is possible that the Liberals and Labour would have worked together in government for a couple of years and that the electoral system would have been changed (to AV). But it was not to be and we can now only speculate on the long-term consequences.

This broad-brush review of the enablers of Lib–Lab co-operation over the past 120 years leads us to several interesting conclusions.

The first is that for only two (and a bit – 1929–31) periods of twenty years in total (out of 116 years) have most of the enablers of co-operation been in place. For most of the period 1918–92, and 2015–19, the parties had major issues of ideology and policy dividing them – not always to the extent of making co-operation impossible, but enough to make working in government difficult or at times impossible.

For most of the periods from 1914 to 1956, 1979 to 1992 and 2015 to 2019, the two parties were also unwilling to work together for strategic reasons – either because of intense competition with each other or for other reasons (including the reliance of many Liberals on informal local Conservative support up to the late 1950s).

For most of the 116 years, too, the larger party was not interested in or was actively opposed to electoral reform. And from 1935 to around 1997, and then from 2010 to 2019, the Liberals/Lib Dems had so few seats that they had limited real clout at Westminster (stuck with between six MPs and twenty-four MPs over this whole period). After 1931, it was only from 1997 to 2015 that the Lib Dems had a solid block of MPs (between forty-six and sixty-two) that would give them more chance of securing a hung parliament and more clout with which to press for electoral reform.

There have also only been limited numbers of years when the larger of the two parties has needed the smaller party to deliver either an outright majority or a comfortable workable majority. This would include: 1910–15, 1923–24, 1929–31, 1950–51, 1964–66, 1974–79. That is only sixteen years out of 116 years.

Having considered the extent to which the two parties were well or badly placed to co-operate over the period 1903–2019, we now conclude by considering the three main means through which that co-operation might be delivered: electoral deals in particular seats ('seats deals'); pacts and coalitions between parties at Westminster; and voting reform. What does the history of the period since 1903 tell us about each?

We start with seats deals, which is where the whole Lib–Lab co-operation story began in 1903 in the Gladstone–MacDonald 'Hospital Pact'. In considering seats deals, we include both those made at a national level, like the 1903 pact, and those struck at more local levels. What are the merits and risks of these types of arrangement?

The last Liberal seat pacts – the results of local arrangements with Conservatives in Bolton and Huddersfield – ended in the early 1960s, and since then the Liberals and Lib Dems have been very sniffy about returning to any arrangement that involves candidates standing down to give another party a free run (with the exception of the need to divide up seats between the Liberals and SDP during the Alliance period).

Tony Blair suggested to Paddy Ashdown in both 1995 and 1998 the possibility of standing down Labour candidates in south-west England, to allow the Lib Dems a straight fight against the Conservatives. Interestingly, George Osborne also floated with the Lib Dems in 2012 a 'coupon election' arrangement for 2015, in which the Lib Dems and Conservatives would have stood down for each other in certain key seats, presumably as part of a 'continuing coalition' offer to voters.[1]

Paddy Ashdown rejected the Blair proposals, perhaps fearing the signal about Lib Dem independence that this would convey,

but also citing the painful local experience of trying to get Liberal/
SDP candidates to stand down in each other's favour in the period
1982–87.

Steel was also, in his memoirs, dismissive about local 'Seats Pacts',
seeing these as anti-democratic and difficult for leaders to manage
or impose.

In some ways, however, it is ironic that the Lib Dems have been
so sceptical of the value of arrangements in which one party stands
down its candidates to give another a 'free run'. Thorpe was absolutely scathing about the 1903 MacDonald–Gladstone Pact, seeing it
as 'an act of uncalled for electoral generosity unforgivable in a Chief
Whip' – an arrangement which let in around thirty Labour MPs
who might not otherwise have been elected.[2] And as we have seen,
the 1903 deal seemed to have been notably successful in 1906, in
delivering a huge Liberal majority based on a relatively modest lead
in the polls. It was also clearly of huge benefit to the smaller party
of the time – allowing a breakthrough for Labour. If seats deals are
such a terrible idea, how is it that they were so successful in 1906
and so valuable for Labour?

Of course, in the longer run, Gladstone–MacDonald almost certainly damaged the Liberal Party but that rather underlines that in certain conditions 'Seats Pacts' can be rather good for at least the smaller
party. And in the period from 1931 to 1956 there is much evidence that
the Liberals only survived at all in Parliament through informal or
formal deals where they were allowed an unchallenged run by the
Conservatives, in certain seats. By the time Grimond was elected Liberal leader in 1956, he was the only one of the six Liberal MPs who had
won his seat at the previous election in a three-cornered fight.

However, the experience of the period since 1903 also serves
to highlight the risks around seats deals being used as a basis for

cross-party co-operation, even in the limited periods where support for this exists.

The circumstances in 1903 (and in the subsequent elections in 1906 and 1910) were a little different from today. The Liberals had failed to field candidates in many constituencies in 1900, so in many of the designated LRC seats the party was not needing to ask existing Liberal candidates to stand aside. Many constituencies also elected two MPs, so it may have been easier to do deals where the parties stood a candidate each. And there were already so called 'Lib–Lab' MPs, so the difficulty in getting local parties to allow LRC candidates a straight fight, and the challenges of getting Liberal voters to support them, were not as great as today. And because the LRC was such a small party in 1903, the seats deal was a less sensitive issue at a national level than such a pact would be today. There is also much evidence that the Liberal and LRC voters were highly aligned and willing to vote for the other party's candidates, so the seats deals in 1906–10 did not appear to drive a significant number of voters into the Unionist political camp.

Meanwhile, the dependence of the Liberal Party on formal and informal deals with Conservatives from the 1920s onwards was not a sign of party strength and good tactics but of weakness. And it must have made many potential Liberal voters and supporters conclude that they needed to choose between one of the other 'major' parties rather than backing candidates of a small party which was being sustained on the life support machine provided by a competitor.

In the 1990s, Paddy Ashdown rejected the possibility of seats deals because he saw them as difficult to deliver, threatening perceived party independence and probably as rather undemocratic. He was also being advised that too great a proximity to Labour might drive wavering former Conservative voters back into that party's fold. Clem Davies was also tempted by seats deals in the

1950s but concerned that these would be too difficult to impose on local Liberal parties.

And the proposal made by George Osborne over a coupon election in 2015 was never going to be acceptable to Nick Clegg or his party, as they judged that getting any closer to the Conservatives would be too damaging to their long-term interests and unacceptable given the growing range of difficult issues that were separating the two parties, including over Britain's role in the European Union, constitutional change, the environment and social policy.

For all these reasons, and despite the example of 1903, seats deals seem unlikely to be a major part of any Lib Dem–Labour co-operation in the future. They can be effective under some circumstances, but there are significant risks both in successfully delivering them and if they undermine the perceived party independence and drive potential swing voters away. They are clearly more likely to work where there is a willingness of voters to unite to defeat one very unpopular party, but under these circumstances, tactical voting is likely to take place anyway, without the need to stand down candidates of one party.

The second issue to consider is the consequences and impact of the Westminster and other national co-operation that the parties have engaged in at different times over the past 120 years. This includes the Lib–Lab co-operation of 1906–14; the minority Labour governments of 1923–24 and 1929–31; the Lib–Lab Pact of 1977–78; the experiences of Westminster co-operation from 1994 to 1999; the Scottish and Welsh coalitions of 1999–2007 and 2000–01 respectively; and the 2010–15 Lib–Con coalition.

Here, the conclusion is clear. In a First Past the Post system, the smaller party's proximity to another larger party in Westminster government is damaging for that smaller party.

Labour was not, of course, in any formal governing arrangement or coalition between 1906 and 1914, but it was seen as being relatively closely aligned to the Liberals, and its seat numbers fell modestly from 1906 to 1910, taking into account the Lib–Lab MPs who joined between the two elections.

In 1923, the Liberals put the first minority Labour government into power and gave it some support until 1924. This was highly damaging, and the Liberals lost 118 seats over the course of the short parliament and saw their vote almost halve from 29.7 per cent to 17.8 per cent. Although the Conservatives were the big winners from this Liberal weakness, the Labour vote share was higher in 1924 than in 1923.

The Liberals repeated this experience between 1929 and 1931, during the second minority Labour government. This time the damage to the smaller party was even greater. The vote share of the official Liberals collapsed from 23.6 per cent to 6.5 per cent, and they lost twenty-six of their fifty-nine seats. Even adding in the 3.7 per cent Liberal National vote and the 0.5 per cent for the 'Lloyd George family group' of Independent Liberals, this still amounted to the total Liberal vote more than halving between the two elections.

The party then steered clear of national pacts, deals and other arrangements until the Lib–Lab Pact of 1977–78. This had an immediate and highly unfavourable impact on the Liberal vote, which fell steeply in local elections, in Westminster by-elections and in the polls. The Liberal vote had been 18.3 per cent in the October 1974 election but fell to around 6–8 per cent over the period of the pact. Even though the pact was terminated around ten months before the May 1979 general election, the Liberal vote did not start to recover until it received an unexpected boost from a spectacular March 1979 by-election win. And in May 1979, the election vote share of 13.8 per cent was still well down on the previous result.

In the run-up to the 1997 election, there was some evidence that the close working relationship between Ashdown and Blair was damaging the Lib Dem vote and that the Lib Dem vote went up during periods where the party was critical of Labour.[3]

Meanwhile, the 2010–15 coalition saw one of the largest declines in party vote share in UK electoral history, with the Lib Dem vote in 2015 sinking from 23 per cent (in 2010) to just 7.9 per cent, and Lib Dem seats dropping from fifty-seven to just eight.

The experience of the two Lib–Lab coalitions in Scotland from 1999 to 2007 was, however, very different from the history of the coalitions, pacts and informal support at Westminster. In both 2003 and 2007, the Lib Dem vote and MSP numbers were highly resilient in the face of what was a very close and public relationship between the two parties. This raises the question of whether the Scottish Lib Dems managed their coalition more effectively than the other examples of Westminster co-operation. Is it proximity by itself that is damaging, or are there ways of working together without the smaller party suffering huge damage?

Scotland was different in several ways that may offer lessons for Westminster, but it was also different in ways that do not.

In all the Westminster arrangements involving the Liberals and Lib Dems, the economic circumstances facing the governments were either highly challenging or difficult, requiring some unpopular decisions to be made. But between 1999 and 2007, the UK government was turning on the spending taps during a benign economic period, which meant the Scottish coalition did not need to deliver the austerity of 1923–24, 1929–31, 1977–78 and 2010–15.

But as the Scottish coalition was also enabled within a PR environment, there was less 'soft' support from tactical voters from other parties to lose in Scotland and the Lib–Lab coalition in Scotland in

1999 was widely expected. Finally, and crucially, between 1999 and 2007, the Lib Dems were not in coalition at Westminster so still appeared at a UK level as an independent national party, one whose support was rising over the period in question. The rising Lib Dem UK vote, combined with Lib Dem independence at Westminster, helped the Scottish Lib Dems survive their coalition in Edinburgh.

It is worth noting that Liberal/Lib Dem losses after periods of party co-operation at Westminster have been far greater than any losses after periods of Labour government where the Liberals/Lib Dems have not been in an arrangement with Labour.

Considering the election results in 1950, 1951, 1966, 1970, October 1974, 2001, 2005 and 2010, we can see that after these periods of Labour government (without Lib–Lab co-operation or pacts) the Liberals/Lib Dems increased their vote share on five occasions, saw it hold steady once (1950) and decline by small amounts just twice (in 1951 and 1970). So, it is not the aftermath of Labour governments that has particularly damaged the Liberals/Lib Dems, it is periods of proximity to other parties in power. These periods of proximity presumably cost the party the support both of those voters who did not like the chosen partner and of those other voters who may have cast their vote as some sort of 'protest' but then found their chosen party in power or soiled by proximity to it.

Given this consistent experience of electoral damage from co-operation with other parties in Westminster government, it is not surprising that since the 1920s, the Liberals and Lib Dems have prioritised electoral reform as a condition for co-operation. This would not only give the party a fairer number of seats in Parliament but would offer some protection from the damage done by coalitions, pacts and overt co-operation with the party in government. The problem for the Liberals/Lib Dems is that, despite trying, they have not been able to make any change to the Westminster system of First Past the Post.

So, what are the lessons of 120 years of failed attempts to deliver electoral reform for Westminster? Over the long period that we are considering, the attitude of the three parties to electoral reform has been strikingly consistent. There are two forms of consistency: firstly, that parties benefiting from the electoral system tend to be not much interested in reform. This includes the pre-1918 Liberal Party, the post-1918 Labour Party (up until very recent times), and the Conservative Party – for all this time.

The second form of consistency has been over the preferred voting system. The Conservatives, not favouring change, have consistently backed the existing First Past the Post system. The Labour Party, generally not wanting too radical a change or to throw a lifeline to the Liberals, has toyed with the Alternative Vote for much of its existence. The Liberals/Liberal Democrats have consistently favoured the Single Transferable Vote and other proportional systems, since being so badly served by FPTP from the 1920s onwards.

Before the First World War, it was Labour that was keenest on reform, though the party always found it a divisive issue. The Alternative Vote was of particular interest to many in Labour, as it seemed to offer another way of working tactically with the Liberals to keep the Unionists out. Switching to AV would mean less need for 1903-type deals, and voters could simply use their second preferences to favour the other party over the Unionists.

By the 1920s, Labour was losing interest in electoral reform. It was the struggling Liberals who now embraced the cause. But from the earliest days, the Liberals did not favour AV. Instead, they backed PR.

The left wing of the Labour Party was very briefly keen on PR – seeing it as a way of breaking free of the need to co-operate with the Liberals. But from the 1920s onwards, this enthusiasm turned to scepticism. Labour was thriving now under FPTP, and even AV seemed to some in Labour to risk leading back to more deals and compromise with one of the two 'capitalist' parties. Some on the left of Labour feared that AV might even facilitate Liberal–Conservative co-operation, which is not implausible in the context of developments in the period from the 1920s to the mid 1950s.

Electoral reform was pushed by Liberals during the short-lived Labour minority government of 1923–24, but there was neither the time to address the issue nor sufficient willingness amongst Labour MPs. But from 1929 to 1931, with a second Labour minority government in power, the issue came back onto the agenda. Labour needed the Liberals. The Liberals needed electoral reform. Both parties had made the reduction of unemployment through government-inspired schemes a key part of their manifestos. And the combined Lab–Lib majority would be enough to survive the odd rebel or defector. In the entire period from 1903 to 2019, there may have been no better opportunity to secure electoral reform. Except there were still multiple problems. MacDonald, quite rightly, did not trust Lloyd George. Labour was deeply divided over electoral reform and took some time even to conclude that it might need to be conceded.

In 1931, AV passed with a majority in the Commons. But it was delayed in the Lords and the Bill was lost when Ramsay MacDonald's administration collapsed and was replaced by the National Government. We can now only speculate on whether AV would finally have been delivered in 1931 or 1932, had the Labour government survived, and if so how this might have changed the future shape of politics in the UK.

In 1951 and 1974, the Liberal Party was offered a coalition by two Conservative Prime Ministers – Churchill and Heath. But neither was willing to offer electoral reform, and the Liberals therefore remained on the opposition benches.

By 1977, David Steel was negotiating a pact to sustain the Labour government, but Labour was so unenthusiastic about PR that the issue of Westminster voting reform does not even appear to have been discussed. Steel instead prioritised PR for direct elections to Europe and for devolved governments in Scotland and Wales. But Labour was divided even on conceding this more limited offer on reform, and ultimately there were large majorities in Parliament against PR.

After the Conservatives' third successive election victory in 1987, interest within Labour in electoral reform grew. Raymond Plant would have backed a proportionate system, including Additional Members, but the leadership intervened to block this and go for the much more limited option of the Supplementary Vote – and a referendum, which was designed to paper over Labour divisions.

Tony Blair's arrival as Labour leader in 1994 marked the beginning of the closest Lib–Lab relationship in history. Blair wanted to 'reunite' the centre-left, but the problem was that Ashdown and Blair had very different visions. In Blair's, the two parties would work increasingly closely together, including in coalition. They would then eventually merge. Ashdown did not rule this out in the long term. But what he argued for was pluralism. His price for co-operation was PR, without which his party would not agree to coalition.

But Blair was never convinced by PR. Initially, he saw it as a distraction from making Labour more 'modern' and electable. But he was also worried that it would reduce his power and be difficult to get through his party. He was also concerned that if the Lib Dems were granted PR, they might go off and forge alliances with other parties. And in 1997, Blair won by such a landslide that PR would have required him to ask many Labour MPs to give up their jobs. Why would they do this? The answer is they would not. And Blair was obsessed with winning and holding power. He was not in the business of giving it away.

It was in 1996 and 1997 that Blair needed to be very honest with Ashdown that he would only ever deliver on AV. Instead, he gave Ashdown the impression that he might support AV Plus – a semi-proportionate system that Ashdown and the Lib Dems were much more likely to favour than pure AV. Ashdown cannot in these circumstances be criticised for pursuing the more proportionate AV Plus system, and he was pragmatic enough to agree to deliver this over two general elections – AV in 2001, and the AMS top-up at the following election.

But Blair was insufficiently candid with both Jenkins and Ashdown about what he might support, and Jenkins was naive in proposing first an undeliverable mix of STV and AV and then a final proposal that would take two parliaments to deliver and required a major system upheaval of the kind which is never popular with incumbent MPs. By the time Ashdown realised that AV was probably all that was deliverable, it was too late, and even Jenkins had publicly ruled out that more limited change.

With the benefit of hindsight, the Lib Dems made a mistake in failing to accept AV in 1997, as a stepping stone to full PR. But it is difficult to be critical of Ashdown. Most in his party, including some of his closest advisers, were telling him he needed to secure PR, not just AV. Some argued that only PR would deliver them into government, while AV would simply allow Blair a bigger majority to govern alone. Ashdown's problem was that Blair did not really think through his own position until it was too late – and in the meantime, he allowed Ashdown to think that AV Plus might be deliverable. It would therefore have made no sense for Ashdown to have given up on that possibility.

A more candid Blair, and a more realistic and less ambitious Ashdown, might have delivered AV in 1998–99, but the moment was lost. By the time the Lib Dems had realised their mistake in rejecting AV as a staging post, and by the time Labour had woken up to its likely loss of power in 2010, the ability of Labour to deliver change had also disappeared. Gordon Brown's conversion to the AV cause came much too late, and by the time the Lib Dems and Labour sat down in May 2010 to discuss the matter, Labour had lost its majority and even combined with all the Lib Dem MPs would not have had a majority in Parliament.

Had Blair and Brown delivered AV by 2010, the result would still have been a hung parliament, but this would almost certainly have resulted in a Lib–Lab coalition, with Brown replaced as Prime Minister by a new Labour leader.

Thus it was that in 2011, the first referendum on electoral reform was granted during a Conservative–Lib Dem coalition, by a Conservative Prime Minister. But though the Lib Dems had made enormous efforts to secure the referendum, they had not adequately worked out whether it would be deliverable. Their much larger coalition partners were strongly opposing change – and probably would have done, whatever guarantees Clegg had extracted from Cameron during the coalition talks. And Labour now had little incentive to expend political effort on a change that might in the short term enable Lib Dem–Conservative co-operation rather than Lib–Lab working.

The referendum was always, therefore, going to be very difficult, if not impossible, to win in the context of 2011, and once lost it exposed the Lib Dems to huge risk at the subsequent general election.

The only blessing for the Lib Dems turned out to be that it was AV and not a proportional system that was rejected.

What next? Well, the Blair–Ashdown era was far from a complete failure as far as electoral reform is concerned. During this period, PR was introduced for elections to the European Parliament, the new Scottish Parliament, the Welsh Assembly and for London government. It is possible that without the close Ashdown–Blair relationship, PR at least for Europe would not have been implemented. But what of Westminster?

One reflection on the history of electoral reform for Westminster is that since the early 1990s, there has been an assumption that this would be delivered after endorsement in a referendum. But it is worth noting that referendums on voting reforms were not held for Scotland, Wales, Europe or London government. Indeed, the driving force for a referendum was always the division in the Labour Party, which the referendum pledge has been used to help paper over. When the issue of using a referendum to make a change in Westminster voting was considered by the Plant Commission, it was rejected.

If a change in voting systems could be properly considered and then agreed upon by one, two or more parties, this proposed change might be inserted as a clear manifesto pledge, and electoral endorsement could be secured through a general election – by either a majority government or by two or more coalition parties securing endorsement for the same system. Public endorsement through either a general election or referendum seems highly desirable and necessary, though the 2019–24 Conservative government used a clause in the 2022 Elections Act to change the voting system for Mayors from the Supplementary Vote to FPTP, without any such public endorsement. It is possible that in the future, the Labour Party may have a clearer and more consistent position on electoral reform, and indeed the 2022 Labour conference saw the party vote to endorse a move to a proportional system, while retaining the constituency link, for the first time.

Another reflection from recent political history relates to the 'base' system for a more proportionate voting system. It seems unlikely that the constituency link will be dropped from the UK electoral system in favour of large STV constituencies. Support for the 'constituency link', where each area has its own local representative, seems strong. But the Jenkins Commission was split on what the system that delivers this constituency link should be, upon which proportionality might be added via 'Additional Members'.

Lord Alexander made a strong case for being wary about AV in his minority report for the Jenkins Commission. While AV had some attractions for both Labour and the Lib Dems, it would almost certainly be simpler and easier to explain to the public a system such as that now used in Scotland and Wales, where FPTP is used to elect constituency MPs, with a 'top-up' of Additional Members to deliver some element of proportionality. And the top-up could be set at a level that would allow majority governments to emerge on the types of vote shares that have tended to lead to majority governments in the past – i.e., 40–45 per cent vote shares, rather than 50 per cent plus.

First Past the Post has the benefit of being (largely) understood by the electorate and is generally supported by most MPs. So, for the most passionate supporters of PR, the benefit of 2011 might appear to be that it has reduced the probability of change to a non-proportional system. These advocates of PR concluded after 2011 that if voting reform ever comes to Westminster, it now seems more likely to be based on a system such as that already used in Scotland and Wales – essentially, FPTP with a modest Additional Member top-up. Whether this conclusion will survive the results of the July 2024 general election, we will consider later.

For much of the past 120 years, the Liberal/Lib Dem and Labour Parties have lacked the key ingredients and enablers to cause them to work together: sufficient alignment on policy and ideology, sufficient proximity of party strategies, the parliamentary arithmetic needed to induce them to work across party lines, the clout and value of the smaller party and the protective blanket of electoral reform or some other mechanism to allow the smaller party to work with the larger without being smothered by it.

But another lesson of the past 120 years is that Labour and the Liberal Democrats have much in common in their value systems, their internationalism, their support for social reform to protect and benefit the more disadvantaged in society, their backing for constitutional reform, their environmental commitments and their respect for personal freedoms and liberties.

Given the Lib Dems' painful experience of informal co-operation, pacts and coalitions, it possible that they will now prioritise independence for as long as it takes to secure a change to a fairer and more proportional system of voting, and until the five enablers of co-operation with Labour are all, or mostly, flashing green. And so will the history and lessons of the past 120 years help shape our politics in the century ahead.

POSTSCRIPT: THE 'LOVELESS LANDSLIDE' OF JULY 2024

When this book was written, it seemed likely that a general election would be held in the autumn of 2024. The results of this would have been available too late to be included here.

But the Prime Minister, to the surprise of his party, the press and political commentators, decided to opt for an early election, and that resulted in what one commentator has described as the 'Loveless Landslide' of July 2024 – a very apt description.

The 2024 general election delivered one of the most dramatic outcomes of any election in UK political history. Many voters were disillusioned and angry with the government and this led to the worst ever general election defeat experienced by the Conservative Party. A parliament of political chaos, with three Prime Ministers and acute economic pain (some of it inflicted very obviously by the short-lived government of Liz Truss) led to voters ruthlessly sweeping away a tired party that had been in power for fourteen years.

The Conservatives lost two-thirds (251) of their seats and were reduced to 121 MPs – fewer even than the 156 of 1906. But in 1906 the Conservative Party still secured 43.4 per cent of the national vote. In 2024, the Conservatives managed a feeble 23.7 per cent – by a considerable margin their worst ever outcome.

Labour was the biggest beneficiary of the Conservative implosion – being returned with a mighty 411 MPs, just under the number achieved by Tony Blair in 1997 (418). But in 1997, Blair banked 43.2 per cent of the national vote. In 2024, Labour achieved just 33.7 per cent – the lowest ever vote share for a majority government. The conclusion is that 2024 witnessed a 'Loveless Landslide' – the election was much more a rejection of the Conservatives than a vote of enthusiasm for Labour. Only in Scotland was there a significant increase in the Labour vote, where the SNP also imploded, losing 80 per cent of their seats and being reduced to just nine MPs.

The Lib Dems were the other big winners from the 2024 election. In 2015, it looked like the coalition might have killed off their prospects for a generation. But, surprising even themselves, the Lib Dems secured seventy-two MPs, their best result for 100 years. Across the south and south-west in particular, the Lib Dems swept away scores of Conservatives, overturning mighty majorities to deliver what might even look like 'safe' Lib Dem seats. The Lib Dems achieved this extraordinary success on just over 12 per cent of the national vote.

In July 2024, Labour won 211 extra seats with just 1.7 per cent more of the vote than in 2019, and the Lib Dems gained sixty-three more MPs for an additional 0.6 per cent of the vote.

What on the earth happened to explain this bizarre outcome?

The big vote gainer of the 2024 election was Nigel Farage's Reform UK party. Many of those who had voted Conservative in 2019 to 'get Brexit done' deserted the Tories, disillusioned by political and economic chaos, declining living standards, surging net immigration and a failing NHS. Reform UK recorded over 14 per cent of the national vote, while securing just five MPs, including Farage. The desertion of these voters helped shatter the 2019 Conservative vote, creating the Labour–Lib Dem landslide.

The other big 'winner' of 2024 was the non-voting category. The turnout of just 59.9 per cent was the second lowest of the past 140 years. Given that the previous lowest turnout of 59.4 per cent was in 2001, when the country was relatively contented after Blair's first-term Labour government, the fact that four in ten voters didn't bother voting in the context of the 'change' election of 2024 may well indicate the most worrying level of voter disengagement and disconnection from politics in the whole era of modern UK democracy.

Indeed, to the extent that the Reform UK vote can also be read in part as a rejection of the current UK political system, it seems fair to conclude that one half of the UK electorate were rejecting 'business as usual' politics by either failing to vote or backing Reform UK. This should trouble all UK political parties but is particularly a warning to the new Starmer Labour government that it must either deliver or risk further disillusion and change in 2028 or 2029, when the next general election is held.

Labour's huge total of 411 MPs should not, therefore, be regarded as any sort of guarantee of another Labour government in 2028/29. If Labour is seen to fail to deliver by the next election, it could instead face a deadly pincer movement with the Lib Dems and Greens (who secured almost 7 per cent of the vote and four MPs in 2024) attacking from the progressive left, while Reform UK scoop up votes from the right. Indeed, Reform UK is now in second place in around 100 seats, of which some ninety are Labour. In the 100 seats requiring the smallest swings for Reform UK to win, fifty-eight seats are held now by Labour. Worryingly for Starmer,

Nigel Farage has now declared that Labour will be his key target over the next few years.

What does all this mean for relations between the Labour Party and the Lib Dems in the parliament to come?

Labour has a huge majority of 174 MPs, and no need for Liberal Democrat support to secure its policy programme. The Lib Dems will remain on the opposition benches and seek to hold the new government to account. This will be much easier given the big increase in Lib Dem seats, which means (with the decline too of the SNP) that they are again back as the third major party in Parliament.

While the Lib Dems will be part of the opposition to Labour, a glance at our five 'enablers of co-operation' show many of them flashing green.

Arguably, the Lib Dem and Labour manifestos of 2024 were more convergent than at any general election since the days of the Labour Representation Committee, 120 years ago. It is difficult to find major areas of fundamental disagreement, except in relatively niche aspects (the Lib Dems did not support Labour's policy of adding VAT to private school fees), and even where parties gave a bigger billing to certain issues (Labour on employment rights and the Lib Dems on social care) it is not difficult to imagine the parties being able to accept each other's policies.

With Labour having junked old left-wing policies on large-scale nationalisation and euroscepticism, both parties have similar agendas underpinned by similar values (internationalism, support for greater equality of opportunity, a liberal attitude to human rights and personal lifestyles and strong support for green policies and tackling climate change). Policy and values convergence is therefore clearly on 'green'.

The second indicator is around willingness to co-operate rather than compete. This is also on green for now, even though the Lib Dems are in opposition to Labour. In the July 2024 election, the Lib Dems and Labour found themselves to be very much complimentary in ousting the Conservatives, with very few seats where the two parties were in contention. This enabled a good deal of tactical voting, where supporters of both parties often backed the other to enable the defeat of a Conservative MP. The Lib Dems did not defeat a single Labour MP in 2024 and of the top fifty of their 2029 target seats, thirty-nine are Conservative-held, one is SNP, and just ten are Labour. This will all have created a degree of positivity in both parties towards the other. How much this will survive a period in which the two parties are on opposite sides of the House of Commons is another matter. We have seen how over the history of the past 120 years it has been difficult for opposition parties to be in 'constructive' mode towards governments for long. They are either part of the government or they are in opposition to it. And in 2028/29, the Lib Dems will be defending many traditionally 'Conservative' seats, where any sense of alignment with Labour could be damaging, particularly if the Labour government is not a success.

Our third indicator of potential scope for co-operation seems firmly on red. This is around the size of the government majority and the extent to which the larger party may 'need' the smaller party. Labour has an immense majority, which appears to make the need for co-operation now or in the near future quite slight. But we have been through a period of extraordinary electoral volatility, and with Labour having secured a miserable 33.7 per cent of the vote (particularly feeble in the political context of 2024), they cannot take for granted that Lib Dem support will not be needed beyond the period of the next general election. This indicator should therefore be evaluated as red/amber in the current context.

Indicator four is flashing green. This is the size and clout of the smaller party. With seventy-two MPs, the Lib Dems have a stronger parliamentary presence than for 100 years. They have real potential clout and are less easy to ignore.

The final indicator is that crucial one of enthusiasm for electoral reform – generally the demand of the smaller party over the lifetime of Liberal/Lib Dem–Labour relations.

The Lib Dems remain committed to electoral reform, even though in the context of 2024 this would hardly have made a difference to them. Their 12.2 per cent of the vote would have produced seventy-nine seats in a pure PR system, versus the seventy-two they secured. But for the Lib Dems, electoral reform is about both securing fairer outcomes in the future and – crucially – about offering protection from the vagaries of FPTP if they are ever again in coalitions.

What is Labour's likely attitude to PR now? The policy was not included in their 2024 election manifesto, despite the recent decision of the Labour Party conference to back PR.

The election result of 2024 seems, on the face of it, to flash very red indeed for the prospects of PR. The election produced (other than for the Lib Dems) one of the most disproportionate outcomes ever – but one that benefited Labour even more dramatically than the Blair landslide of 1997. This time, Labour banked 63 per cent of the MPs for just 33.7 per cent of the vote. A pure PR system would have removed 191 of those 411 seats and handed them to the other parties. Under pure PR, Reform UK would have secured ninety-three MPs, instead of five. The Greens would be on around forty-two MPs, not four. The SNP would be on sixteen, not nine. And the Conservatives would have 154 MPs, not 121.

It seems difficult to believe that Labour will be enthusiastic about change to a system that would have handed so many of its present total of seats to other parties – including Reform UK, which could be a deadly future competitor. It has ever been thus. The problem delivering electoral reform is that it is tough to do without a big majority but seems unappealing to a winning party when it has just benefited from the occasional largesse that FPTP offers.

But for this very reason, Labour might be unwise to take a short-term view of the case for electoral reform. That was the mistake made from 1997 to around 2009, by when it was too late to deliver the change, which might have prevented Labour's loss of power in 2010.

Labour's majority in 2024 looks large but is very shallow. With just 33.7 per cent of the vote, they have little buffer. Just a small decline in support, or upswing in the Conservative vote, could quickly wipe away their majority, however huge it now looks.

The Labour government faces two immediate challenges. The most important and pressing is how it persuades a sceptical electorate that it really can make a difference and meet the many challenges that the country faces. Can it convert the 'Loveless Landslide' into a parliament of real progress and delivery? Can it therefore at the next election hold its existing support, avoid a loss of votes to its five major competitors and start to motivate and re-engage with the 40 per cent of voters who didn't bother to support any party in 2024? Can it also win over some of those who backed Reform UK and who might once have been considered natural Labour voters?

The second question is how can Labour work with others who have similar values and policies? Over the past 100 years, the right in British politics has been represented by the Conservative Party, which has been highly successful in holding power. The shattering of the right in 2024 helped remove the Conservatives from power, though it is far too simplistic to view all those who voted Reform UK in 2024 as right-wing voters. Over the parliament ahead, the Conservative Party will likely be preoccupied with considering how it can rebuild its alliance of right voters – and it is too early to know how or whether this can be done.

It is for those in the Labour Party and the Lib Dems to consider now if and how the centre and left of politics can create its own alliances and co-operation over the years ahead. For much of the past 120 years, as we have seen, such a question might have made little sense. For long periods before the 1960s, and indeed in the 1970s and 1980s, the Liberal Party was as far distant from Labour as it was from the Conservatives. From the vantage point of 2024, though, these two parties look much more natural potential partners than enemies. But in the short term, Labour may be tempted to stick with the electoral system that has just delivered them an outsize majority and denied much representation to Reform UK. And the Lib Dem leadership has good reason to be cautious of getting too close to a Labour Party that isn't traditionally popular in the seats the Lib Dems have just taken from the Conservatives.

Will these two parties, with much in common today in terms of policies and values, remain competitors, pulled apart by electoral interests?

Or will leaders in both parties find the keys, the practical mechanisms, for unlocking the door of partnership that seems currently sealed shut by an electoral system that tends to embed division and political partisanship, rather than co-operation? To this question, the history of the past 120 years offers clues but no certainty.

APPENDIX 1: KEY LANDMARKS IN LIB–LAB RELATIONS

January 1874: First Lib–Lab MPs elected.

July 1892: First three Independent Labour Party MPs elected.

May 1894: Ramsay MacDonald refused selection as a Liberal parliamentary candidate; stands instead for ILP.

August 1895: All twenty-eight ILP candidates defeated in the general election.

February 1900: Labour Representation Committee (LRC) formed.

October 1900: Two LRC MPs elected in the general election.

July 1903: LRC wins the Barnard Castle by-election – securing its first seat against both Liberal and Unionist candidates, while receiving some Liberal support.

September 1903: MacDonald–Gladstone 'Hospital Pact' agrees to give the LRC a straight fight with the Unionists in around thirty seats, with no Liberal candidates.

February 1906: Twenty-nine LRC MPs elected, including Ramsay MacDonald in Leicester. Labour group formed in Parliament.

1909: Lib–Lab MPs join Labour group in Parliament.

January 1910: General election results in a decline in Labour MPs from forty-six to forty. Labour group moves across to take up seats on government benches.

Autumn 1911–Summer 2012: Ramsay MacDonald receives approaches from senior Liberals over possible future Lib–Lab coalition.

March 1914: Lloyd George offers Ramsay MacDonald a new Lib–Lab election pact, including a post-election policy programme, on behalf of the 'Inner Cabinet'.

May 1915: Labour joins Asquith's coalition government.

December 1916: Labour joins Lloyd George's coalition.

1918: Labour adopts new Party Constitution, including Clause IV commitment to public ownership.

December 1918: General election sees the end of organised Lib–Lab co-operation in key seats.

January 1924: Liberal MPs enable the formation of the first (minority) Labour government under Ramsay MacDonald.

May 1924: Labour Cabinet gives support to a Liberal Bill on PR, but Labour MPs insist on a free vote.

July 1929: Second Labour minority government includes the prospect of electoral reform in the King's Speech.

December 1929: Ramsay MacDonald establishes the Ullswater Conference to consider electoral reform.

March 1930: Labour Cabinet agrees to back an Electoral Reform Bill.

September 1930: Labour Cabinet agrees to offer the Liberals support for AV.

June 1931: AV Bill passes the Commons stages.

August 1931: Labour government collapses, coalition formed.

1950–51: Churchill offers Lib–Lab pacts in up to sixty constituencies.

October 1951: Churchill offers Liberals a coalition, but this is rejected over lack of electoral reform.

November 1956: Jo Grimond elected Liberal leader, adopts strategy of seeking realignment of centre-left by working with Labour.

November 1960: Liberals stand a candidate in Bolton East by-election, effectively ending long-running Lib–Con pacts in Bolton and Huddersfield and restoring Liberal independence.

May 1964: Harold Wilson proposes a Speaker's Conference to consider electoral reform.

February 1974: Hung parliament, Liberals reject Heath coalition offer over lack of electoral reform.

March 1977: Lib–Lab Pact to sustain Labour in office.

December 1977: Majority of Labour MPs fail to support PR for direct elections to the European Parliament, a key plank of the Lib–Lab Pact.

July 1978: Lib–Lab Pact ends.

March 1981: Foundation of the SDP and beginning of Alliance attempt to replace Labour as the main opposition party.

June 1983: SDP–Liberal Alliance wins only twenty-three seats in general election against Labour's 209 and misses the opportunity to replace Labour.

October 1990: Labour votes to establish the Plant Commission to consider electoral reform.

May 1992: Lib Dem leader Paddy Ashdown delivers his Chard Speech after fourth Conservative election win, proposing realignment of centre-left and co-operation with Labour.

March 1993: Plant Commission backs Supplementary Vote, after leadership pressure not to propose a more proportionate system.

April 1995: Tony Blair drops Clause IV commitment to public ownership.

November 1995: Blair suggests to Ashdown giving the Lib Dems an unopposed fight against the Conservatives in key seats in southwest England. Ashdown rejects this.

March 1996: Blair tells Ashdown he may back AV.

April 1996: Robin Cook tells Ashdown it will be difficult to move Blair beyond AV, but worth trying 'AV Plus'.

July 1996: Blair agrees privately with Ashdown to back a two-question referendum, and he is minded to support change on the first and AV on the second.

December 1996: Blair tells Ashdown it is possible he might back AV Plus.

March 1997: Cook–Maclennan Constitutional Committee reports.

May 1997: Labour manifesto promises to establish an Independent Commission on electoral reform to recommend a proportional alternative to FPTP. Blair's public position remains 'not persuaded'.

July 1997: Joint Lib–Lab Cabinet Committee announced.

March 1998: Blair and Ashdown plan November 1998 coalition, following Jenkins Report on voting reform. Blair promises to back Jenkins if his recommendations are as expected.

September 1998: Blair proposes to Ashdown not standing Labour candidates against Lib Dems in twenty key Lib Dem seats. Rejected by Ashdown.

September 1998: Blair tells Ashdown he can no longer press ahead with referendum on electoral reform or coalition.

October 1998: Jenkins Report on electoral reform is published, but with Labour distancing itself from conclusions.

May 1999: Lib–Lab coalition government formed in Scotland after first elections for the Scottish Parliament.

June 1999: First elections to the European Parliament under PR. Lib Dem seats rise from two to ten.

August 1999: Paddy Ashdown replaced by Charles Kennedy as Lib Dem leader.

October 2000: Lib Dem–Labour coalition government formed in Wales.

September 2001: Joint Cabinet Committee suspended by Kennedy/Blair.

June 2007: Gordon Brown invites Ashdown to join Labour Cabinet. Ashdown rejects this.

February 2010: Commons votes for AV referendum by 31 October 2011, as Brown seeks to keep open post-election Lib–Lab options.

April 2010: Labour manifesto promises referendum on AV by October 2011.

May 2010: Hung parliament results in Lib–Con coalition.

May 2011: AV referendum: AV rejected.

September 2015: Labour elects Jeremy Corbyn.

September 2022: Labour Party conference supports shift to PR system, while maintaining constituency links.

APPENDIX 2: KEY ENABLERS OF LIB–LAB CO-OPERATION

Code:

G = Green; enabling co-operation
A = Amber; co-operation difficult but not impossible
R = Red; co-operation made difficult

	1903–14	1914–31	1931–56	1956–74	1974–79	1979–92	1992–99	1999–2019
Policy Alignment: (Sufficient?)	G	A	R	A	R	R	G	A
Willingness: (Larger party enthusiasm?)	G	G (29/31)	R	R	G	R	G	R
Size of smaller party: (Large enough to have clout?)	G	G	R	R	R	R	G	A
Electoral reform: (Larger party prepared to consider?)	R	G (29/31)	R	R	R	R	G	R
Majority size: (Small enough to require third-party help/ insurance?)	G	G	R	G	G	R	R	R

BIBLIOGRAPHY

PRIMARY SOURCES

2010

'Liberal Democrat–Labour Party Discussions', 9 May 2010, 7.45 p.m., Labour's Proposals for Coalition. Author's records

'Heads of Agreement, Liberal Democrat–Labour Party Discussions', 9 May 2010, Liberal Democrat Proposals for Coalition. Author's records

Minutes of Liberal Democrat–Labour Coalition Talks, May 2010. Author's records

'A Partnership For Renewal', 5 May 2010, Liberal Democrat Draft Coalition Agreement. Author's records

'Post-Election Strategy: Recommendations', 16 March 2010: Advice from Danny Alexander MP, Chris Huhne MP, David Laws MP, Andrew Stunell MP to Nick Clegg MP. Author's records

1992–2000

'Rekindling the Spirit of Devolution: The First Partnership Agreement for the National Assembly of Wales', Draft 2 (February 2000). Author's records

'A Partnership for Scotland', Drafts 1–5 of the Coalition Agreement for the first Scottish Parliament (May 1999). Author's records

'Statement of Co-operation', Labour's first draft proposal for a Scottish coalition (May 1999). Author's records

Private letter to Paddy Ashdown from David Laws, Policy Director, on areas for policy co-operation with Labour, 5 November 1998

Paddy Ashdown, Liberal Democrat Conference Speech, 24 September 1998

Private letter from David Laws, Liberal Democrat Policy Director, to Paddy Ashdown MP, 25 July 1998. Author's records

Private letter from Chris Rennard, Liberal Democrat Chief Executive, to Paddy Ashdown MP, before a Blair–Ashdown meeting, March 1998. Author's records

'Maximising Distinctiveness through the Policy Review', private paper from David Laws, Policy Director, to Paddy Ashdown MP (1997)

Paddy Ashdown, 'The Chard Speech', 9 May 1992

Paddy Ashdown, Unpublished Diaries, 1990–1999

1977

National Archives, PREM16/1399, Joint Statement by the Prime Minister and the leader of the Liberal Party, 23 March 1977

National Archives, PREM 16/1399, Note of a meeting, 12.30 p.m., 22 March 1977

National Archives, PREM 16/1399, Handwritten Note, Expressing Views of Michael Foot, 22 March 1977

Books and Articles

Paul Adelman, *The Rise of the Labour Party: 1880–1945* (1996)

Paddy Ashdown, *The Ashdown Diaries Volume One: 1988–1997* (2000)

Paddy Ashdown, *The Ashdown Diaries Volume Two: 1997–1999* (2001)

Paddy Ashdown, *A Fortunate Life* (2009)

Ed Balls, *Speaking Out: Lessons in Life and Politics* (2016)

Peter Bartram, *David Steel: His Life and Politics* (1981)

Lewis Baston and Ken Ritchie, *Don't Take No for An Answer* (2011)

Caroline Benn, *Keir Hardie* (1992)

Tony Benn, *Conflicts of Interest: Diaries 1977–80* (1990)

John Bew, *Citizen Clem* (2016)

David Blaazer, *The Popular Front and the Progressive Tradition* (1992)

Tony Blair, *A Journey* (2010)

Neal Blewett, *The Peers, the Parties, and the People: The General Elections of 1910* (1972)

Vernon Bogdanor, *The Strange Survival of Liberal Britain* (2022)

Duncan Brack, Robert Ingham, Tony Little, *British Liberal Leaders* (2015)

Duncan Brack and Tony Little, *Great Liberal Speeches* (2001)

Gordon Brown, *My Life, Our Times* (2017)

Kenneth D. Brown, *The Unknown Gladstone: The life of Herbert Gladstone, 1854–1930* (2018)

James Callaghan, *Time and Chance* (1987)

John Campbell, *Lloyd George: The Goat in the Wilderness, 1922–1931* (2013)

John Campbell, *Roy Jenkins: A Well-Rounded Life* (2014)

Peter Clark, *The Men of 1924: Britain's First Labour Government* (2023)

David Cloke, 'The 1918 Coupon Election and its consequences', *Journal of Liberal History* (2018)

Chris Cook, *A Short History of the Liberal Party: 1900–92* (1993)

F. W. S. Craig, *British Electoral Facts: 1832–1987* (1989)

Richard Crossman, *The Crossman Diaries: 1964–1970* (ed. Anthony Howard) (1979)

Jon Cruddas, *A Century of Labour* (2024)

John Curtice, 'So How Well Did We Do? A critical look at the Liberal Democrat performance in the 1997 election', Liberal Democrat History Group Newsletter (September 1997)

John Curtice, 'The 2001 Election: Implications for the Liberal Democrats', *Journal of Liberal Democrat History* (Autumn 2001)

John Curtice, 'Disappointment or Bridgehead? The Liberal Democrats in the 2005 Election', *Journal of Liberal History* (Autumn 2005)

John Curtice, 'The 2010 Election: has the mould of British politics finally cracked?', *Journal of Liberal History* (Autumn 2010)

John Curtice, 'The 2015 Election Campaign and Its Outcome', *Journal of Liberal History* (Autumn 2015)

John Curtice, 'The 2017 Election: A Missed Opportunity?', *Journal of Liberal History* (Autumn 2017)

John Curtice, 'Gambling on Brexit: The Liberal Democrat Performance in the 2019 General Election', *Journal of Liberal History* (Winter 2019–20).

Iain Dale, *Conservative Party General Election Manifestos: 1900–1997* (2000)

Iain Dale, *Labour Party General Election Manifestos: 1900–1997* (2000)

Iain Dale, *Liberal Party General Election Manifestos: 1900–1997* (2000)

Iain Dale, *The Prime Ministers* (2020)

Iain Dale, *British General Election Campaigns 1830–2019* (2024)

George Dangerfield, *The Strange Death of Liberal England* (1997)

Bernard Donoughue, *Downing Street Diary: Volume Two* (2009)

Roy Douglas, *The History of the Liberal Party: 1895–1970* (1971)

Mark Egan, '1945 and All That…', *Liberal Democrat History Group Newsletter* (June 1997)

'Fabian Manifesto 1892' (1892)

Jo Grimond, *Memoirs* (1979)

Roy Hattersley, *David Lloyd George: The Great Outsider* (2010)

Robert Hazell, 'Liberal Democrats in coalition: constitutional reform', *Journal of Liberal History* (Autumn 2016)

Denis Healey, *The Time of My Life* (1989)

Simon Heffer, *Sing as We Go: Britain Between the Wars* (2023)

Kevin Hickson and Jasper Miles, *James Callaghan: An Underrated Prime Minister?* (2020)

Greg Hurst, *Charles Kennedy: A Tragic Flaw* (2006)

Robert Ingham and Duncan Brack, *Peace, Reform and Liberation: A History of Liberal Politics in Britain 1679–2011* (2011)

Roy Jenkins, *Pursuit of Progress* (1953)

Roy Jenkins, *Partnership of Principle* (1985)

Roy Jenkins et al., 'The Report of the Independent Commission on the Voting System' (1998)

Charles Kennedy, *The Future of Politics* (2000)

John Maynard Keynes, 'Liberalism and Labour', in *Essays in Persuasion* (1931)

Jonathan Kirkup, *The Lib–Lab Pact: A Parliamentary Agreement, 1977–1978* (2016)

David Laws, *22 Days in May* (2010)

David Laws, *Coalition* (2016)

Keith Laybourn and Jack Reynolds, *Liberalism and the Rise of Labour, 1890–1918* (1984)

Liberal Industrial Inquiry of 1928, 'Britain's Industrial Future' (1928)

Caron Lindsay, 'Liberal Democrats in Coalition: The Scottish Record', *Journal of Liberal History* (Summer 2014)

Graham Lippiatt, 'Working with others: the Lib–Lab Pact', *Journal of Liberal History* (Autumn 2008)

Graham Lippiatt, 'Decline and Fall: The Liberal Party and the elections of 1922, 1923 and 1924', *Journal of Liberal History* (Spring 2014)

Michael McManus, *Jo Grimond: Towards the Sound of Gunfire* (2001)

Peter Mandelson, *The Third Man* (2010)

V. Markham Lester, *H. H. Asquith: Last of the Romans* (2019)

David Marquand, *Ramsay MacDonald* (1997)

David Marquand, *The Progressive Dilemma: From Lloyd George to Blair* (1999)

Michael Meadowcroft, 'The 1924 Labour Government and the Failure of the Whips', *Journal of Liberal History* (Autumn 2018)

Alistair Michie and Simon Hoggart, *The Pact: The Inside Story of the Lib–Lab Government, 1977–1978* (2015)

Jasper Miles, *The Labour Party and Electoral Reform* (2023)

Kenneth Morgan, *The Age of Lloyd George* (1971)

David Owen, *Time to Declare* (1991)

Ian Packer, *Liberal Government and Politics: 1905–15* (2006)

Martin Pugh, *Speak for Britain: A new history of the Labour Party* (2010)

Andrew Rawnsley, *Servants of the People: The Inside Story of New Labour* (2000)

Chris Rennard, *Winning Here: Memoirs Volume 1* (2018)

John Rentoul, *Tony Blair: Prime Minister* (2001)

Peter Rowland, *The Last Liberal Governments: The Promised Land, 1905–1910* (1968)

Peter Rowland, *The Last Liberal Governments: Unfinished Business, 1911–1914* (1971)

Conrad Russell, *An Intelligent Person's Guide to Liberalism* (1999)

G. R. Searle, *The Liberal Party: Triumph and Disintegration, 1886–1929* (1992)

Adrian Slade, 'What might have been', interview with John Pardoe, *Journal of Liberal History* (Autumn 2002)

Michael Steed, 'Did the Great War really kill the Liberal Party?', *Journal of Liberal History* (Summer 2015)

David Steel, *A House Divided: The Lib–Lab Pact and the Future of British Politics* (1980)

David Steel, *Against Goliath* (1989)

Neil Stockley, '1974 Remembered', *Journal of Liberal Democrat History* (Spring 2000)

Neil Stockley, 'The 1979 General Election', *Journal of Liberal History* (Spring 2020)

Mark Stuart, *John Smith: A Life* (2005)

Margaret Thatcher, *The Path to Power* (1995)

Andrew Thorpe, *A History of the British Labour Party* (2015)

Jeremy Thorpe, *In My Own Time* (1999)

David Torrance, *A History of the Scottish Liberals and the Liberal Democrats* (2022)

David Torrance, *The Wild Men: The Remarkable Story of Britain's First Labour Government* (2024)

Jim Wallace, 'Comparing Coalitions', *Journal of Liberal History* (Autumn 2015)

David Walter, *The Strange Rebirth of Liberal England* (2003)

Alun Wyburn-Powell, *Clement Davies: Liberal Leader* (2003)

NOTES

CHAPTER 1

1   Roy Douglas, *The History of the Liberal Party: 1895–1970* (1971), p. xii

2   Caroline Benn, *Keir Hardie* (1992), p. 146

3   George Dangerfield, *The Strange Death of Liberal England* (1997), p. 70

4   Benn, 1992, p. 57

5   Ibid. p. 91

6   Kenneth D. Brown, *The Unknown Gladstone: the life of Herbert Gladstone, 1854–1930* (2018), p. 80

7   Douglas, 1971, p. 68

8   David Marquand, *Ramsay MacDonald* (1997), p. 76

9   Paul Adelman, *The Rise of the Labour Party: 1880–1945* (1996), pp. 112–13

10   Kenneth Morgan, *The Age of Lloyd George* (1971), p. 139

11   Marquand, 1997, p. 79

12   Brown, 2018, p. 100

13   G. R. Searle, *The Liberal Party: Triumph and Disintegration 1886–1929* (1992), p. 72

14   Marquand, 1997, p. 80

15   Ibid. p. 84

16   Quoted in Marquand, 1997, p. 91

17   Adelman, 1996, p. 35

18   Duncan Brack in Dale et al., *British General Election Campaigns, 1830–2019*, p. 202

19   Douglas, 1971, p. 74)

20   Vernon Bogdanor, *The Strange Survival of Liberal Britain* (2022), p. 456

21   Searle, 1992, p. 74

22   Iain Dale, *British General Election Campaigns, 1830–2019* (2024), p. 202

23   Roy Hattersley, *David Lloyd George: The Great Outsider* (2010), p. 29

24   Adelman, 1996, p. 45

25   Neal Blewett, *The Peers, the Parties, and the People: The General Elections of 1910* (1972), p. 317

26   Martin Pugh, *Speak for Britain: A new history of the Labour Party* (2010), p. 71

27   Bogdanor, 2022, p. 536

28   Blewett, 1972, p. 265

29   Pugh, 2010, p. 80

30   Marquand, 1997, p. 142

31 Ibid.
32 Ibid. p. 143
33 Bogdanor, 2022, p. 733
34 Jasper Miles, *The Labour Party and Electoral Reform* (2023), p. 18
35 Marquand, 1997, p. 159
36 Ibid. p. 160
37 Ibid. p. 161
38 Peter Rowland, *The Last Liberal Governments: Unfinished Business, 1911–1914* (1971), p. 354
39 Tanner, Searle, pp. 116–117

CHAPTER 2

1   Morgan, 1971, p. 47 and 150
2   Bogdanor, 2022, p. 557
3   Hattersley, 2010, p. 406
4   V. Markham Lester, *H. H. Asquith: Last of the Romans* (2019), p. 320
5   In Robert Ingham and Duncan Brack, *Peace, Reform and Liberation: A History of Liberal Politics in Britain 1679–2011* (2011), p. 177
6   Douglas, 1971, p. 118
7   Ibid. p. 123
8   Searle, 1992, p. 152
9   Pugh, 2010, p. 134
10 Searle, 1972, p. 153
11 Morgan, 1971, p. 196
12 Ibid. pp. 79–197
13 Campbell, *Lloyd George* (2013), p. 53
14 Douglas, 1971, p. 160
15 Campbell, 2013, p. 43
16 Campbell, 2013, p. 77
17 David Torrance, *The Wild Men: The Remarkable Story of Britain's First Labour Government* (2024), p. 96
18 Ibid. p. 9
19 Dutton in Ingham and Brack, 2011, p. 188
20 John Maynard Keynes, 'Liberalism and Labour', in *Essays in Persuasion* (1931), pp. 297–8
21 Campbell, 2013, p. 111
22 Hattersley, 2010, p. 599
23 Campbell, 2013, p. 222
24 Ibid. p. 243
25 Morgan, 1971, p. 104
26 Marquand, 1997, p. 527
27 Ibid. p. 530
28 Campbell, 2013, p. 262
29 Pugh, 2010, p. 211
30 Marquand, 1997, p. 533
31 Campbell, 2013, p. 275
32 Ibid. p. 280
33 Douglas, 1971, p. 213
34 Searle, 1992, p. 162
35 Campbell, 2013, p. 284
36 Marquand, 1997, p. 602
37 Campbell, 2013, p. 293
38 Ibid. p. 295
39 Ibid. p. 300

CHAPTER 3

1 Campbell, 2013, p. 314
2 Douglas, 1971, p. 231
3 John Bew, *Citizen Clem* (2016), pp. 128–9
4 Alun Wyburn-Powell, *Clement Davies: Liberal leader* (2003), p. 142
5 Douglas, 1971, p. 252
6 Wyburn-Powell, 2003, p. 143
7 Wyburn-Powell in Brack et al., 2015, p. 346
8 Douglas, 1971, p. 253
9 Ibid. p. 253
10 *The Times*, 26 January 1950
11 Wyburn-Powell, 2003, p. 172
12 Letter to G. Murray, 11 May 1950
13 Wyburn-Powell, 2003, p. 189
14 Ibid. p. 191
15 Ibid.
16 Ibid. p. 192
17 Ibid. p. 193
18 Ibid. p. 209

CHAPTER 4

1 Michael McManus, *Jo Grimond: Towards the Sound of Gunfire* (2001), p. 146
2 Jo Grimond, *Memoirs* (1979)
3 McManus, 2001, p. 144
4 Ibid. p. 144
5 Grimond, 1979
6 Quoted in Jonathan Kirkup, *The Lib–Lab Pact: A Parliamentary Agreement, 1977–1978* (2016)
7 Douglas, 1971, p. 281
8 Richard Crossman, *The Crossman Diaries: 1964–1970* (ed. Anthony Howard) (1979), p. 126

CHAPTER 5

1 Jeremy Thorpe, *In My Own Time* (1999)
2 Ibid.
3 David Steel, *Against Goliath* (1989)
4 Ibid.
5 Ibid.
6 Alistair Michie and Simon Hoggart, *The Pact: The Inside Story of the Lib–Lab Government, 1977–1978* (2015), p.183
7 Steel, 1989
8 Bernard Donoughue, *Downing Street Diary: Volume Two* (2009)
9 Michie and Hoggart, 2015
10 Ibid. p. 54
11 National Archives, PREM16/1399
12 National Archives, PREM 16/1399, handwritten note
13 Michie and Hoggart, 2015, p. 62
14 Grimond, 1979
15 Ibid. p. 250
16 Ibid. p. 250
17 Benn, 1990
18 Donoughue, 2009
19 Michie and Hoggart, 2015, p. 6

20 National Archives, PREM16/1399, 23 March 1977
21 Margaret Thatcher, *The Path to Power* (1995)
22 Michie and Hoggart, 2015, p. 71
23 Ibid. p. 164
24 Donoughue, 2009, p. 214
25 Michie and Hoggart, 2015, p. 143
26 Kirkup, 2016
27 Steel, 1989
28 Grimond, 1979, p. 254
29 Denis Healey, *The Time of My Life* (1989), p. 403
30 Michie and Hoggart, 2015, p. 176
31 Donoughue, 2009, p. 331
32 Chris Rennard, *Winning Here: Memoirs Volume* 1 (2018), p. 20
33 Ibid. p. 22
34 Michie and Hoggart, 2015, p. 187
35 Benn, 1990, p. 91
36 Thatcher, 1995
37 Adrian Slade, 'What might have been', interview with John Pardoe, *Journal of Liberal History* (Autumn 2002)
38 Graham Lippiatt, 'Decline and Fall', *Journal of Liberal History* (Autumn 2008)

CHAPTER 6

1 John Campbell, *Roy Jenkins: A Well-Rounded Life* (2014), p. 204
2 Roy Jenkins, *Partnership of Principle* (1985), p. 41
3 Campbell, 2014, p. 609
4 Jenkins, 1991
5 Rennard, 2018, p. 105
6 Ibid. p. 106
7 Paddy Ashdown, *The Ashdown Diaries Volume One: 1988–1997* (2000), p. 42
8 Ibid. p. 120
9 Ibid. p. 107
10 Ibid. p. 120
11 Ibid. pp. 7 and 17
12 Miles, 2023, p. 81
13 Ibid. p. 159

CHAPTER 7

1 Rennard, 2018, p. 170
2 Miles, 2021, p. 89
3 Ibid. p. 91
4 Ibid. p. 228
5 *New Statesman*, July 1996
6 Ashdown, 2000, p. 273
7 Philip Gould, *The Unfinished Revolution* (1999), p. 27
8 Ashdown, 2000, p. 287
9 Ibid. p. 312
10 Ibid. p. 357
11 Ibid. p. 318
12 Ibid. p. 421
13 Ibid. p. 421
14 Ibid. p. 422
15 Ibid. p. 449

16 Rennard, 2018, p. 213
17 Ashdown, 2000, p. 482
18 Ibid. p. 482
19 Ibid. p. 484
20 Ibid. p. 488
21 Rennard, 2018, p. 221
22 Ashdown, 2000, p. 507
23 Ibid. p. 507
24 Ashdown, 2000, p. 524
25 Marquand, 1999, p. vii
26 Andrew Rawnsley, *Servants of the People* (2000), p. 1
27 John Curtice, 'So How Well Did We Do? A critical look at the Liberal Democrat performance in the 1997 election', Liberal Democrat History Group Newsletter (September 1997)
28 Ibid.
29 Ibid.
30 Ibid.
31 Paddy Ashdown, *The Ashdown Diaries Volume Two: 1997–1999* (2001), p. 28
32 Ibid. p. 28
33 Ibid. p. 30
34 Ibid. p. x
35 Ibid. p. 36
36 Ibid. p. 37
37 Peter Mandelson, *The Third Man* (2010), p. 257
38 Ashdown, 2001, p. 106
39 Ibid. p. 106
40 Ibid. p. 107
41 Ibid. p. 131
42 Rennard, author's papers, 1998
43 Rennard, 1998
44 Ashdown, 2001, p. 178
45 Rennard, 2018, p. 245
46 Roy Jenkins et al., 'The Report of the Independent Commission on the Voting System' (1998)
47 Ibid. p. 29
48 Miles, 2021, p. 111
49 Rennard, 2018, p. 248
50 Ashdown, 2001, p. 252
51 Ibid. p. 259
52 Ibid. p. 259
53 Ibid. p. 309
54 Ibid. p. 322
55 Rennard, 2018, p. 249
56 Ibid. p. 249
57 Interview with the author, 17 April 2024
58 Dutton, 2011
59 David Torrance, *A History of the Scottish Liberals and the Liberal Democrats* (2022), p. 193
60 Tony Blair, *A Journey* (2010)
61 Ibid. p. 119
62 Ibid. p. 120
63 John Rentoul, *Tony Blair: Prime Minister* (2001), p. 490
64 Mandelson, 2010, p. 565
65 Ibid. p. 259
66 Rentoul, 2001, p. 499

CHAPTER 8

1 Greg Hurst, *Charles Kennedy: A Tragic Flaw* (2006), p. 128
2 John Curtice, 'The 2001 Election: Implications for the Liberal Democrats', *Journal of Liberal History* (Autumn 2001)
3 Conrad Russell, *An Intelligent Person's Guide to Liberalism* (1999), p. 122
4 Paddy Ashdown, *A Fortunate Life* (2009), p. 374
5 Ibid. p. 375
6 Miles, 2021, p. 131
7 Miles, 2021, p. 133
8 John Curtice, 'The 2010 election: has the mould of British politics finally cracked?', *Journal of Liberal History* (Autumn 2010)
9 David Laws, *22 Days in May* (2010), pp. 35–6
10 Miles, 2021, p. 139
11 Laws, 2010, p. 153
12 Laws, 2010, p. 156
13 Lewis Baston and Ken Ritchie, *Don't Take No for An Answer* (2011), p. 21
14 Mandelson, 2010, pp. 542–4
15 Blair, 2010, p. 681
16 Ed Balls, *Speaking Out* (2016), p. 319
17 Michie and Hoggart, 2015, p. 3
18 David Dutton, 'Comparing Coalitions', *Journal of Liberal History* (Autumn 2015)

CHAPTER 9

1 Laws, *Coalition* (2016), pp. 134–5
2 Douglas, 1971, p. xii
3 Curtice, 1997

INDEX